Stephen Crane's Blue Badge of Courage

Stephen Crane's
Blue Badge of Courage

George Monteiro

Louisiana State University Press / Baton Rouge / MM

Designer: G. Weston
Typeface: text: Bembo, display: New Berolina
Typesetter: Coghill Composition, Incorporated
Printer and binder: Thomson-Shore, Inc.

Library of Congress Cataloging-in-Publication Data

Monteiro, George.
    Stephen Crane's blue badge of courage / George Monteiro.
        p.   cm.
    Includes bibliographical references and index.
    ISBN 0-8071-2578-4 (cloth : alk. paper)
        1. Crane, Stephen, 1871–1900—Views on temperance.   2. Temperance societies—
United States—History—19th century.   3. Temperance—United States—History—
19th century.   4. Crane, Stephen, 1871–1900—Childhood and youth.   5. Temperance
in literature.   I. Title.
    PS1449.C85 Z745   2000
    813'.4—dc21   00-040572

Title page illustration: Stephen Crane at the age of twenty-two
Photograph by Corwin Knapp Linson. Collection of Stanley and Mary Wertheim. Used by permission.

To
Brenda, Steve, Emily, Kate, Dave

Contents

Illustrations

Acknowledgments

Daniel Hoffman, John Berryman, and Robert W. Stallman were my first guides to understanding the complexities and beauties of Stephen Crane's writing. Working in quite different ways, each of them produced work that to this day remains remarkably stimulating and always insightful. I am thankful for their encouragement of my own efforts, support that seemed always to come at the right moment in my life.

David H. Hirsch was my great friend for nearly four decades. I miss our long conversations over lunch that no matter how they started out always turned to the consideration of writers and their work.

I thank Brenda Murphy for reading the manuscript carefully and criticizing it thoughtfully. To Kate, Steve, and Emily, who grew up listening to my talk about Stephen Crane, I offer them, belatedly, my apologies.

Some of the material of this book has appeared, in modified form, in Louis H. Leiter and Neil D. Isaacs's *Approaches to the Short Story* and in the journals *American Literary Realism, Arizona Quarterly, Dionysos, Georgia Review, Journal of Modern Literature, Modern Fiction Studies, Prairie Schooner,* and *Stephen Crane Studies.* Those materials are used here with editorial consent.

Stephen Crane's Blue Badge of Courage

Introduction

If "Realism" is only half of life as the body is only part of the Man, how can a book or a play presenting only the outside of things be true to nature and life? It is easy to picture a lean and slippered pantaloon bobbling along the crowded street; then on the paper one may see his bent back, the wrinkles in his leathery cheeks, the faded rustiness of his once black coat, the cracks in his dirty linen, the knotted veins, the enlarged knuckles of his old hands. But it takes a Balzac to show the tragedy in the man's soul—not by pasting a label on the man's breast, but by making his soul live before you.

—*New York Tribune* (1891)

The more emotions we allow to speak in a given matter, the more different eyes we can put on in order to view a given spectacle, the more complete will be our conception of it, the greater our "objectivity."

—Friedrich Nietzsche, *The Genealogy of Morals* (1887)

Stephen Crane's Blue Badge of Courage is intentionally unfashionable. Its stated subject does not mask a "truer" subject, nor does it serve as a pretext for writing about something else. Stephen Crane is not employed to serve as a "window" on nineteenth-century American life or as a precursor for twentieth-century art. The book does not set up Crane's fiction as a tool for digging away at the culture of his times. Nor is it about nineteenth-century cultural proscriptions that are now widely considered to have been destructive excesses in human behavior. More specifically, although there is a good deal in this study about the texts employed by workers in the temperance movement in their attempts to educate, cajole, or coerce the intemperate into mending their ways, this is not a book about the Woman's Christian Temperance Union (WCTU) or any other institutionalized temperance group fronted as a study of Stephen Crane. Nor is it a book about American theories and practices of literary realism taking off from an initial concern with Crane's conscious or unconscious commitment to what he thought William Dean Howells, Hamlin Garland, and he himself considered to be the beautiful war for realism. While all these have been or might reasonably be the goals of other studies, they are not the goals of this one. Simply put, the goal of *Stephen Crane's Blue Badge of Courage* is to bring news about Stephen Crane and his literary work. Therefore, all other subjects or avenues of investigation—no matter how worthy in themselves or attractive as ventures or adventures to literary theorists or cultural historians— are introduced and entertained, examined and applied, as materials necessary for a fuller understanding of Crane's creative work. The value of what has been unearthed and is now introduced into the evenhanded and disinterested discussion of Crane lies solely in its potentially illuminating applicability to Crane's literary texts. *Stephen Crane's Blue Badge of Courage* is author and text centered. Informed analysis, one hopes, and not deconstruction, which has always seemed to me mean-spirited in its application, both to text and author, in denying to both of them the right to a donnée, to vision and intelligence. Crane deserves, in its fullest reach, the empathetic analysis the scholar can bring to the task when he reads him honestly. He is no whipping boy, cat's paw, straw man, or MacGuffin. Least of all is he, not even restively, an example of anybody's honorific or demonic ideology.

My more specific subject is Stephen Crane's imaginary. I propose that an important component is the terminology, imagery, and overall discourse of the temperance movement, of the legions of men and women who organized a fearsome war upon intemperance—upon the manufacture and sale of alcoholic drink and tobacco. That language was, capaciously, a histrionic language of demonism and apocalyptics that is itself largely derived from Holy Scripture, Christian hymns, sermons, and homilies. It spoke of monsters, beasts, reptiles, of maelstroms, cataclysms, and the woes and chromatic horrors of delirium tremens. It employed the moral language of Good and Evil, of social responsibility, criminal addiction, and the restoration of personal integrity. It offered water to the thirsty in place of rum. It offered commission in the cold-water army in place of the false camaraderie of the saloon. It offered family communion in place of the pernicious familiarity of the obligatory barroom "treat."

Even more precisely, I am interested in Crane's imagination and how it unfolded in his writing more than I am in sketching in the details of the material culture of his time. For instance, it is, of course, of some interest to know how, in Crane's time, popular amusements of various stripes exploited and promoted an interest in the unusual, the freakish, of what was considered to be the startlingly abnormal. But I wish more to discover the specific literary implications of Crane's having included references to those popular interests (among many other references in a given work) or reflected, consciously or even unconsciously, those public interests. Crane was not primarily interested in telling his readers that they shared a distasteful interest in "monsters," but in investigating what considering a disfigured human being to be a "monster" might lead to in

2

a small, largely homogenous community. That is why, as one astute reader of "The Monster" noticed immediately, although Doctor Trescott "says least and seldom appears," he is "the central figure of the drama."[1] Crane's intention was to tell a moral tale about human behavior in the most efficient way possible. Since he was a writer who believed that words conveyed impressions—that were durable as well as instantaneous—language was of course his aesthetic, as well as his moral, medium.

Since from the beginning Stephen Crane committed himself to an aesthetics that called for writing only about what he had experienced and to a writer's epistemology that required him to be true to what he saw, he started out with personal answers to what constituted literary realism. His interest was always in what he or an individualized character saw and felt in a given situation. He knew, too, that such an individual could not help but bring preconceived notions to his perceptions and feelings. Furthermore, he counted himself among those individuals who were the chosen subjects of his fiction. Surely, Michael Davitt Bell is fundamentally correct when he writes, "Crane apparently recognized that if environment shapes lives it does so, above all, by predetermining perception, by granting so much authority to the styles in which others' perceptions have been expressed that these styles come to constitute, in effect, the only experience there is."[2] What is missing here, however, is the acknowledgment of one important component. Although Bell offers an insightful disquisition on the disparity in linguistic abilities between the narrator of *Maggie* and the Bowery denizens he anatomizes, he stops short of saying what is the most glaring truth about his characters: although their heads are full of predetermining styles of perception, they do not possess even the workaday language to express, let alone criticize and potentially modify, the received mythologies and large melodramatic images that suffuse their thoughts and control the way they handle the merest tasks of daily living. Crane never denies that there is something apart from human perception that others have called reality. His writer's task was not to question or affirm its existence. His concern was clear. He was interested in the realities of individual human perceptions and their attendant effect on personal psychology and behavior. It is no wonder that Crane is not a player in any "social constructive" reading of Amy Kaplan's sort of the American literary realists against themselves.[3] It is precisely because Crane's writing does not address realism as a metaphysical problem or, more precisely, an epistemological one apart from the perceptions of individual human beings that

1. "Droch" [Robert Bridges], "Stephen Crane's 'The Monster,' " *Life*, 32 (Sept. 1, 1898), 166.
2. Michael Davitt Bell, *The Problem of American Realism: Studies in the Cultural History of a Literary Idea* (Chicago and London: University of Chicago Press, 1993), 139.
3. Amy Kaplan, *The Social Construction of American Realism* (Chicago and London: University of Chicago Press, 1988).

renders arguments about the historical accuracy of *The Red Badge of Courage* largely beside the point.

Far more fruitful ventures into the way Crane's precocious novel can be seen as an intervention in the battle over literary realism are Donald Pease's detailed charting into the way Crane structures the novel to reveal the way the incidents of battle fulfill Henry Fleming's psychological fears or expectations and, to a more limited extent, Amy Kaplan's "The Spectacle of War in Crane's Revision of History," which offers the novel idea that Crane's view of war as spectacle anticipated later twentieth-century media presentation of war as, well, spectacle.[4] J. C. Levenson's analysis of Crane's realism in *The Red Badge of Courage* offers a fresh and sound way to approach the matter: "The extremes of inner and outer view, and the instability that arises from the jumps back and forth and in between, would be found objectionable by Norris and others, but Crane's method has a function in the text," he writes. "It establishes the young soldier in a recognizably modern world where both external and internal experience are in flux and where the two flow into one another, so that the boundary between them is hard to determine."[5] Levenson's generalization seems to me just and perceptive, locating Crane precisely and fruitfully in the literary realism disputes of his time.

In a letter written in the spring of 1894, Crane expressed his pleasure at discovering that he was on the side of the literary realists of his day. "I discovered that my creed was identical with the one of Howells and Garland," he marveled, "in this way I became involved in the beautiful war between those who say that art is man's substitute for nature and we are the most successful in art when we approach the nearest to nature and truth, and those who say—well, I don't know what they say."[6] Much has been made of this general statement of allegiance, with its naming of William Dean Howells and Hamlin Garland, to the cause of literary realism. What Crane meant specifically by it is anyone's guess, with some guesses being better than others. Surely he did not mean that the three of them—Howells, Garland, and himself—shared a literary style. Certainly, in 1894 at least, they were drawn to similar social subject matter that was alien to the interest of those "others" who, Crane insisted, were keeping

4. Donald Pease, "Fear, Rage, and the Mistrials of Representation in *The Red Badge of Courage*," in *American Realism: New Essays*, ed. Eric J. Sundquist (Baltimore and London: Johns Hopkins University Press, 1982), 155–75; Amy Kaplan, "The Spectacle of War in Crane's Revision of History," in *New Essays on The Red Badge of Courage*, ed. Lee Clark Mitchell (Cambridge, Eng.: Cambridge University Press, 1986), 77–108.

5. J. C. Levenson, "*The Red Badge of Courage* and *McTeague*: Passage to Modernity," in *The Cambridge Companion to American Realism and Naturalism: Howells to London*, ed. Donald Pizer (Cambridge, Eng., and New York: Cambridge University Press, 1995), 160.

6. *The Correspondence of Stephen Crane*, ed. Stanley Wertheim and Paul Sorrentino (New York: Columbia University Press, 1988), I, 63.

his and Garland's work out of the "big" magazines. Hence his work might appear in Benjamin Orange Flower's *Arena*, a socialist journal published in Boston, but not in the more socially conservative *Atlantic Monthly*, also published in Boston. It was his "realism," he thought, that editors held against him. Yet he could write no other way, as he explained to the editor of *Demorest's Family Magazine* in 1896: "It has been a theory of mine . . . that the most artistic and the most enduring literature was that which reflected life accurately. Therefore I have tried to observe closely, and to set down what I have seen in the simplest and most concise way. I have been very careful not to let any theories or pet ideas of my own be seen in my writing."[7]

He did have theories, however, about the sort of personal realism that he was after. In fact, over the stretch of his career (though the impulse weakened later in the decade, in novels such as *Active Service* and the unfinished *The O'Ruddy*, though not, significantly, in the great short stories such as "The Open Boat," "The Blue Hotel," and "The Upturned Face") Crane remained a realist of the psyche who discovered for himself, early on, the aesthetic and epistemological uses of impressionism. He understood this and explained it as clearly as he could in 1896: "A man is born into the world with his own pair of eyes and he is not at all responsible for his quality of personal honesty. To keep close to my honesty is my supreme ambition. There is a sublime egotism in talking of honesty. I, however, do not say that I am honest. I merely say that I am as nearly honest as a weak mental machinery will allow. This aim in life struck me as being the only thing worth while. A man is sure to fail at it, but there is something in the failure."[8] It was this commitment to rendering honestly what he saw through his own eyes that led him to his own brand of literary impressionism as the means to the kind of psychological realism he espoused. At his best, he achieved extraordinary results, as his friend and fellow writer Joseph Conrad discerned. In December 1897, and immediately apropos of "The Open Boat," published six months earlier, Conrad complimented Crane: "The boat thing is immensely . . . [and] fundamentally interesting to me. Your temperament makes old things new and new things amazing. . . . You are an everlasting surprise to one. You shock—and the next moment you give the perfect artistic satisfaction. Your method is fascinating. You are a complete impressionist. The illusions of life come out of your hand without a flaw. It is not life—which nobody wants—it is art—art for which everyone—the abject and the great hanker—mostly without knowing it."[9] The "illusions of life"

---

7. Ibid., 230.

8. Ibid., 195–96.

9. Ibid., 315. See also David Shi, who writes: "Crane knew that literal realism was impossible. . . . His objective was not to produce an *imitation* of life but to offer a vivid *impression* of life as he saw and experienced it. He knew that realistic fiction at its best represented a translation of life rather than a transcription" (*Facing Facts: Realism in American Thought and Culture, 1850–1920* [New York and Oxford: Oxford University Press, 1995], 225).

that came out of Crane's hand without a flaw, as Conrad undoubtedly knew, were not restricted to immediate and somewhat naked sense impressions but extended to impressions informed and energized by knowledge, dreams, illusions, and preconceptions alike.

Stephen Crane's Blue Badge of Courage looks into the way Crane fabricated for his readers impressions of battle, bouts of dissipation, Western showdowns, and shipwreck by drawing on personal experience, not always of those very matters or situations, of what he knew at first hand. Specifically, it looks into the sometimes ingenious ways Crane used his knowledge of the mythologies, practices, and language of the temperance workers in his own family, particularly his mother and father, who were deeply committed to the temperance movement.

If there is a basic theme in this study of Stephen Crane's literary world it is that the imagination displayed in his early and mature work was strongly potentiated by what he appropriated for his writing from certain childhood experiences at school, at church, and at home. Those experiences sometimes gave him subject matter, but more often they provided him with an outlook in extremis conveyed by words and images he derived from the temperance reader and the Sunday school text. Combined with his schoolbooks, these at times complementary texts fed the otherwise secular imagination of this fourteenth child of a Methodist minister and an official of the Woman's Christian Temperance Union.

The primary evidence for the analyses offered in this study is textual. The news I hope to bring relates to how certain cultural facts—the war on intemperance, the promotion of war and the way it was conducted, the myth of a violent, whiskey-soaked West—helped to shape his work. These and other cultural facts provided him with substance for literature, a substance that, given his originally skeptical and preternatural irony, was investigated, judged, formulated, and turned into the unique formulations and colors of Crane's poetic fiction and parablelike poems. I have tried to keep in mind the poet Elizabeth Bishop's cautionary observation that "it takes probably hundreds of things coming together at the right moment to make a poem and no one can ever really separate them out and say this did this, that did that."[10] But I suspect that some of the things that go into the making of a piece of writing are more important than others, and I have tried to single out some of those more important "things." To recognize them will help us understand how Crane got at the kind of realism that moved through appearance to reveal the soul.

The critical account that follows does not proceed chronologically. Crane wrote much in a career lasting less than a decade, and in the rush and variety

10. *Conversations with Elizabeth Bishop*, ed. George Monteiro (Jackson: University Press of Mississippi, 1996), 88.

of his writing throughout the 1890s Crane returned frequently to his first themes. Of central importance to any study of Crane's creative mind is the recognition that when he went out into the world—be it to school in Easton, Pennsylvania, or Syracuse, to the Tenderloin district of New York City, to the mines in Scranton, to spend winter in Nebraska or spring in Mexico, to cover wars in Greece or Cuba—he saw reality with certain familial imperatives in place. Even the powerful alchemy of Crane's artistry could not entirely remove the strong traces of the religious rhetoric and principles of his family, particularly those motivating his mother's WCTU tactics or his father's social gospel sermons. On the contrary. His family's rhetoric and principles stood him in good stead, not as primary guides to conduct but as a fund of informed experience that, as a writer committed to the realities of impressionism, he could draw upon to write about situations and characters he had not yet directly experienced. He knew, too, that his own personally devised brand of impressionism called for drawing on the full range of a rich and supple language. The almost indelible sources of that language, for a good portion of his literary career, were the informed experiences of school, church, and, above all, home. No one should ever accuse Crane of attempting (and failing) to write a prose that approximates transparency before the reality he would reflect in his fiction, poetry, or journalism.

From the start students of Crane's writing have been aware that his work was strongly marked by the cultural imperatives of his religious inheritance. Insufficiently emphasized, however, is the extent to which Crane put to use the theatricality inherent in the way that his family went about its work. Crane expanded on this insight into his family by viewing most if not all of human life theatrically, in the multiple senses that existence was in itself theatrical, that men behaved theatrically, and that the writer Crane was—and it did not contradict his notions of literary realism—was one who needed to theatricalize his narratives and fables. This he did, not only in the way he perceived his characters-in-action but in the style he forged for telling their stories.

1

Far from the Tree

The Publication House established in New York by the National Temperance Society does honor to the liberality and zeal of its founders. It is already a power in the land.

—Rev. J. T. Crane, *Arts of Intoxication* (1870)

If any man hereafter says I can't hold liquor, he lies. I am a liquor holder from Holdersville.

—Stephen Crane (1895)

On the first day of November 1871, the Reverend Jonathan Townley Crane recorded in his diary: "This morning, at 5.30′ our fourteenth child was born. We call him Stephen."[1] It was a rare family confidence, for usually the Reverend Crane's notations referred to the details of his religious and social ministry. Sketchy as they are, his diaries offer revealing glimpses into an interestingly active life.

Many of the concerns of his youngest son's writing are anticipated in his father's journals. The Reverend J. T. Crane writes of war and Sunday schools. He preaches to "colored people," supports "Negro Suffrage," and opposes the use of tobacco. He records his attendance at a State Temperance Convention in New Brunswick in 1865 and at the National Temperance Convention in Saratoga Springs in 1873. Statistics linking crime with drink get his attention. Of 477 prisoners in the New Jersey state prison, 310 are under twenty-five years of age, he notes, and "384 were led into crime by means of drinking alcoholic liquors." "Among these 384," he exults, "not one was a pledged Temperance man when he fell into crime."[2]

---

1. Thomas A. Gullason, ed., "A Family Portfolio: 2. Extracts from the Reverend Crane's Newly Discovered Two-Volume Journal," in *Stephen Crane's Career: Perspectives and Evaluations*, ed. Thomas A. Gullason (New York: New York University Press, 1972), 20.
2. Ibid., 12, 14, 19–20.

Mary Helen Peck Crane thought her husband's temperance work to be of paramount importance. In the biographical sketch she prepared for the Pennington Seminary after his death (he had served the school as its principal for nine years), she rehearsed his credentials as a social activist: "He was a pioneer in the temperance cause in New Jersey, serving as corresponding editor of the *Reformer*, a temperance sheet published in Trenton. During his vacations, while canvassing for students, he lectured and preached on the subject from Haverstraw to Cape May. In company with other brethren, he went annually before legislative committees to plead for prohibitory laws, and used often to express himself in favor of woman being given the ballot that she might better protect her home."[3] It is understandable that Mrs. Crane would emphasize the temperance aspect of her husband's life, given her own work for the Woman's Christian Temperance Union conducted at all levels—local, state, and national. She was friendly with Frances E. Willard, the much-admired president of the WCTU, who had been a guest in her home.[4] When Miss Willard compiled *A Woman of the Century*, in 1893, she profiled the late Mrs. Mary Helen Peck Crane as a "church and temperance worker."

She was the only daughter of Rev. George Peck, D.D., of the Methodist Episcopal Church, the well-known author and editor. She became the wife of the late Rev. Jonathan Townley Crane, D.D., when twenty years of age, and was the mother of fourteen children. She was a devoted wife and mother and was energetic in assisting her husband in his work in the church and among the poor. Mrs. Crane was an ardent temperance worker and, as her children grew up, she devoted much time to the work of the Woman's Christian Temperance Union. Mrs. Crane delivered addresses on several occasions before the members of the New Jersey Legislature, when temperance bills were pending, and she greatly aided the men who were fighting to secure good laws. As the pioneer of press-work by women at the Ocean Grove Camp Meeting, she did valuable work, and her reports for the New York "Tribune" and the New York Associated Press, during the last ten years of the great religious and temperance gatherings at the noted Mecca of the Methodists, are models of

3. Mrs. Helen Crane, "Rev. Jonathan T. Crane, D.D.," *Pennington Seminary Review*, 1 (June 1889): 1–5; reprinted in Gullason, *Stephen Crane's Career*, 29–35. Quotation comes from page 32 of the latter.
4. Stanley Wertheim and Paul Sorrentino, *The Crane Log: A Documentary Life of Stephen Crane, 1871–1900* (New York: G. K. Hall, 1994), 43. It was probably his knowledge of this fact that prompted Thomas Beer to invent the Crane quotations to the equally unlikely "Miss Harris," including this one: "Frances Willard . . . is one of those wonderful people who can tell right from wrong for everybody from the polar cap to the equator. Perhaps it never struck her that people differ from her. I have loved myself passionately now and then but Miss Willard's affair with Miss Willard should be stopped by the police" (*Stephen Crane: A Study in American Letters*, intr. Joseph Conrad [New York: Knopf, 1923], 205).

their kind. For about ten years she was the State superintendent of press for New Jersey of the Woman's Christian Temperance Union. She wrote several leaflets that were of great value to the press-workers of the local unions. For over a half-century Mrs. Crane was an active member of the Methodist Episcopal Church. She led the life of a sincere Christian and died 7th December 1891, after a short illness contracted at the National convention of the Woman's Christian Temperance Union in Boston.[5]

Examples of Mary Crane's writings on behalf of temperance causes are ample. She had her customary say against "worldly amusements" in an 1884 piece, for instance, lashing out against the drunkard: "In the little back room in the drug store our young men may be initiated into drinking habits, and take their places just as surely among the moderate drinkers ultimately to swell the great army one hundred thousand strong, who go to a drunkard's death every year, as in the open saloon," she wrote.[6] But later, toward the end of her life, she complains, in a letter to the *New Jersey Tribune*: "Foggy as the afternoon was I went to the Reform Club meeting in the Third Presbyterian church, Jersey City. Judging by the attendance at that meeting temperance sentiment is not very strong in that rum-ridden city. Scarcely enough to save it from the fate of Sodom. I saw more men around any one of a dozen saloons which I passed in going to the meeting than were present."[7]

The Cranes' fourteenth and last child was introduced to his parents' religious convictions and militant social causes at a tender age, though that task fell largely to his older sister Agnes. "Stevie" was not yet four when she took him to Sunday school[8] and to Methodist camp. Melvin Schoberlin describes what Stephen saw and heard at Camp Tabor: "The preacher stamped and raised his clenched hand to his head, and dashed it down, and, in a voice of thunder, gave a terrific description of the final conflagration. 'O sinner, sinner,' thundered the preacher, 'are you determined to take hell by storm? Are your bones iron, and your flesh brass, that you plunge headlong into the lake of fire?' There was an unbroken roar of fervent supplication, while the awful voice of the preacher

5. *A Woman of the Century: Fourteen Hundred-Seventy Biographical Sketches Accompanied by Portraits of Leading American Women in All Walks of Life*, ed. Frances E. Willard and Mary A. Livermore (Buffalo, Chicago, and New York: Charles Wells Moulton, 1893), 213–14.

6. Mrs. M. H. Crane, "Change of Base," *Ocean Grove Record* (Mar. 15, 1884), 3; reprinted in Gullason, *Stephen Crane's Career*, 36.

7. Mary Helen Crane, letter to *New Jersey Tribune* (Feb. 16, 1887), 2; holograph copy in Schoberlin Research Files, Stephen Crane Collection, George Arents Research Library for Special Collections, Syracuse University Library, Syracuse, New York.

8. Paul Sorrentino, "Newly Discovered Writings of Mary Helen Peck Crane and Agnes Elizabeth Crane," *Syracuse University Library Associates Courier*, 21 (Spring 1986), 125.

resounded above this tempest of prayer." It is small wonder that the frightened child "clung to his sister's skirt, and wept."[9]

Crane was a few years older when he bought his first beer while in Asbury Park with his mother, who was there to attend a temperance gathering. Post Wheeler recalls the incident in his 1955 memoirs in a scene that could have come right out of *Maggie: A Girl of the Streets*, tough talk and all. The young Wheeler's mother had taken him to hear Miss Frances Willard. He remembered that the "celebrated . . . secretary of the W.C.T.U.," dressed in "gray, with a white scarf that fell from the back of her head down to her waist," looked like "some kind of a nun." Wheeler's mother met with "another W.C.T.U. lady speaker of note," one "who had come from as far away as New Jersey to the 'rally.' Her name was Mrs. Jonathan Crane and she had brought her youngest son with her." It was the younger Stevie who introduced Wheeler to cigarettes. Stevie also treated himself to his first beer, a bit of daring and nerve that deeply impressed Wheeler. Walking up to "a fat Pennsylvania Dutchman," who, beside the exit gate, had "set up a keg of beer on an up-turned box on which stood a row of glass mugs, with a sign which said: *Beer 10 cents*," Stevie took a dime from his pocket "with an air of purpose." "My blood chilled. 'What you going to do?' I asked in a hollow undertone." There was no answer. Stevie "set down the dime on the box and said, 'Gimme one.' " Surveying "Stevie's diminutive figure," the Dutchman hesitated, but with his "fingers" closed on the "eloquent coin." " 'You gimme a beer or gimme back my dime!' said Stevie in a shrill falsetto." But when "a mug with a dab of foam in it" is placed before him, the brash child regards it scornfully. " 'That ain't half full!' " he says indignantly. " 'You fill it up.' " The Dutchman turned the tap then and Stevie drank slowly, while Wheeler "watched in stupe-faction." They walked through the gate. " 'How does it taste?' " asked Wheeler. " ' 'Tain't any better'n ginger ale,' he said. 'I been saving that dime for it all afternoon.' " Wheeler's awe at his young friend's temerity did not abate. "Beer! Right in the crowd, too," he marveled. How did he dare do it? " 'Pshaw! . . . Beer ain't nothing at all,' " Stevie blustered. " 'How was I going to know what it tasted like less'n I tasted it? How you going to know about things at all less'n you *do* 'em?' "[10]

No doubt the adult who recalled this beer-drinking episode seventy-five years after the fact had the advantage of having read the mature Crane's work,

9. Quoted in Melvin H. Schoberlin, "Flagon of Despair: Stephen Crane," unpublished manuscript, Schoberlin Collection, Syracuse University Library, Syracuse, New York; requoted in Sorrentino, "Newly Discovered Writings," 124 n. 30.

10. Post Wheeler and Hallie Erminie Rives, *Dome of Many-Coloured Glass* (Garden City: Doubleday, 1955), 20–22.

for he draws the "right" conclusion about his character. It is as if he has shaped his narrative to illustrate Crane's persistent need to test things out for himself.

Yet it is also true that the young Crane (especially) did not allow his lack of any direct knowledge of a thing or situation to deter him from writing about such things or experiences. When he fell short on direct experience, he created "experiential" knowledge by resorting to analogy.[11] He extrapolated from what he knew to write about what he, strictly speaking, had not encountered. What use did the writer make, incidentally, of Wheeler's chagrin and cowardice, when, faced with Stevie's "unanswerable logic" and thinking of "the blue ribbon" on his jacket (gained by signing a pledge card numbering him among those "who never, no, never, would taste the damnable devil's brew that beckoned to a drunkard's grave"), the older boy pulled off the blue ribbon and hid it in his pocket?[12]

Crane's mother was still highly active in temperance work when the Woman's Temperance Publishing Association put out its *White Ribbon Birthday Book* in 1887. The quotation for November 1, Stephen Crane's birthday, might have amused her rebellious son. It affirms "that the American mother who to-day being pressed on every side by the aggression of King Alcohol, confronts American men, the infant in her arms her only sceptre, the motherhood upon her brow her only crown, and cries to them for protection of her kingdom, the home."[13] That same month, with his mother participating in the National Convention of the WCTU in Nashville, Stevie Crane, who had just turned sixteen, suddenly left Pennington Seminary, which his father had once headed. His reason for doing so, he later explained, was that they had called him "a liar."[14] Within months he began his professional career as a reporter by digging up and contributing New Jersey shore items to his brother Townley's news agency.[15] Two years later, after trying out two colleges, he was plying his writer's trade in New York City.

---

11. Of relevance here is Patrick K. Dooley's discussion of the ways William James's meditations on "knowledge about" and "knowledge by acquaintance" offer insights into Crane's epistemology and aesthetics (*The Pluralistic Philosophy of Stephen Crane* [Urbana and Chicago: University of Illinois Press, 1993], especially chapters 2 and 4).

12. Wheeler and Rives, *Dome of Many-Coloured Glass*, 22, 20.

13. *The White Ribbon Birthday Book*, ed. Anna A. Gordon (Chicago: Woman's Temperance Publishing Association, 1887), 230. The quotation is attributed to Elizabeth Cleveland.

14. Wertheim and Sorrentino, *Crane Log*, 39.

15. James B. Colvert, *Stephen Crane* (San Diego: Harcourt Brace Jovanovich, 1984), xii; Wertheim and Sorrentino, *Crane Log*, 44.

The Destructive Element

Some of my best work is contained in short things which I have written for various publications, principally the New York Press in 1893 or thereabout.

—Stephen Crane (1896)

New York was essentially his inspiration, the New York of suffering and baffled and beaten life, of inarticulate or blasphemous life; and away from it he was not at home, with any theme, or any sort of character. It was the pity of his fate that he must quit New York, first as a theme, and then as a habitat; for he rested nowhere else, and wrought with nothing else as with the lurid depths which he gave proof of knowing better than any one else.

—William Dean Howells, "Frank Norris" (1902)

Early in 1896 Stephen Crane explained to the editor of *Leslie's Weekly* that of two books he published in 1895, "I am much fonder of my little book of poems, *The Black Riders*. The reason, perhaps, is that it was a more ambitious effort. My aim was to comprehend in it the thoughts I have had about life in general, while *The Red Badge* is a mere episode in life, an amplification."[1] Yet Crane's distinction has not distracted his readers from the fact that, as one critic reminds us, "He never knowingly wrote a line that didn't speak the truth as he felt it—an aesthetic creed of great seriousness."[2] One consequence of agreeing with this critic is that when read attentively there is almost nothing in Crane's writing—novel, story, reportage, play, or poem—that will not yield news of

1. *The Correspondence of Stephen Crane*, ed. Stanley Wertheim and Paul Sorrentino (New York: Columbia University Press, 1988), I, 232–33.
2. Daniel Hoffman, "Talking About Poetry with W. D. Ehrhart," in *Words to Create a World: Interviews, Essays, and Reviews of Contemporary Poetry* (Ann Arbor: University of Michigan Press, 1993), 200.

the way Crane thought about the mysteries of human existence. Sometimes those thoughts were voiced in dialogues (seemingly one-sided) with the other voices of his time.

1

Poem IV of *The Black Riders and Other Lines* begins in the midst of things, as it were, as if the poem were an answer to a question or a response to a statement made by some unknown speaker. It is printed in caps (as are all the poems in this book), perhaps, as has been ventured, to "suggest scare headlines":[3]

> YES, I HAVE A THOUSAND TONGUES,
> AND NINE AND NINETY-NINE LIE.
> THOUGH I STRIVE TO USE THE ONE,
> IT WILL MAKE NO MELODY AT MY WILL,
> BUT IS DEAD IN MY MOUTH.[4]

Crane's poem may be regarded as a reaction to the sentiment expressed in the following lines constituting stanzas one, two, and six of a hymn by Charles Wesley, often placed first in Methodist hymnals.

> O for a thousand tongues, to sing
> My great Redeemer's praise;
> The glories of my God and King,
> The triumphs of his grace!
>
> My gracious Master and my God,
> Assist me to proclaim,
> To spread through all the earth abroad,
> The honors of thy name.
>
> . . . .
>
> Hear him ye deaf; his praise, ye dumb,
> Your loosened tongues employ;
> Ye blind, behold your Saviour come;
> And leap, ye lame, for joy.[5]

Or Crane's lines might be regarded as an answer to Frances E. Willard's "Saloons Must Go!"—a temperance song that also adapts the imagery of Wesley's hymn:

---

3. Christopher Benfey, *The Double Life of Stephen Crane* (New York: Knopf, 1992), 127.

4. Stephen Crane, *The Black Riders and Other Lines* (Boston: Copeland and Day, 1895), 4.

5. *Hymnal of the Methodist Episcopal Church* (New York: Phillips & Hunt/Cincinnati: Walden & Stowe, 1883), 5.

Listen to the tread of many feet,
From home and playground, farm and street;
They talk like tongues, their words we know:
Saloons, saloons, saloons, must go![6]

In *The Black Riders and Other Lines* appears a poem, numbered XLVIII:

> ONCE THERE WAS A MAN,—
> OH, SO WISE!
> IN ALL DRINK
> HE DETECTED THE BITTER,
> AND IN ALL TOUCH
> HE FOUND THE STING.
> AT LAST HE CRIED THUS:
> "THERE IS NOTHING,—
> "NO LIFE,
> NO JOY,
> NO PAIN,—
> "THERE IS NOTHING SAVE OPINION,
> "AND OPINION BE DAMNED."[7]

There is something puzzling about this poem until we read it against temperance texts such as this one—"You are told that public opinion seems to demand the saloon. As a White Ribbon I ask, 'Whose public opinion? That of the home?' 'Oh, no!' The home is solidly against it."[8] Or when it is read against this one—"Public opinion . . . is a mighty engine for good if we can array it on our side. He who despises it must be either more or less than man; he must be puffed up by a conceit which mars his usefulness, or he must be too abject to be reached by scorn."[9] Or, to take a third example: "The work that opens up for us is to help create a public opinion which shall no longer grant indulgence to a hollow mockery of virtue, but demand an equal standard of morality for both sexes."[10] While in the third of these passages there is a more general reference to the need for the equal treatment of women, in the other two temperance speakers exhort their listeners to align themselves with proper public opinion so as to better promote the war against intemperance. Crane's poem extends the temperance workers' message beyond mere alcoholic drink to the

6. Frances E. Willard, "Saloons Must Go!" in *Frances E. Willard Recitation Book, Werner's Readings and Recitations, No. 18* (New York: Edgar S. Werner, 1898), 178–79.

7. Crane, *Black Riders*, 51.

8. Frances E. Willard, "The Widening Horizon," in *Frances E. Willard Recitation Book*, 91.

9. Canon F. W. Farrar, "Public Opinion," in *Readings and Recitations, No. 2*, ed. L[izzie] Penney (New York: National Temperance Society and Publication House, 1878), 26.

10. Anna Rice Powell, quoted in *The White Ribbon Birthday Book*, ed. Anna A. Gordon (Chicago: Woman's Temperance Publishing Association, 1887), 38.

larger question of life. Narrow temperance views are the implied target of Crane's poem. It helps to have it placed in such a context. But the influence of the second passage may extend beyond poem XLVIII of *The Black Riders*. Its language seems to be echoed in the Nebraska story "The Blue Hotel" (emphasis added): "The *conceit* of man was explained by this storm to be the very *engine* of life."[11] The extent to which Crane's imagination was steeped in the figures and tropes and details of the war on alcoholic drink and general intemperance that was being waged all around him during his childhood by his father and, especially, his mother can be indicated by an examination of poem XII of *The Black Riders*.

"AND THE SINS OF THE FATHERS SHALL
BE VISITED UPON THE HEADS OF THE CHIL-
DREN, EVEN UNTO THE THIRD AND FOURTH
GENERATION OF THEM THAT HATE ME."

WELL, THEN, I HATE THEE, UNRIGHTEOUS
    PICTURE;
WICKED IMAGE, I HATE THEE;
SO, STRIKE WITH THY VENGEANCE
THE HEADS OF THOSE LITTLE MEN
WHO COME BLINDLY.
IT WILL BE A BRAVE THING.[12]

The source of Crane's epigraph is Exodus 20:5, and the reference to "image" recalls Old Testament imprecations against worshiping graven images and honoring false gods. Interestingly enough, Crane's father had used as an epigraph to a chapter titled "Alcohol: The Hereditary Effect" a variant of the same text from Exodus: "Visiting the iniquities of the fathers upon the children unto the third and fourth generation."[13] Yet the poem seems to address a picture, perhaps a lithograph or engraving hanging on a wall at home or at church. When he was only three his sister Agnes was already taking Stevie to Sunday school.[14] In fact, when he was enrolled in the primary class at St. Paul's, he "received a gaudy-tinted lithograph each Sunday in reward."[15]

11. Stephen Crane, "The Blue Hotel," in *Tales of Adventure*, Volume V of *The University of Virginia Edition of the Works of Stephen Crane*, ed. Fredson Bowers, intr. J. C. Levenson (Charlottesville: University Press of Virginia, 1970), 165.

12. Crane, *Black Riders*, 13.

13. Rev. J. T. Crane, *Arts of Intoxication: The Aim, and the Results* (New York: Carlton & Lanahan/ San Francisco: E. Thomas/Cincinnati: Hitchcock & Walden, 1870), 172.

14. Paul Sorrentino, "Newly Discovered Writings of Mary Helen Peck Crane and Agnes Elizabeth Crane," *Syracuse University Library Associates Courier*, 21 (Spring 1986), 125.

15. Melvin H. Schoberlin, "Flagon of Despair: Stephen Crane," unpublished manuscript, Schoberlin Collection, Syracuse University Library, Syracuse, New York. II-3, quoted in Sorrentino, "Newly Discovered Writings," 125 n. 34.

Frances E. Willard had complained that improper pictures could be seen even on the walls of the houses of temperance people. "I see on the wall pleasant pictures of fruits and flowers, and among the clustering leaves, I see the mantling wine-cup with its ruddy glow and enticing look. Such pictures are not safe to present before the eyes of children. Far better to show them the rude but picturesque 'iron-bound bucket,' or the homely but honest picture of 'the cold-water society,' if it should even represent three horses drinking from a trough."[16] Miss Willard's personal complaint was backed up by official action. From the beginning it was part of the Woman's Christian Temperance Union's plan of work to place engravings "and similar pictures on the walls of every school room."[17] It was the fifth of nine recommendations in a "Plan of Work" adopted at the first national WCTU convention. That there existed a temperance-supporting engraving captioned with the words of Exodus 20:5 makes sense. It would have been consonant with the generalization that "the lust for strong drink is hereditary," as one temperance worker put it, but that no "father has a right to bequeath such a legacy of damnation to his offspring."[18]

2

Early in his career, under the auspices of his brother Townley, Stephen Crane reported news from the New Jersey seaside towns for the *New York Tribune*. On August 21, 1892, the *Tribune* printed Crane's now notorious piece on the parade of the Junior Order of United American Mechanics in Asbury Park on the previous Wednesday afternoon. The piece contrasted the marching members of the order with the "bona fide Asbury Parker" in attendance. The marchers formed "the most awkward, ungainly, uncut and uncarved procession that ever raised clouds of dust on sun-beaten streets." The procession was "composed of men, bronzed, slope-shouldered, uncouth and begrimed with dust. Their clothes fitted them illy, for the most part, and they had no ideas of marching. They merely plodded along, not seeming quite to understand, stolid, unconcerned and, in a certain sense, dignified—a pace and a bearing emblematic of their lives." These are men with "tan-colored, sun-beaten honesty" in their faces. "Such an assemblage of the spraddle-legged men of the middle class, whose hands were bent and shoulders stooped from delving and

16. Frances E. Willard, "The Great Evil," in *Readings and Recitations, No. 5*, ed. L[izzie] Penney (New York: National Temperance Society and Publication House, 1884), 69.

17. Anonymous, *A Brief History of the Woman's Christian Temperance Union*, 2nd ed. (Evanston: Union Signal, 1907), 95.

18. Rev. T. L. Cuyler, "Boys—and the Bottle," in *Readings and Recitations, No. 2*, ed. L[izzie] Penney (New York: National Temperance Society and Publication House, 1878), 19.

constructing, had never appeared to an Asbury Park summer crowd, and the latter was vaguely amused."[19]

During the summer there existed two Asbury Parkers. There was the aforementioned bona fide Asbury Parker, "a man to whom a dollar, when held close to his eye, often shuts out any impression he may have had that other people possess rights. He is apt to consider that men and women, especially city men and women, were created to be mulcted by him." And there were the summer visitors that made Asbury Park "a resort of wealth and leisure, of women and considerable wine." Oddly, this is the only reference to anything alcoholic in the piece.[20] But there is a point in mentioning wine this once, for it was well-known that the Junior Order of United American Mechanics (JOUAM) excluded from their membership any person engaged in the sale of "alcoholic or spirituous beverages."[21] "The Height of the Season at Asbury Park," however, a piece published in the *Tribune* a week earlier than the parade story that is generally attributed to Crane reports: "One of those drug stores that really exist for the sole purpose of selling liquors in this 'no license' town was raided last Monday evening, and the proprietor, clerk and some dozen patrons were arrested. The affair caused no little excitement in town, and no small inconvenience to those unfortunate ones who were arrested to appear as witnesses. Some women, unhappily, were in the party, but were not put under arrest."[22] Mentioning that women were complicit in purchasing liquor might be a sly thrust aimed at the WCTU's conviction of woman's moral superiority.

Crane's parade piece evoked a strenuous complaint from the leadership of the JOUAM. E. A. Canfield, in a letter published in the *Tribune* on August 24, 1892, called the unsigned piece a "slur" on "a National political organization" of "American-born citizens." He defined the organization's principles and "main objects": "to restrict immigration, and to protect the public schools of the United States and to prevent sectarian interference therein," and to "demand that the Holy bible be read" in the "public schools, not to teach sectarianism but to inculcate its teachings." Although the organization's position on temperance goes unmentioned, JOUAM presents its membership as "bound together to protect Americans in business and shield them from the depressing

---

19. Stephen Crane, "Parades and Entertainments," in *Tales, Sketches, and Reports*, Volume VIII of *The University of Virginia Edition of the Works of Stephen Crane*, ed. Fredson Bowers, intr. Edwin H. Cady (Charlottesville: University Press of Virginia, 1973), 521–22. The piece, unsigned, appeared in the *New York Tribune* on August 21, 1892, 22.

20. Crane, "Parades and Entertainments," 521–22.

21. Anonymous, "Modern Fraternities Closed to Liquor Dealers," in *World Book of Temperance* (Abridged ed.), comp. by Dr. and Mrs. Wilbur F. Crafts (Washington, D.C.: International Reform Bureau, 1908), 38. This list includes only twelve other groups.

22. Stephen Crane, "The Height of the Season at Asbury Park," in *Tales, Sketches, and Reports*, 562. The piece, unsigned, was published in the *New York Tribune* on August 14, 1892, 8.

effects of foreign competition."[23] Canfield had discerned that Crane's irony was not directed entirely at the two classes of Asbury Parkers. The *Tribune* apologized—its owner, Whitelaw Reid, was on the national Republican ticket as vice-presidential candidate—and fired Townley Crane, the writer's older brother, who ran the press bureau covering the shore resorts. Stephen Crane's own reporting from the Jersey shore had come to an end as well. He would henceforth concentrate on New York City.

3

Intemperance "has emptied churches just as it has filled brothels," railed one temperance worker. "It has caused hospitals, asylums, and jails, and it has filled graveyards long before their time." "If to-night its victims could leave their dens, their dungeons, and their graves," he continues, "and hold up their bony, or skeleton, or bloated hands, stretching them out in all their ghastliness, it would be a sight to make Heaven weep. Death, famine, and despair, the accumulated harvest from brewery and still, would be massed in a horrifying portraiture of shuddering, trembling souls, against whom heaven's gates are closed, and who, hearing the awful declaration, 'No drunkard shall enter,' would seek hell as a refuge."[24] This was one important aspect of the vision that the young Stephen Crane carried with him when he went out into the streets of New York to conduct his personal surveys of how it was with the denizens of poverty. Such apocalyptic views, always pinpointing intemperance as the cause of human misery, were part and parcel of the moral climate of Jonathan Townley Crane and Mary Helen Peck Crane's household during Stephen's tender and formative years. It was a dark vision of human sinfulness tied to drink that Crane managed to test in the complicated maze of social and economic facts during the deep economic crisis of the early 1890s. Published in the October 1894 issue of the *Arena*, B. O. Flower's Boston-based journal of social protest, "The Men in the Storm" offers an extraordinary example of how Crane successfully wrenched himself free from the temperance worker's view of the hapless men in the streets. Though he saw clearly the need to leave behind the temperance worker's harsh judgments and often mistaken assessments of the facts, he continued to employ the apocalyptic imagery and the scriptural language so freely appropriated by the temperance movement.

As was his wont, Crane "researched" the facts that went into "The Men in the Storm." Scouring New York City's Bowery for evidence of the effects of

---

23. Quoted in *Tales, Sketches, and Reports*, 909.

24. O. H. Tiffany, "An Evil Waste," in *Readings and Recitations, No. 4*, ed. L[izzie] Penney (New York: National Temperance Society and Book Publication House, 1882), 73.

economic depression, Crane doggedly courted those experiences that would enable him to write authentically about the poor. In an example of stunt-journalism, pioneered in America by the *New York World*'s Nellie Bly in the 1880s, he temporarily turned himself into a Bowery outcast to get the "feel" of the situation he would write about.[25] His friend the painter Corwin K. Linson recalled the event.

> At the end of February [1894] there came a driving blizzard, and after a bitter night I found Steve in bed in the old League Building looking haggard and almost ill. All the others were out, getting ferocious appetites but little else. Pulling a manuscript from under his pillow, he tossed it to me and settled back under cover to watch. It was that bread-line classic, "The Men in the Storm," which Hamlin Garland had suggested for the Bacheller Syndicate. I wondered if these two real friends knew what it cost Steve in vital force to get that story; exposure in rags to that icy cold, standing in the pelting storm studying the men as they gathered in almost interminable succession—and no sleep until it was written.

When Linson asked him why he had not worn warmer clothing to protect himself from the blizzard he was able to describe so incisively, Crane snapped back characteristically, and perhaps self-righteously, "How would I know how those poor devils felt if I was warm myself?"[26]

The story projects its theme in its title: man's exposure to nature's violence. Only in retrospect, perhaps, does one realize that the title serves, in muted fashion, to imply a second theme of equal importance: man's exposure to the subtle violence measured out by society. It opens with a description of snow sweeping into the street. "The blizzard began to swirl great clouds of snow along the streets," he writes,

> sweeping it down from the roofs and up from the pavements until the faces of pedestrians tingled and burned as from a thousand needle-prickings. Those on the walks huddled their necks closely in the collars of their coats and went along stooping like a race of aged people. The drivers of vehicles hurried their horses furiously on their way. They were

25. Michael Robertson notes that "Joseph Pulitzer's *World*, New York City's largest newpaper in 1894, included at least one experiment in virtually every Sunday newspaper during the months before Crane published his two experiments." Crane's contribution to "this well-worn genre," following his "Men in the Storm" piece, was in pairing complementary pieces: "An Experiment in Misery" and "An Experiment in Luxury" (*Stephen Crane, Journalism and the Making of Modern American Literature* [New York: Columbia University Press, 1997], 95–96).

26. Corwin K. Linson, *My Stephen Crane*, ed. Edwin H. Cady (Syracuse: Syracuse University Press, 1958), 58.

made more cruel by the exposure of their positions, aloft on high seats. The street cars, bound up-town, went slowly, the horses slipping and straining in the spongy brown mass that lay between the rails. The drivers, muffled to the eyes, stood erect and facing the wind, models of grim philosophy.[27]

On this day all men are at the mercy of the storm. But personal situations within society vary greatly, and that fact suggests that as individuals men are less than equal in their vulnerability to natural violence. Those whose poverty renders them most vulnerable drift together solipsistically on a darkening side street. As they wait, the pathos of their being outcasts spirals toward tragedy. The hours pass, without even the glimmer of an internal light to dispel their unspeakable fear that the doors will never open. By turns, the men huddle like animals trying to keep warm, and then, despairing, "surged heavily against the building in a powerful wave of pushing shoulders." Crane details the psychology of a swelling mob of beaten and confused men: their personal and collective ambiguity; a herd behavior that is stuttering, unsure, and abortive. Anticlimactically, after long exposure, the men are released from the grip of the storm. As each one approaches the open door, all vexation melts away from his face.

In this sense "The Men in the Storm" makes the simple and time-worn point that those human beings who "have not" differ ipso facto, at least within the reaches of society, from those who "have." To call attention to this discrepancy, hitherto implicit, Crane resorts to a symbol. The symbolic "affluence" of the individual looking out at the huddling unemployed from the window of a "*dry*-goods" (emphasis added) store was all too apparent to Crane's readers. The cut of his beard alone, causing him to look like the royal wastrel of fin de siècle England, the Prince of Wales, was enough to damn him. Nevertheless, the explicit cry of the Bowery outcasts is not for an equitable share of wealth or even for a fair share of necessities; it asks only for relief from the white swirl of the blizzard. As Crane distinguishes, the men ask not to be taken *into* the shelter but only to be let *out* of the storm.

If these men are socially and economically exploited, however, it follows as well from Crane's more comprehensive point of view that their sheepish bewilderment has a cause that goes beyond that immediate human exploitation. Accessibility to shelter is a social and economic matter, to be sure; but the storm itself is natural and, in a different sense, metaphysical. "In this half-darkness," writes Crane, in a passage that moves from one explanation to the other,

the men began to come from their shelter places and mass in front of the doors of charity. They were of all types, but the nationalities were mostly

27. Stephen Crane, "The Men in the Storm," in *Tales, Sketches, and Reports*, 315–22.

American, German and Irish. Many were strong, healthy, clear-skinned fellows with that stamp of countenance which is not frequently seen upon seekers after charity. There were men of undoubted patience, industry and temperance, who in time of ill-fortune, do not habitually turn to rail at the state of society, snarling at the arrogance of the rich and bemoaning the cowardice of the poor, but who at these times are apt to wear a sudden and singular meekness, as if they saw the world's progress marching from them and were trying to perceive where they had failed, what they lacked, to be thus vanquished in the race.

Almost in passing Crane slips in the notion that contrary to what the temperance worker may think these men are not drunkards. They are men of "temperance." The clue to their plight lies in the last words of the quoted passage—"vanquished in the race." Echoing the Old Testament, they weld this passage to a later paragraph, which Crane begins: "The crushing of the crowd grew terrific toward the last. The men, in keen pain from the blasts, began almost to fight. With the pitiless whirl of snow upon them, the *battle* for shelter was *going to the strong*" (emphasis added). In the spirit of the Methodism in which he was raised (but, contradictorily, not that of the temperance movement), Crane alludes to the Book of Ecclesiastes. "The race is not to the swift, nor the battle to the strong," warns the Preacher. "Neither yet bread to the wise, nor yet riches to men of understanding, nor yet favour to men of skill," he adds, "but time and chance happeneth to them all." With example after example, the Preacher nails down his definition of human experience, but he ends, surprisingly, with consolation for the poor: "The sleep of the labouring man is sweet, whether he eat little or much: but the abundance of the rich will not suffer him to sleep." Crane scorns such attempts at placation. His Prince of Wales figure in the shop window exudes not insomnia but comfort. Indeed, the very sight of the men outside, the author tells us, "operated inversely, and enabled him to more clearly regard his own environment, delightful relatively." As for the "labouring" poor, they are lulled into remaining impassive, continuing to fix dull eyes upon the windows of the haven that remains closed to them. The Preacher notwithstanding, the race within society does indeed go to the swift and the battle to the strong. "Theologians had for a long time told the poor man that riches did not bring happiness," wrote Crane on another occasion, "and they had solemnly repeated this phrase until it had come to mean that misery was commensurate with dollars, that each wealthy man was inwardly a miserable wretch." And whenever "a wail of despair or rage had come from the night of the slums they had stuffed this epigram down the throat of he who cried out and told him that he was a lucky fellow."[28]

28. Stephen Crane, "An Experiment in Luxury," in *Tales, Sketches, and Reports*, 293–301. This companion piece to "An Experiment in Misery" is less than effective because Crane obviously could not conduct the kind of experiment among the rich that could make him feel convincingly like one of them.

Above all, however, "The Men in the Storm" conveys Crane's conviction that the nature of human experience is antinomic. He focuses on the difficulties inherent in a world in which social and economic responsibility exists in the face of a philosophic naturalism that denies the relevance of that responsibility. Every man's fate, as Crane sees it, is to be a social animal and at the same moment, almost incomprehensibly, a naturalistic being totally at loose in the universe. That is, Crane sees humanity as locked into participating in two incompatible environments. In the one, man's social milieu, he is responsible for his every move; in the other, the naturalistic-cosmic, he is determined and hence without responsibility for his behavior. The men in the storm are dual victims, of society and of nature. Crane at one and the same moment both agrees and disagrees with the boy's old friend in "An Experiment in Luxury" that "nobody is responsible for anything."[29]

Crane began his career as a student of natural and social violence, and he remained a student of the varieties of violence to the last. In "The Men in the Storm," however, it was not the public violence of warfare that concerned him, nor was it primarily the snarled impersonal violence fostered by the ways of American society. Crane's experience in working the "bread-lines" caused him to qualify his view that society was man's principal, bedrock assailant. Blowing wind and deadening cold, with men rocking together quietly in the snow-laden air, turned out to be something more than ready-made symbols for a piece of straight social commentary or, even, temperance rhetoric. Rather, they revealed to the author that there was somehow an affinity between man's two assailants: nature and society.

The "young man" of "An Experiment in Misery," a sketch first published in the New York Press in 1892, is Crane as young reporter. His mission is to report on his experience impersonating a homeless down-and-outer in New York City. "In the sudden descent in style of the dress of the crowd he felt relief, and as if he were at last in his own country." He attaches himself to a man he calls only the "assassin." For giving him three of the seven cents it takes to get a bed for the night, the young man is led by the "assassin" to a flophouse where they stay the night. The next morning, when the assassin claims, "th' on'y thing I really needs is a ball"—"Me t'roat feels like a fryin' pan," he complains—the young man stakes him, for three cents, to a breakfast consisting of a bowl of coffee and a roll.[30]

The young man defines inadvertently his difficulty as a writer. On his leather-covered cot "cold as melting snow," he "lay[s] carving biographies for these men from his meager experience." It's a metaphor for the overall difficulty Crane faced as a young writer trying to write first about New York slum

---

29. For a reading of the "explicit" theme of "class struggle" in "An Experiment in Luxury," see Robertson, *Stephen Crane*, 192–93.

30. Stephen Crane, "An Experiment in Misery," in *Tales, Sketches, and Reports*, 283–93.

life and then about fighting and military life during the American Civil War. Committed to writing out of experience, he nevertheless could not and would not put off his writing until he had had that experience.

In this one-night experiment Crane underwent initiation to the vicissitudes that provided him with ample substance for his piece in the *New York Press.* This experience would also come in handy for later work, sometimes in surprising ways. At the flophouse, for instance, within the reach of his hand lay one poor wretch, "with yellow breast and shoulders bare to the cold drafts. One arm hung over the side of the cot and the fingers lay full length upon the wet cement floor of the room. Beneath the inky brows could be seen the eyes of the man exposed by the partly-opened lids. To the youth it seemed that he and this corpse-like being were exchanging a prolonged stare and that theother threatened with his eyes. He drew back, watching his neighbor from the shadows of his blanket edge. The man did not move once through the night, but lay in this stillness as of death, like a body stretched out, expectant of the surgeon's knife." The confrontation between two bodies—one alive and the other "dead"—would resonate, with descriptive hints from scenes of drunkards from temperance literature, in the famous corpse-in-the-glen scene of *The Red Badge of Courage.*

Indeed, it was precisely a "literary" experience of the intemperate down-and-outer that Crane took with him into the streets. Once there, however, he soon learned things that were lacking in his temperance readings—that, for instance, this underworld is redolent with stink. It everywhere assails his nostrils with "strange and unspeakable odors" that attack him "like malignant diseases with wings." "Exhalations" come at him "from a hundred pairs of reeking lips." One saloon entrance itself is a devouring maw. "A saloon stood with a voracious air on a corner. A sign leaning against the front of the doorpost announced: 'Free hot soup to-night.' The swing doors snapping to and fro like ravenous lips, made gratified smacks as the saloon gorged itself with plump men, eating with astounding and endless appetite, smiling in some indescribable manner as the men came from all directions like sacrifices to a heathenish superstition." Within, the saloon offers its free lunch, which might well be, as was the custom, "usually well salted to inspire drinking," with the saloon "bouncer" "generally on hand to discourage hearty appetites."[31]

On a substratum of observed details, Crane builds a surrealistic superstructure that reeks with the kind of overheated judgment natural to temperance writing. The saloon is the incarnation of evil and temptation. "Caught by the delectable sign, the young man allowed himself to be swallowed." Even the beer the bartender draws for him is surrealistically threatening. "A bartender

31. Mark Edward Lender and James Kirby Martin, *Drinking in America: A History* (New York: Free Press/London: Collier Macmillan, 1982), 104.

placed a schooner of dark and portentous beer on the bar. Its monumental form upreared until the froth a-top was above the crown of the young man's brown derby."[32] The saloon overwhelms him, the very foam on the schooner of beer threatens to engulf him. One would think it a stretch to link these images with Crane's later poem "A man adrift on a slim spar," if Crane did not end "An Experiment in Misery" in this intriguing way. "He confessed himself an outcast, and his eyes from under the lowered rim of his hat began to glance guiltily, wearing the criminal expression that comes with certain convictions." Outcast, rim, hat, guilt, drink, froth (from the earlier passage), and (a Crane standby) assassin—all are echoed or somehow reflected in the poem, the first and penultimate stanzas of which read:

> A man adrift on a slim spar
> A horizon smaller than the rim of a bottle
> Tented waves rearing lashy dark points
> The near whine of froth in circles.
> > God is cold.
> . . . .
> A horizon smaller than a doomed assassin's cap,
> Inky, surging tumults
> A reeling, drunken sky and no sky
> A pale hand sliding from a polished spar.
> > God is cold.[33]

The young reporter's one-day experiment in the Bowery had taught him—before the fact—what it must be like to drown, a castaway, at sea.

If the eventful years that followed the publication of "The Men in the Storm" and "An Experiment in Misery" brought their own tests and confirmations, the young Stephen Crane, as we have seen, was already in the early 1890s a formidable interpreter of the way it was with man in society and nature. The messages of the castaway in the New York blizzard and the seven-cent flophouse bed Crane would rediscover anew in the sea around an open boat and, with a howling violence, in the snow swirling around a saloon on the Great Plains.

---

32. Compare this passage with the one describing the child Jimmie as he reaches up to get the pail of beer at the saloon: "Straining up on his toes he raised the pail and pennies as high as his arms would let him. He saw two hands thrust down and take them. Directly the same hands let down the filled pail and he left" (Stephen Crane, *Maggie: A Girl of the Streets (A Story of New York)* [1893], Norton Critical Edition, ed. Thomas A. Gullason [New York: Norton, 1979], 10).

33. Stephen Crane, "A man adrift on a slim spar," in *Poems and Literary Remains*, Volume X of *The University of Virginia Edition of the Works of Stephen Crane*, ed. Fredson Bowers, intr. James B. Colvert (Charlottesville: University Press of Virginia, 1975), 83.

3

Transcendental Histrionics

[We] do not forget that all homes have not a Christian mother to be the priestess of their altar fires. Alas, some women are intemperate, and many women need missionary work done in their own hearts; many children are orphaned or worse than motherless.

—Frances E. Willard, *Woman and Temperance* (1883)

Last Christmas they gave me a sweater,
  And a nice warm suit of wool,
But I'd rather be cold and have a dog,
  To watch when I come from school.

—Stephen Crane, "I'd Rather Have" (*ca.* 1879–80)

Listen my children and you shall hear
Of the midnight ride of a pail of beer.

—Folk rhyme (1890s)

1

Crane's early story "A Dark Brown Dog" was not published during his life-time. It appeared posthumously in *Cosmopolitan* in 1901 and was first collected in book form in 1921 when Vincent Starrett included it in *Men, Women and Boats,* a volume in Boni and Liveright's Modern Library. The story has been aptly called a study in "the formation of the slum sensibility."[1]

Among Crane's critics, the story has been most admired by John Berryman

---

1. Milne Holton, *Cylinder of Vision: The Fiction and Journalistic Writing of Stephen Crane* (Baton Rouge: Louisiana State University Press, 1972), 65 n.

and Patrick K. Dooley. "One of the perfectly imagined American stories," writes Berryman, it is a study of "the relation of tyranny and adoration."[2] Dooley sees the story as evidence of Crane's "distinctive" and "exceptional" ability "to empathize with non-human hopes, desires, pains, and pleasures." "The reader is persuasively initiated into the dog's consciousness," he continues, "including canine nightmares."[3]

Berryman's account of what takes place in "A Dark Brown Dog" conveys a sense of his unique insight into Crane's imagination. He begins by quoting from the story:

> A child was standing on a street-corner. He leaned with one shoulder against a high board fence and swayed the other to and fro, the while kicking carelessly at the gravel. . . . After a time, a little dark brown dog came trotting with an intent air down the sidewalk. . . . In an apologetic manner the dog came close, and the two had an interchange of friendly pattings and waggles. The dog became more enthusiastic with each moment of the interview, until with his gleeful caperings he threatened to overturn the child. Whereupon the child lifted his hand and struck the dog a blow upon the head. This thing seemed to overpower and astonish the little dark brown dog, and wounded him to the heart. He sank down in despair at the child's feet.

Berryman then summarizes—"He follows the baby home and enters the family, where he suffers Eastern sufferings, until the child learns to protect him when he can," followed by further quotation: "So the dog prospered. He developed a large bark, which came wondrously from such a small rug of a dog. . . . The scene of their companionship was a kingdom governed by this terrible potentate, the child; but neither criticism nor rebellion ever lived for an instant in the heart of the one subject. Down in the mystic, hidden fields of his little dog-soul bloomed flowers of love and fidelity and perfect faith." "One day the father comes home drunk," Berryman briefly resumes his summary, "and the child dives under the table." Then more quotation:

> [The dog] looked with interested eyes at his friend's sudden dive. He interpreted it to mean: Joyous gambol. He started to patter across the floor to join him. He was the picture of a little dark brown dog en route to a friend. The head of the family saw him at this moment. He gave a huge howl of joy, and knocked the dog down with a heavy coffee-pot. The

---

2. John Berryman, *Stephen Crane* (New York: William Sloane, 1950), 69.

3. Patrick K. Dooley, *The Pluralistic Philosophy of Stephen Crane* (Urbana and Chicago: University of Illinois Press, 1993), 81.

dog, yelling in supreme astonishment and fear, writhed to his feet and ran for cover. The man kicked out with a ponderous foot, [strikes him again with the pot, and flings him] with great accuracy through the window. The soaring dog created a surprise in the block. . . . [And it takes the child a long time to reach the alley,] because his size compelled him to go downstairs backward, one step at a time, and holding with both hands to the step above.[4]

Alert to elements of parody in Crane's work, Eric Solomon nevertheless finds none in "A Dark Brown Dog." Here he finds that "Crane's humor totally desert[s] him, and this story of a child and his dog does try to jerk tears."[5] But Crane's parody manifests itself in different ways, and it may have several targets.

Crane's story is revisionist. In "A Dark Brown Dog" he has "reworked" stereotypical texts he had encountered elsewhere. Note, first, that the death of the child's dog results immediately from the father's drunkenness. Temperance readers and manuals are replete with stories in which a father's alcoholism leads to death—not only of pets but, commonly, of children.[6] More often than not, the death of a daughter or son will lead the father to deep remorse and redemption simply by his forsaking spirits for clear, cold water.

"The Wine-Cup," frequently anthologized in textbooks, brought the temperance message home to schoolchildren. A prince—about whom it was said, "show him a wine-cup, he would soon lay down his scepter"—ignores his old teacher's imploring words to stop wasting his life "among this drunken crew." When the wise man cautions him—"Remember what the oracles have said: / 'What most he loves who rules this Cretan land, / Shall perish by the wine-cup in his hand' "—the prince answers violently:

> "Prophet of ill! no more, or you shall die.
> See how my deeds shall give your words the lie,
> And baffle fate, and with all who hate me—so!"
> Sheer through the casement, to the court below,
> He dashed the half-drained goblet in disdain,
> That scattered as it flew a bloody rain.
> His courtiers laughed.
>   But now a woman's shriek

---

4. Berryman, *Stephen Crane*, 69–70.

5. Eric Solomon, *Stephen Crane: From Parody to Realism* (Cambridge, Mass.: Harvard University Press, 1966), 48.

6. It was also a staple of what today might be called crossover fiction such as T. S. Arthur's *Ten Nights in a Barroom and What I Saw There* and Walt Whitman's *Franklin Evans; or, The Inebriate: A Tale of the Times*, as well as temperance songs such as "I Have Drank My Last Glass" and "Oh, Let Me In" in *Temperance Battle Songs!*, comp. S. W. Straub (Chicago: S. W. Straub, 1883), 50–51, 56–58.

Rose terrible without, and blanched his cheek.
He hurried to the casement in affright,
And lo! his eyes were blasted with a sight
Too pitiful to think of. Death was there,
And wringing hands, and madness, and despair.
There stood a nurse, and on her bosom lay
A dying child, whose life-blood streamed away,
Reddening its robe like wine! It was his own,
His son, the prince that should have filled the throne
When he was dead, and ruled the Cretan land,—
Slain by the wine-cup from his father's hand![7]

All the necessary and (fictionally) sufficient circumstances for the drunkard's redemption are here. In Crane's story, however, there is no sign of imminent personal redemption. Indeed, the father's drinking is part of the child's slum environment; and to most of the people in this environment the death of this dog, it can be safely inferred, offers no cause for real concern. The mode of its death—the dog's careening down through the skies—is a different matter. It attracts public attention and bemusement.

But it is not merely this and other redemptive temperance texts that lie behind "A Dark Brown Dog." The same school readers that presented "The Wine-Cup" also presented "Only a Dog," headnoted as "one of the most touching *true* 'dog stories' ever told." "It was a case of love at first sight," begins the narrative. "He was a beautiful shepherd dog, of no breed that I have ever encountered either before or since. His color was buff, shading to white underneath, and set off by two long pointed collars of dark-gray hair upon his shoulders." The dog's face, his "crowning glory," was the "the most esthetic shade of 'old gold,'" and was set off by a black nose-tip, two little black eyebrows, a pair of sensitive and inquisitive yellow ears, and the most human, intelligent, loving brown eyes." When she first saw him, his face was "lighted up with a smile of joy at seeing a party of friendly people approaching him"; and when she called him, he "came bounding across the field, with his plumy tail waving, his brown eyes shining, and such an expression of good-will to men, that then and there the conquest was made, and I became his abject slave and adorer." The author successfully negotiates for the dog, and within a week the dog fully understands he is the little girl's "exclusive property." Although "he accepted the rest of the family as near and dear relations, he never for one moment doubted in his loyal little heart to whom he owed the most devoted love and

7. Stoddard, "The Wine-Cup," in *Swinton's Fifth Reader and Speaker* (New York and Chicago: Ivison, Blakeman, 1883), 404–8. As "The Cup-Bearer," the story appears in *The Juvenile Temperance Reciter* (New York: National Temperance Society and Publication House, 1880), 53–55.

allegiance." He followed his young mistress from room to room about the house, accompanied her in her walks, slept in her room at night, and "was never for one moment separated from" her by "any act of his own will." The dog has an honored place in the household. He was "so obedient and sympathetic, that all, from the aged father whose silver hairs were indeed 'a crown of glory,' to the youngest grandchild who visited the parental home, regarded him as a true and faithful friend and a beloved companion."

The rest of the narrative tells how the dog pays special attention to the father in the father's illness and then how the father reciprocates by attending to the dog when it falls mortally ill. The narrator remembers how one afternoon her father "came down to shake hands with the little patient, and to speak a word of sympathy to him." The dog "looked up at him with love shining from his dimmed eyes, and gave his little feeble paw, and wagged his bushy tail with unusual vigor. It was their last meeting." The father dies that very night, and two days later—"when amid the grief of the whole city, and the tolling bells, and weeping heavens, we committed to earth all that was earthly of one of God's saints"—the dog died.[8]

If one wished to do so, it would be possible to demonstrate that Crane's story can be used to "answer" this "true story"—almost point by point by contrast and reversal—except for the dog's natural character, its friendliness, devotion, and loyalty to human beings. Whereas the author of "Only a Dog" sees nothing but human kindness and constant consideration toward the animal, Crane sees a substantial pattern of cruelty and violence—emanating directly from the child who "possesses" him but obviously reflecting the general cruelty of the family and social environment that has shaped him. All that shines golden in the girl's narrative turns dark brown in Crane's story.

Such textbook stories—epitomizing the subgenres of the inspiring dog story and of the cautionary temperance tale—contributed to Crane's own imagining of the reality of life in the New York slums. In this respect "A Dark Brown Dog" can be considered something of a trial run at depicting and judging the full-blown Bowery world of Maggie Johnson and the rest of her family.

2

Crane's readers have sometimes been puzzled by what they have considered to be his failure to provide explicit details surrounding Maggie Johnson's last appearance in the flesh on the night she walks down to the East River (chapter 17). The question usually posed is whether Maggie's death is a suicide or a murder. The appearance of the "chuckling and leering" man who follows

8. Alice Bacon, "Only a Dog," in *Swinton's Fifth Reader,* 79–87.

Maggie down to the river in the first edition of *Maggie* (published at Crane's expense in 1893) offers one kind of circumstantial evidence. Crane's description of the strange man could have come right out of the pages of a temperance reader describing a dissipated drunkard—"blear-eyed, bloated, sensual," old before his time.[9] "When almost to the river the girl [Maggie] saw a great figure. On going forward she perceived it to be a huge fat man in torn and greasy garments. His grey hair straggled down over his forehead. His small, bleared eyes, sparkling from amidst great rolls of red fat, swept eagerly over the girl's upturned face. He laughed, his brown, disordered teeth gleaming under a grey, grizzled moustache from which beer-drops dripped. His whole body gently quivered and shook like that of a dead jelly fish. Chuckling and leering, he followed the girl of the crimson legions."[10] Crane does not tell us whether this huge, fat man, described so as to inspire disgust in the reader, is to be the prostitute Maggie's final john, her last would-be or actual customer. Is he her murderer or just a voyeur who stalks her? Does his presence have anything to do with her suicide? Or is he merely a witness to that suicide?

Crane's decision to drop this figure when the book was reissued by a commercial press three years after its first appearance largely takes away any clear indication that Maggie was murdered—at least on the night described in chapter 17. In the 1896 edition she moves steadily toward the dark waters of the river and, so far as the reader can tell, in the final moments of the chapter is very much alone. Indeed, she has been rejected by a series of men as she moves toward the river—and, quite possibly, suicide. If she does commit suicide out of despair, does it not make more sense—poetic or fictional—to have her do so out of a sense of abandonment by her family, by her friend Pete, and by society at large reflected in her conscious solitariness at the end? But there might also have been a certain theatrical necessity for the drunken follower in the first place, one that became unnecessary to Crane's slightly changed intentions for his work when it was reissued by Appleton in 1896.

There might be still another reason for Crane's decision to drop Maggie's "chuckling and leering" follower. He might well have learned of the existence of just such a "watcher" on one of the East River piers. This "watcher"—not a murderer but a good Samaritan—was the subject of a Sunday journal feature,

9. John B. Gough, "Who Did It?" in *Readings and Recitations, No. 3*, ed. L[izzie] Penney (New York: National Temperance Society and Publication House, 1879), 74. See also Charles Mackay, "The Dream of the Reveler," in *Readings and Recitations, No. 3*, 38.

10. Stephen Crane, *Maggie: A Girl of the Streets (A Story of New York)* (1893), Norton Critical Edition, ed. Thomas A. Gullason (New York and London: Norton, 1979), 1–58. This text is to be preferred, in my opinion, to the eclectic text (a combination of the 1893 and the revised 1896 versions) that is constructed by the textual editor of *Bowery Tales*, Volume I of *The University of Virginia Edition of the Works of Stephen Crane*, ed. Fredson Bowers, intr. James B. Colvert (Charlottesville: University Press of Virginia, 1969).

shortly after *Maggie*'s first appearance and within two years of the Appleton edition. The *New York Recorder* in November 1894 published a story with this headline: "PIER OF THE SUICIDES / Three Hundred Have Sought to Use It as the Stepping-Off Place to Oblivion / AT THE FOOT OF MISERY STREET / Or rather Cherry, Which Is Synonymous—A Man with Broken Legs Who Had a Passion for Life-saving and Who Has Prevented Many from Suicide at This Pier."[11] "THE PIER of the suicides!" is "right in the centre of the busy whirl of commerce."

Statistics show that drowning is the favorite method employed by suicides, and the reports prove that in this city Pier 55, East River, leads all other places in its number of attempted suicides. This pier adjoins the Grand Street Ferry on the south, and it is perhaps especially fitting that it should be at the end of old Cherry street, which from end to end has more misery in it than any other street in the city. Grand and Cherry streets practically unite at the river front. There is a great stream of travelers over the Grand Street Ferry from early morning until late at night, and the discontented ones seem to gravitate naturally to Pier 55 to seek relief from their troubles. . . . The water which sweeps around Corlears Hook, just below the pier, is always rough, and its very appearance is so dark and forbidding that it seems as if it must destroy all the notion of peace and rest which the suicide seeks in exchange for misery and trouble. But conditions probably are looked at differently by those who wish to die.

The statistics for the past ten years show that three hundred persons have "gone to this pier bent on suicide," 90 percent of them going at night, with the "midnight hour" being the "favorite time." Yet how many people have actually killed themselves "by jumping into the river from this pier only the silent waters which give up their dead from time to time can tell," for "the tide runs so swiftly that a person jumping from the pier would be carried far away in a short time, and few bodies have been found near by." Yet even the "known death record has been comparatively small," it is boasted, owing to the "alertness and watchfulness" of a "life-saver" who spends "most of his time" watching from "a little shanty at the entrance of the pier, which at one time was a sort of oyster saloon." "Saving human lives amounts to a passion with him, and for many years, at any time of the day or night, in Winter or Summer, he has always

11. Anonymous, "PIER OF THE SUICIDES / Three Hundred Have Sought to Use It as the Stepping-Off Place to Oblivion / AT THE FOOT OF MISERY STREET / Or rather Cherry, Which Is Synonymous—A Man with Broken Legs Who Had a Passion for Life-saving and Who Has Prevented Many from Suicide at This Pier," *New York Recorder* (Nov. 11, 1894), 14.

been ready to risk his own life to save others." This lifesaving Samaritan admits that he "can't help saving lives" any more than he "can stop eating," and he supposes that someday he will lose his "life trying to help some poor fellow." "I'm always on the watch on the pier, and I can pick out a suicide at a glance," he says. "I can see them going down the pier from my shanty in the bright light, and I go after them and turn them away. I've taken over 200 people off the pier who would have jumped into the river, and I've heard some very pitiful stories from their lips to show that they had nothing to live for."

If Crane's *Maggie* did not have precedence, having been published for the first time in 1893, one might be tempted to see the *Recorder's* piece on the vigorous lifesaving work going on at the "pier of the suicides" as a source for the chapter detailing Maggie's last night. One imagines Crane weighing the irony inherent in the one-sided celebration of those who would frustrate the determined suicide from enacting her "final" desire for death and then deliberately transforming the good Samaritan of the pier at Cherry Street, ever vigilant for signs betraying the intentions of those bent on suicide, into the leering, abetting voyeur who chuckles at Maggie as she walks down to the river. It was not within Crane's idea of the prevailing reality of the city as he saw it to write a story extolling the virtues of any lifesaving vigilantes. He was simply not interested in contributing to what he would have found to be the distortions—moral and social—of such uplifting journalism.

But in looking at the fate of Maggie and of the Johnson family overall, Crane was not able, finally, to keep to his notions of a realism that depended on what he saw. As he was not sufficiently aware himself, that peculiar, personal vision he so much counted on to keep him to the literary realism he so much admired was itself colored by his deeply moralistic upbringing. Who was this Maggie, this flower that "blossomed in a mud puddle" but a creature out of the temperance tracts and readers that Stephen's own mother, herself an avid and highly placed worker for the WCTU and a friend of Frances E. Willard, brought into the Crane household during her youngest child's most impressionable years? No one has suggested a close biographical source for Maggie (or for anyone in the Johnson family). And no wonder. Maggie's true source was not the streets and the slum tenements of New York but the pages of books. In the 1950s Marcus Cunliffe offered numerous possibilities—including the Reverend Thomas De Witt Talmage's earnest books and Charles Loring Brace's portentous *The Dangerous Classes of New York*.[12] To these suggestions later scholars have added Jacob Riis's *The Children of the Poor and How the Other Half Lives,* as well as work in Benjamin Orange Flower's journal, the *Arena*.[13] Missing in this mix is the temperance reader.

12. Marcus Cunliffe, "Stephen Crane and the American Background of *Maggie*," *American Quarterly*, 7 (Spring 1955), 35–44.

13. Much of this material is reproduced in Gullason's Norton Critical Edition of *Maggie*.

What such readers provided Crane that other books dealing with the social conditions of the poor did not was their mode as practical handbooks for performance. They advocate theatricality by encouraging recitation and acting. These collections provide texts tailored in length and style for use at meetings. Sermons, speeches, narratives, and poems are simply scripts for the temperance workers' theater of reform. Each temperance meeting offers an opportunity for performance; every gathering hall is potentially a stage. It is a safe bet that the temperance meeting gave the young Crane some of his earliest experiences of "theater."

The suggestion that Crane's early encounters with the rhetorical appeals of temperance recitations shaped his vision of New York slum reality does not imply that Crane espoused either the stated values of the temperance workers or their hopeful view that some sort of millennia would play out first in the lives of individual drunkards and their families and then in the society at large. What is more likely is that the young literary realist—ironic and skeptical though he was—adopted the temperance workers' familiar paradigms, twisting and turning them so as to accommodate his view of reality without always seeing how the mediation of those paradigms and that rhetoric also worked to shape (and occasionally limit) his ability to see the reality around him. Annie Herbert's poem "Mulligan's Gospel" is a case in point:

> I've a rare bit of news for you, Mary Malone,
> And truth, 'tis strangest that ever was known;
> You remember I told you, a twelvemonth ago,
> How a soul came from heaven to Poverty Row?
> If an angel had troubled the waters that bore
> Such little white craft to our turbulent shore,
> No mortal could tell—but that innocent child,
> Like a dove without wings nestling down and tender,
> With eyes veiling pictures of Paradise splendor,
> Came into the tenement crazy and evil,
> And the hard life so pitiless, rough, and defiled,
>   Over to Mulligan's.

> It is strange to our eyes, but perhaps you have seen
> A vine clasp its tendrils of delicate green
> Round a desolate rock, or a lily grow white
> With its root in the tarn and its face in the light
> Or when night and the storm wrapt the sky in a shroud,
> A star shaken out from the fold of a cloud?
> So this little one came, but it never seemed right,
> There were children enough, heaven knows! in that Babel

34

Cadets for the Tombs from the bold whisky rabble,
Choked out from the love that is heaven's own light,
Rank weeds of the soil, cropping out for a fight,
     Over to Mulligan's.

There was many a banquet in Mulligan Hall,
When the revelers feasted on nothing at all,
And a king at the board giving knighthood of pains,
And orders of crosses and clanking of chains.
Tim held as a law the most perfect in life
The strong tie that bound him to Nora, his wife;
But blinded by drink, when his passion ran high,
He beat her, of course, with a fury inhuman,
And she such a poor, patient, bit of a woman;
Well for her, a soft voice answered low to her cries,
And her sun never set in the baby's blue eyes,
     Over to Mulligan's.

It was twelve months or more from the time she was
    born,
As I sat at my window one sunshiny morn,
"Just come over," the voice of Tim Mulligan said;
"I belave in me sowl that me baby is dead!"
He had held a wild revel late into the night,
And the wee frightened dove plumed her pinions for
    flight.
This the man saw at last, with a sudden dismay,
"God forgive me," he cried, "sure she'd niver be
    stayin'
Wid the cursin' and drink whin me lips shud be
    prayin','"
And the priest came and went, little dreaming that day
How the priesthood of angels was winning its way,
     Over to Mulligan's.

Then the sweetest, the saddest, the tenderest sight,
Lay the child like a fair sculptured vision of light,
Hands clasped over daisies, fringed lids over tears,
That never would fall through life's sorrowful years.
"Ah, mavourneen!" moaned Tim, "it's foriver I'll think
That the saints took yez home from the demon of drink;
And mayhap"—here he shivered decanter and bowl,

"She will see me up there wid the mother of Jesus,
And sind down the grace that from sin iver frees us."
So the leaven that spread from one beautiful soul,
Through that turmoil of misery leavened the whole,
    Over to Mulligan's.

Now a thing the most wonderful, Mary Malone,
And truth, 'tis the strangest that ever was known;
Mr. Mulligan met me to-day on the street,
And he looks like a man, from his head to his feet.
Though his clothes are but coarse, they are comely and
    trim
And no man dares to say, "Here's a health to ye, Tim."
He will soon rent a cottage, and live like the best;
And the gossips do say with wise lifting of fingers,
It is all for sweet charity's sake that he lingers
In the Row where God's peace settled down in his
    breast,
When a soft weary wing fluttered home from the rest,
    Over to Mulligan's.[14]

The somewhat generic situation depicted in this poem is echoed in *Maggie*. Its image of the baby anticipates Crane. If Maggie, unlike the baby in the poem, survives to adulthood, her younger brother Tommie, like the baby in the poem, does not. In the poem, the dead child lay "like a fair sculptured vision of light, / Hands clasped over daisies . . ."—a scene replicated ironically in *Maggie*. While the poem's baby is sweet, sad, and tender, *Maggie*'s Tommie, hardly angelic, is described as a "red, bawling infant." Yet, he too "went away in a white, insignificant coffin, his small waxen hand clutching a flower that the girl, Maggie, had stolen from an Italian." The poem's babe was like "a vine [that] clasp[s] its tendrils of delicate green / Round a desolate rock, or a lily grown white / With its root in the tarn and its face in the light"; while, in Crane's novella, it is Maggie, who "blossomed in a mud puddle," growing up "to be a most rare and wonderful production of a tenement district, a pretty girl." The engine of existence "over to Mulligan's" is reveling and drinking, times when, "blinded by drink," Mulligan's "passion ran high," and he beat his wife, "of course, with a fury inhuman, / And she such a poor, patient, bit of a woman." Crane transforms that hint into the drunken brawls of the Johnsons in which Maggie's father and mother smash furniture and batter each other. It

14. Annie Herbert, "Mulligan's Gospel," in *Readings and Recitations, No. 2*, ed. L[izzie] Penney (New York: National Temperance Society and Publication House, 1878), 40–42.

is as if Crane subscribes to the temperance generalization that "it aint a bit wickeder for a woman than for a man; but 'twould seem worse to have our mothers drunk, than it does to have our fathers."[15] A piece entitled "The Destroyer" restates the argument: "If a man is made in the image of God's intellect, a woman is made in the image of God's heart. A tender woman is tenderest to her child. Is there anything that can unmother a woman, that can pluck the maternal heart out of her, and put in its place something that is powerful and fiendish? Is there any other agent on earth, or even in the world of the damned, that can so transform a mother's heart into something for which thought itself can not find similitude? Satan himself can not do it; but rum can."[16] There can be no mistaking the irony with which Crane, in the final chapter, evokes the factitious compassion for Maggie expressed by her mother. Eating away "like a fat monk in a picture," she finishes her coffee before shedding her first sentimental tear at the news that her daughter is dead. Now she will "fergive her." Now she will condescend to send for Maggie's body for burial. Only after her daughter's death will the mother allow her prodigal daughter to come home. It will be recalled that when the brother Jimmie had attempted earlier to bring home the "fallen" Maggie, explaining that his desire had nothing to do with "dis prod'gal bus'ness anyway," the mother had responded, " 'It wasn't no prod'gal dauter, yeh damn fool. It was prod'gal son, anyhow.' " This exchange will remind readers of the New Testament (Luke 15:11–32), but to Crane's contemporaries it might as readily have recalled the popular temperance song "The Prodigal Girl."

> How oft do we sing of the prodigal son,
> Who has fallen in sin and disgrace,
> And plead with him gently to give up his ways.
> And to seek a kind father's face;

---

15. Mary Dwinell Chellis, "Polly's Temperance Speech," ibid., 13.

16. Rev. H. M. Scudder, "The Destroyer," in *Readings and Recitations, No. 1*, ed. L[izzie] Penney (New York: National Temperance Society and Publication House, 1877), 52–53. Drunken mothers are not as common in temperance literature as are drunken fathers, but one example is worth quoting.

How intoxicating drinks destroy the natural affection and change the once affectionate mother into a demon!

A minister was called on to visit a dying man. The wife was partially intoxicated, and expressed a fear that he was following her "poor girl." On further examination of the apartment the minister saw the corpse of a fine girl, whose hair had been closely cropped. Enquiring the reason, he was informed by the wretched mother that she had "sold the girl's hair for eighteenpence." A mother had actually stripped her daughter's corpse of the hair, and having sold it, spent the money in drink, and was evidently under the influence of liquor by the bedside of a dying husband (Rev. J. B. Wakeley, "The Cruel and Unnatural Mother," in *The American Temperance Cyclopædia of History, Biography, Anecdote, and Illustration* [New York: National Temperance Society and Publication House, 1875], 24–25).

How willing and ready we stand to forgive—
Tho' tainted with the world's mad whirl; But
Who stands with out-stretched arms to receive
An unfortunate prodigal girl?
    Rescue the prodigal girl,
    Some mother's unfortunate child;
    Go, save her to-day, and do not delay,
    But rescue the prodigal girl.

The second verse expresses sentiments close to Crane's, whose personal view of Maggie fits these lines to a T.

Why judge her so harshly, we know not the cause
Of her pitiful, wayward career,
Perhaps for the love and the trust of false friends,
She has paid the price so dear;
We know not the yearning of the spirit within—
Of the longings of a heart grown wild; Oh,
Waken the conscience of a sin-tossed soul,
And save the poor prodigal child.[17]

The news about Maggie's death is brought to the mother by Maggie's surviving brother, the "prodigal son" Jimmie. Even though in some ways Jimmie is the incarnation of his dead father's spirit—especially in his drunkenness—he has, in his bumbling way, felt concern for Maggie. Yet his own life gives truth to the widespread notion among temperance workers "that the lust for strong drink is hereditary." "But what father," asks one such worker, "has a right to bequeath such a legacy of damnation to his offspring?"[18] It was not for nothing that Crane's mother once chaired the WCTU's national committee on juvenile work.[19]

For it was one of Crane's intentions in *Maggie* to demonstrate that heredity was not everything, that environment counted for a great deal.[20] Frances E. Wil-

17. Emmet G. Coleman, "The Prodigal Girl," in *The Temperance Songbook: A Peerless Collection of Temperance Songs and Hymns for the Women's Christian Temperance Union, Loyal Temperance Legion, Prohibitionists, Temperance Praise Meetings, Medal Contests, etc.*, ed. Emmet G. Coleman (New York: American Heritage Press, 1971), 8–9.

18. T. L. Cuyler, "Boys—and the Bottle," in *Readings and Recitations, No. 2*, 19.

19. Anonymous, *A Brief History of the Woman's Christian Temperance Union*, 2nd ed. (Evanston: Union Signal, 1907), 14.

20. Consider June Howard's conclusion that *Maggie*, though "structured in part by progressive deterioration," is not "particularly concerned with heredity" (*Form and History in American Literary Naturalism* [Chapel Hill and London: University of North Carolina Press, 1985], 96).

lard, who on at least one occasion was a guest of the Cranes in Asbury Park,[21] cautioned in 1883 in *Woman and Temperance* that "the science of heredity" was "not enough," for "girls, equally with their brothers inheriting the taste for stimulants, seldom develop it; hence in the environment we must seek for farther explanation."[22] If in *Maggie* the son Jimmie seems to get his penchant for drink from his father and mother, the daughter Maggie is not so determined. Maggie demonstrates no inherited taste for alcohol. In several copies of the 1893 edition of *Maggie* (including Hamlin Garland's), Crane inscribed the message that his story "tries to show that environment is a tremend[ous] thing in the world and frequently shapes liv[es] regardless. If one proves that theory," he continues, "one makes room [in] Heaven for all sorts of souls, notably an occasional street girl, who are not confidently expected to be there by many excellent people."[23] His tale could be viewed as a "corrective" to his father's conservative position, so clearly echoed in his sermon against the notion of an all-embracing "determinism," that human beings are responsible for their own actions. "Every man, whether we choose to call him virtuous or vicious," argued the Reverend Crane, "is only one little wheel in the universal enginery, which is driven by blind, resistless, external force, unknown and unknowable."[24]

There is more than one story told in *Maggie*—the mother's, Jimmie's, and Pete's (the seducer who victimizes Maggie and is himself victimized by others), but the principal story remains, of course, the tragic one of the doomed girl who "blossomed in a mud puddle." Immediately after Pete has spurned her but before she—in Jimmie's terms (in the 1896 edition)—"go[es] on d' toif," Maggie in her confused wanderings comes upon "a stout gentleman in a silk hat and a chaste black coat, whose decorous row of buttons reached from his chin to his knees." Maggie "had heard of the Grace of God and she decided to approach this man. . . . But as the girl timidly accosted him, he gave a convulsive movement and saved his respectability by a vigorous side-step. He did not risk it to save a soul." To which, Crane adds wryly: "For how was he to know that there was a soul before him that needed saving?" Here Crane reflects the sentiments of temperance writing even more directly than is his wont because it suits his anticlerical bias. "It is easy enough to stand on the platform and make a speech," chided the Reverend T. De Witt Talmage, "but to go down where men are suffering and dying, and help to lift them up, that is the question. . . . Here is a man who has fallen into a ditch, and we come along with our best clothes on;

---

21. Stanley Wertheim and Paul Sorrentino, *The Crane Log: A Documentary Life of Stephen Crane, 1871–1900* (New York: G. K. Hall, 1994), 43.

22. Frances E. Willard, *Woman and Temperance; or, The Work and Workers of the Woman's Christian Temperance Union* (Hartford: Park Publishing, 1883), 237.

23. *The Correspondence of Stephen Crane*, ed. Stanley Wertheim and Paul Sorrentino (New York: Columbia University Press, 1988), I, 52, 53.

24. Quoted in Wertheim and Sorrentino, *Crane Log*, 20.

we look down at him and we say: 'Isn't it a pity? I wish I could help that man out. Get a pry; I wish I had on my other clothes'—when, if we had the Grace of God in our hearts, we would stoop right down and take him out. No, we must not soil our patent-leathers; we must look after our respectability; we must do everything relating to the Kingdom of God in the most elegant shape, or not do it at all." For the clergyman—Talmage's or Maggie's—it is the practical dictates of God's Grace that fall before the entrapping notions of social respectability. Talmage's message is clear: "We must get off our stilts as Christian ministers and Christian reformers, and walk side by side with men in the great and awful struggle of this life."[25] But the failure with Maggie (and prostitutes overall) goes further. As early as 1877 the WCTU had created a Committee for Work with Fallen Women (later renamed the Department for the Suppression of the Social Evil). The early program "allied its goals with gospel temperance, with saving the prostitute from her life of sin by converting her to evangelical Christianity and teetotalism."[26] No help there for the likes of Maggie Johnson.

But how "realistic" was Crane's imagined parable about Maggie, that pearl of great price that is lost in the demi-world of New York and whose life ends in the East River? In *People We Pass: Stories of Life Among the Masses of New York City*, Crane's contemporary Julian Ralph writes fiction about those beings identified by Talmage as "lost" to a neglectful ministry. *Maggie* can be compared with Ralph's story "Dutch Kitty's White Slippers," which anticipates *Maggie* in premise, argues Thomas Connery, though not in outcome. When Ralph's Kitty, a tenement girl, faces ruin after taking up with "the dance hall/beer hall crowd," she does not take up prostitution or fall into despair. Unlike the doomed Maggie, Kitty escapes ruin by "running to her boyfriend, who takes her back with warmth and understanding, in contrast to Maggie's boyfriend, Pete, who doesn't care for her and slams the door in her face." "Crane's view is a harsh one," observes Connery, but Ralph's perspective not only "rings as true as Crane's" but is perhaps more typical. "Maggie, despite her brutal treatment and harsh fate, is a beautiful white flower amid crude, thorny weeds and in that she is a creation of Crane's imagination," writes Connery, "while Kitty is typical of so many tenement girls who work long hours six days a week, dance away Saturday night, and eventually marry another tenement inhabitant and doom themselves to a life of taking care of babies in crowded living situations and with a low income, and maybe a husband who drinks too much."[27]

Connery's suggestion that Ralph's view of New York's tenement reality was

25. Rev. T. De Witt Talmage, "True Help," in *Readings and Recitations, No. 3*, ed. L[izzie] Penney (New York: National Temperance Society and Publication House, 1879), 19, 20.

26. Ruth Bordin, *Woman and Temperance: The Quest for Power and Liberty, 1873–1900* (Philadelphia: Temple University Press, 1981), 110.

27. Thomas Bernard Connery, "Fusing Fictional Technique and Journalistic Fact: Literary Journalism in the 1890s Newspaper" (Ph.D. diss., Brown University, 1984), 122.

at least as valid as Crane's is well taken. Indeed, more young women factory workers of the time probably ended up married to drunkards and living in a tenement full of children than walking the streets in the trade. It is something of this sort, perhaps, that Alan Trachtenberg has in mind when he suggests that *Maggie* is "a complicated piece of parody written with a serious regard for the task of rendering a false tale truly."[28] Yet it should be reiterated that Maggie is not created entirely out of whole cloth, if not from directly observed experience. As we have seen, there are hints in the temperance readings for Crane's conception of Maggie as a contradictorily pure product of the slums.

But to understand fully what Crane was about in *Maggie*, one has also to take into account the use to which Crane puts the popular theater of his day. Earlier students of Crane's work have sensed that Crane's novella has some relationship to the theater. For instance, the action of the book has been divided into three acts with "an appended conclusion," and, in another instance the structure of *Maggie* has been discussed briefly as that of "the familiar 'play within the play,' " in which much of the action is presented as having been "witnessed."[29] And a third critic sees the tenement neighbors of the Johnsons functioning as a "chorus." But there is something even more theatrical at play in the way Crane presents his material. It is as if it were all intended for performance, almost as if, that is, *Maggie* were a dramatic script incompletely turned into narrative.

3

It will be recalled that on weekends Maggie's Pete takes her to the Central Park Menagerie and the Museum of Art. Weeknights, however, he takes her to the theater. Crane offers a somewhat generic account of what they see on the stage: "plays in which the brain-clutching heroine was rescued from the palatial home of her guardian, who is cruelly after her bonds, by the hero with the beautiful sentiments. The latter spent most of his time out at soak in pale-green snow storms, busy with a nickel-plated revolver, rescuing aged strangers from villains." Through Maggie's eyes and her limited awareness, Crane offers a wry criticism of the melodramas playing the New York theaters in the early 1890s. As Crane undoubtedly knew, his father had also eyed the theater warily. In *Popular Amusements* (1870) Jonathan Townley Crane devoted a chapter to the theater, warning against its potentially deleterious effects on the uninformed, impressionable mind. He concludes that chapter by asking several rhetorical questions:

28. Alan Trachtenberg, "Experiments in Another Country: Stephen Crane's City Sketches," in *American Realism: New Essays*, ed. Eric J. Sundquist (Baltimore and London: Johns Hopkins Press, 1982), 145.

29. Solomon, *Stephen Crane*, 35–44; Janet Overmyer, "The Structure of Crane's *Maggie*," *University of Kansas City Review*, 29 (Autumn 1962), 71–72.

By what blindness, by what mode of self-delusion, can virtuous women be induced to patronize an institution which lives on the ruins of virtue? How can they sit among the spectators, and look upon wanton exhibitions and shameless exposures of person, such as would anywhere else crimson every modest cheek with shame or redden it with the consciousness of insult? How can they sit among the crowd, while eager eyes are looking down wolfishly upon the brother, the lover, or the husband who sits by their side, and foul hearts are wondering whether he ever comes to this place alone, and whether he is beyond the reach of their subtile arts? How can virtuous women consent ever to set foot within the walls of a theater, when they know that the very air is thick with infamy and death, and when every one who sees them there knows that they know it?[30]

It would be instructive to know just how much direct experience the Reverend Crane had with the theater of his day. Certainly his account of what he has heard or imagined as going on in the theater suggests that he was entirely unfamiliar with the professed values of melodrama in which the virtuous are ultimately saved and the villainous brought to some sort of justice. We do know that the minister's son did see a good deal of theater, knew the playwrights, and hung around with actors such as Franklin Garland, Hamlin's brother. He did not spend his time on the direct, sordid lures of a consciously wicked theater, if, indeed, such a theater existed. His quarrel with the theater of his day, broadly put, lay in its failure to present life realistically, a consequence of which was that it warped the minds of its uninformed, impressionable audiences. An awed Maggie takes it all in uncritically. Crane cynically calls it "transcendental realism."

> Maggie lost herself in sympathy with the wanderers swooning in snow storms beneath happy-hued church windows. And a choir within singing "Joy to the World." To Maggie and the rest of the audience this was transcendental realism. Joy always within, and they, like the actor, inevitably without. Viewing it, they hugged themselves in ecstatic pity of their imagined or real condition.
>
> The girl thought the arrogance and granite-heartedness of the magnate of the play was very accurately drawn. She echoed the maledictions that the occupants of the gallery showered on this individual when his lines compelled him to expose his extreme selfishness.

And Maggie's reaction reflects that of "the loud gallery," which was "overwhelmingly with the unfortunate and the oppressed." The audience "encour-

30. Rev. J. T. Crane, *Popular Amusements* (Cincinnati: Hitchcock and Walden/New York: Carlton and Lanahan, 1870), 57–58.

aged the struggling hero with cries, and jeered the villain, hooting and calling attention to his whiskers. When anybody died in the pale-green snow storms, the gallery mourned. They sought out the painted misery and hugged it as skin." Even "shady persons in the audience revolted from the pictured villainy of the drama. With untiring zeal they hissed vice and applauded virtue."

Crane then sketches out the lines of the typical melodrama:

> In the hero's erratic march from poverty in the first act, to wealth and triumph in the final one, in which he forgives all the enemies that he has left, he was assisted by the gallery, which applauded his generous and noble sentiments and confounded the speeches of his opponents by making irrelevant but very sharp remarks. Those actors who were cursed with villainy parts were confronted at every turn by the gallery. If one of them rendered lines containing the most subtle distinctions between right and wrong, the gallery was immediately aware if the actor meant wickedness, and denounced him accordingly.
>
> The last act was a triumph for the hero, poor and of the masses, the representative of the audience, over the villain and the rich man, his pockets stuffed with bonds, his heart packed with tyrannical purposes, imperturbable amid suffering.

Such plays always had the same stirring effect on Maggie. They raised her spirits. "The theatre made her think." She "rejoiced at the way in which the poor and virtuous eventually surmounted the wealthy and wicked. . . . She wondered if the culture and refinement she had seen imitated, perhaps grotesquely, by the heroine on the stage, could be acquired by a girl who lived in a tenement house and worked in a shirt factory."

If the nature and tenor of Crane's objections to melodrama are vastly different from those of his father, their intentions, not surprisingly, are uniformly moral. To set matters straight (in the world and on the stage) is Crane's intention in *Maggie*. Its action is intended to counteract such hope-filled but misguided views of life, theatrical constructs in which obligatory snowstorms are conventionally pale-green.

If on a larger social canvas of his narrative Crane speaks on behalf of the girl of the streets, in the specifics of craft he works closely with what the theater of his day offers him. *Maggie*'s readers have often commented on the episodic nature of the book, that it is constructed out of loosely connected scenes without the usual explicit connective tissue. For some readers this is seen to be the book's principal weakness, attributable to its author's artistic immaturity. But this episodic narrative can be looked at differently, as a series of theatrical scenes. The book opens with exposition that "translates" into a set of stage directions. (The verb tenses have been put in the present.) "A very little boy stands upon a heap of gravel for the honor of Rum Alley. He is throwing stones at howling urchins from Devil's Row who are circling madly about the heap and pelting at him. His infantile countenance is livid with fury. His small body is writhing in the delivery of great, crimson oaths." We move right into dialogue, into action: " 'Run, Jimmie, run! Dey'll get yehs.' "

Take a second example—from the opening to chapter 11, in which Jimmie and his friend search out Pete in the shrinelike bar he tends. (Again verb tenses have been changed from past to present.)

On a corner a glass-fronted building sheds a yellow glare upon the pavements. The open mouth of a saloon calls seductively to passengers to enter and annihilate sorrow or create rage.

The interior of the place is papered in olive and bronze tints of imitation leather. A shining bar of counterfeit massiveness extends down the side of the room. Behind it a great mahogany-appearing sideboard reaches the ceiling. Upon its shelves rest pyramids of shimmering glasses that are never disturbed. Mirrors set in the face of the sideboard multiply them. Lemons, oranges and paper napkins, arranged with mathematical precision, sit among the glasses. Many-hued decanters of liquor perch at regular intervals on the lower shelves. A nickel-plated cash register occupies a position in the exact centre of the general effect. The elementary senses of it all seem to be opulence and geometrical accuracy.

Across from the bar a smaller counter holds a collection of plates upon which swarm frayed fragments of crackers, slices of boiled ham, dishevelled bits of cheese, and pickles swimming in vinegar. An odor of grasping, begrimed hands and munching mouths pervades.

Pete, in a white jacket, is behind the bar bending expectantly toward a quiet stranger. "A beeh," says the man.[31]

Crane's conscious theatricality potentiates style and structure. This is clearly so in chapter 17—the account of Maggie's so-called last night. Readers have admired this chapter for its daring telescoping into one evening of events a different literary realist would have spread out over days or even months, for Maggie's tableaulike passage through the streets and down the social scale is indicated by the decreasing social status of the men she encounters (and solicits) as she makes her way toward the East River. Granted that in a piece of prose fiction such a technique borders on the experimental or, at least, the extraordi-

31. For the argument that in this scene and elsewhere Crane "developed a language of food in order to give an impression of being 'inside' the social topic, of seeing deeper than the surface," see Henry Golemba, " 'Distant Dinners' in Crane's *Maggie*: Representing 'The Other Half,' " *Essays in Literature*, 21 (Fall 1994), 235–50.

nary. If one looks at the chapter in terms of the theater and its way of doing things, one can readily see how that chapter could be immediately transposed to the stage. In Maggie's movement toward her fate as a suicide, the stages of her downward journey—the human reminders of her rejection—would pass before us on the stage. The final "leering" and "chuckling" fat man would serve to enhance the terror of her final solitude. By 1896, however, the theatrical basis for the 1893 *Maggie* seemed less imperative, and Crane, enjoying a great success as a novelist after the appearance in book form of *The Red Badge of Courage*, no longer saw, perhaps, a fictional reason for embodying the horror attendant on Maggie's doom in the grotesque voyeur haunting the East River piers. It might also be the reason why he softened some of the dialect.[32]

At the time of its first publication Crane's corrective literary vision of life in the New York City slums had few readers. It was praised, however, by several readers of prominence. Hamlin Garland championed the work. He was instrumental, moreover, in persuading B. O. Flower, the editor of the *Arena,* to invite Crane to contribute to his socialist journal. William Dean Howells, ever on the lookout for new writers, chimed in with an enthusiastic review. Predictably, however, Crane's radically moral parable failed to reach the theater audience whose taste for the "transcendent realism" of the day's melodrama he had so skillfully anatomized.

4

Only once has *Maggie* been turned into a produced play and never into a movie, though it has been foreshortened into the balloons and drawings of the comic book.[33] Ten years after it was first published, however, Crane's novella was "rewritten" (with its meaning subverted) as a short story. In 1903 the *National Magazine*, which maintained an interest in Crane in the first few years after his death (in 1902, for example, it reprinted a ten-line poem extolling Crane's heroism), published a short story unmistakably emanating from Crane's novella. "Maggie of the 'Dump': An Incident of the Coal Famine" runs to some two thousand words. While its title echoes that of Crane's first

---

32. This explanation does not address directly the objection: "Still less forgivable is the Appleton destruction of Crane's experiments in rendering dialect" (Joseph Katz, "The *Maggie* Nobody Knows," *Modern Fiction Studies*, 12 [Summer 1966]: 212). In rendering such dialect, however, Crane should not be granted primacy. Actors and playwrights such as Edward Harrigan had anticipated him in his own day.

33. *Maggie, Girl of the Streets*, by Arthur Reel, was first produced by the Drama Committee, New York City, on January 17, 1976; "The World of Story: The Champion of Rum Alley [*Maggie: A Girl of the Streets*, Chapter I]," in *The World Around Us: Fishing Classics Illustrated Publication, No. 34* (June 1961) (New York: Gilberton World-Wide Publications, 1961), 49–53.

book, its subtitle plays off the subtitle of Crane's second book, *The Red Badge of Courage*, which Crane describes as *An Episode of the American Civil War*.[34] This *Maggie* offers, belatedly, an answer to Crane's hard-nosed realism. Like Crane's heroine, this Maggie is a "young street girl or girl of the street." Both Maggies are poor, though unlike Maggie Johnson, Maggie Sullivan does not take to the streets for a living. Like Crane's Maggie, her avatar speaks the dialect of the slums: "Ye'd steal fr'm yer mother, Frenchy. Didn't I seen ye tryin' t' swipe it? Yer jes touch it, 'f ye dare, an' I'll fix ye, see!" Both works open with an altercation among children. In the sketch the argument is between the fourteen-year-old Maggie and "Frenchy," who has just tried to "pinch" the bag of cinders and coal she has picked at the dump.

Crane's novella and this sketch diverge crucially, however, in the judgment each makes of the way poverty and the overall environment affect the poor. If Crane's *Maggie* deplores the failure of love and charity in Maggie's Lower East Side world, the sketch celebrates their triumph even in the midst of the "coal" famine. The second Maggie picks fuel not only for her family but mainly for an old crippled woman living alone. The narrator visits the old woman, "Mother Martin," who tells him of the love Maggie and she have for each other. Unlike the curses that Crane's Maggie gets from her own mother, who will forgive her only in death ("I'll fergive her! I'll fergive her!"), this second Maggie is blessed by Mother Martin ("May th' howly Virgin bless her . . . An' hivin receive her"). It is obvious that Mother Martin is a sentimental reincarnation of the "snarled and leathery" old woman who lives on the floor below the Johnsons. That crone—"with her aged limbs, twisted from rheumatism, [she] had kicked the breath out of a huge policeman"—turns out to be the only one willing to take in the "fallen" Maggie when her mother casts her out. " 'So,' she cried, ' 'ere yehs are back again, are yehs? An' dey've kicked yehs out? Well, come in an' stay wid me teh-night. I ain' got no moral standin.' "

Unlike Crane's *Maggie*, the sketch concludes with a statement of its moral, lest the reader fail to infer it from the dramatized events. "When I left that humble home that day it was with a kindlier feeling in my heart for all the world," writes the narrator; "and I thought that it was indeed true that the milk of human kindness still flowed in human hearts; that all was not greed and indifference to others' needs; that there were not only 'sermons in stones,' but also in the children of the slums, and that there is 'good in everything.' " Character in this melodramatic world, triumphing over environment, is a far cry from Crane's ironic, exasperated, and sometimes angry pessimism. This second

34. Henry D. Muir, "Stephen Crane," *National Magazine*, 17 (Nov. 1902), 247; M. Oakman Patton, "Maggie of the 'Dump': An Incident of the Coal Famine," *National Magazine*, 17 (Mar. 1903), 752–55. Muir's poem had appeared in his *Songs and Other Fancies* (Chicago: Privately printed, 1901), 107.

Maggie harks back to the Maggies of the New York theater. Edward Harrigan's *Reilly and the 400*, produced in New York in 1891, features the song "Maggie Murphy's Home," which, in its first and last stanzas, runs:

> Behind a grammar school-house
>   In a double tenement,
> I live with my old mother,
>   And always pay the rent.
> A bed-room and a parlor
>   Is all we call our own,
> And you're welcome every evening,
>   At Maggie Murphy's home.
>
> .   .   .   .
>
> I walk through Hogan's alley,
>   At the closing of the day,
> To greet my dear old mother,
>   You'll hear the neighbors say—
> Oh! there goes little Maggie,
>   I wish she were my own;
> Oh, may blessings ever linger
>   O'er Maggie Murphy's home![35]

The sounds made by Harrigan's Maggie Murphy are not those of Crane's Maggie Johnson, and it is a sure bet that Harrigan's Hogan's Alley is cleaner and safer than Crane's Rum Alley. It is not for nothing that the tenement Maggie Murphy shares with her mother is located right behind, not a saloon or a sweatshop but a grammar school house. Competing against such bouncy portrayals of the poor New York Irish, *Maggie: A Girl of the Streets (A Story of New York)* by the unknown "Johnston Smith" was certain to fail.[36]

Crane had seen right through the moralistic theatricality of the temperance worker, just as he had seen through the dangerously soupy morality ladled out in the theater. *Maggie* was too harsh for its time, even though it, too, was not the entirely disinterested, objective piece of realism its author (along with Howells, Garland, and Flower) took it to be.

35. Edward Harrigan, "Maggie Murphy's Home," in *Harrigan and Braham's Songs from "Reilly and the 400 Hundred"* (New York: Benedict Popular Publishing, [1891?]), 6–7.

36. For a different contemporary rewriting of Crane's first novel—this time by a champion of Howellsian realism—see Lawrence J. Oliver's "Brander Matthews' Re-visioning of Crane's *Maggie*," *American Literature*, 60 (Dec. 1988), 654–58.

4

The Drunkard's Progress

Thus alcohol stands indicted as an impostor. He who is fully under its influence may be happy after a fashion, but his enjoyment is based upon a mockery. He feels like a giant, while he is really shorn of his natural force. He drivels the veriest nonsense, while he thinks he reasons better than Plato. His maudlin attempts at smartness are the feeblest and the flattest of human utterances; but they seem to him wit almost superhuman. When he is so far gone as to stammer in his speech and totter in his gait, and be helpless in mind and body, his sense of his wisdom, his strength, his greatness, and his goodness is at its highest point.

—Rev. J. T. Crane, *Arts of Intoxication* (1870)

Much has been said about our negligence in rendering our homes attractive, and our cuisine appetizing; and not always without reason. We therefore recommend that in our unions essays be read on the science and art of making home outwardly wholesome and attractive, books on that subject be circulated, and all possible efforts be made to secure a more scientific attention to the products of the kitchens, and a higher aesthetic standard for the parlor.

— WCTU "Plan of Work" (1874)

And we cry till our bitter crying the nation alarms
For the sons Intemperance is stealing out of our arms!

—Josephine Pollard, "Stolen; or, the Mother's Lament" (1882)

1

There are nine steps in "The Drunkard's Progress," according to a nineteenth-century temperance print. Step 1 depicts the young man taking "a glass with a friend." In step 2 the incipient drunkard takes "a glass to keep the cold out." In step 3 he has had "a glass too much." In step 4 he is "drunk and riotous." With step 5, he attains "the summit"; sitting down now with "jolly compan-ions," he is the "confirmed drunkard." Now begins the descent. With step 6 he comes to "poverty and disease." At step 7 he is "forsaken by friends." Step 8, taken in "desperation," leads him into "crime." In Step 9 he turns his gun on himself and blows his brains out, committing, as the label says, "death by suicide." Although not every one of the steps corresponds exactly with the steps of George Kelcey's rise and fall as a drinker, the correspondence overall is close enough to suggest that Crane had one such temperance paradigm in mind when he constructed the plot of *George's Mother.*

When we consider what might be called the work's ethos, moreover, we find that it has strong affinities with the documented principles of the Ameri-can temperance movement. What I have in mind, particularly, are two docu-ments dating from the early years of the Woman's Christian Temperance Union that can be brought to bear on *George's Mother.* The first document is "Which Shall Win?"—a piece by Frances E. Willard, the WCTU's longtime president. The second one is the text of a resolution passed by the WCTU at its second national convention. In tandem they provide a useful perspective on Crane's intentions in the second of his Lower East Side novellas.

Miss Willard, quoted from an 1877 temperance reader, argues:

> The grog-shop is a two-edged sword, and cuts both ways at once. It is a rotating machine for the snaring of souls. It catches our young men and boys before they reach the church and Sabbath-school—while they are on their way—and they never reach its doors, or else it catches them as they return, and mars or neutralizes the blessed lessons there imparted. Between the two there is the old "irrepressible conflict" over again. It is war to the knife, and the knife to the hilt, and only one can win. And in the warfare, we of Christ's army are outnumbered. There are twelve sa-loons to every church; twelve bar-keepers to every minister. The church opens its blessed doors two or three days in the week; the saloon grinds on and on with its mill of destruction all the days of every week; all the months of every year. . . . They have studied carefully the tastes, tenden-cies, and preferences of our boys and young men, their natural and inno-cent taste for variety, fondness for amusement, preference for young company, and they pander to all these in ways that take hold upon death.[1]

Miss Willard, soon to be the WCTU's president, was present at its second con-vention, held in Cincinnati in 1875, which passed the following resolution:

---

1. Frances E. Willard, "Which Shall Win?" in *Readings and Recitations, No. 1,* ed. L[izzie] Penney (New York: National Temperance Society and Publication House, 1877), 9–10.

"That since women are the greatest sufferers from the liquor traffic, and realizing that it is to be ultimately suppressed by means of the ballot, we, the Christian women of this land, in convention assembled, do pray Almighty God, and all good and true men, that the question of the prohibition of the liquor traffic shall be submitted to all adult citizens, irrespective of race, color or sex."[2] Among the suffering women, of course, were wives, mothers, and daughters. "Do you hear the cry of the women— / Of the women whose hearts are broken?" asks one temperance poem calling for the dawning of a better day, "Of a day when wives' and mothers' sadness / Shall be all forgotten in their gladness."[3] The suffering of one daughter in a home of alcoholics Crane undertook to dramatize in *Maggie: A Girl of the Streets*. The suffering of a temperance-worker mother he undertook in *Maggie*'s companion piece, *George's Mother*. "Our women believe that special efforts should be made to help the mother in her unequal warfare with the dram-shop for the preservation of her boy," wrote Frances E. Willard in 1888, "[for] it is plainly perceived by them that something is wrong in the popular division of responsibility by which, although the father may be a moderate drinker, the failure of the boy to grow up good and pure is adjudged to be his mother's fault."[4] Many of Crane's readers have seen *George's Mother* as a try at adjusting this moral balance in the mother's favor and have stopped right there. But other readers have looked more deeply for evidence of Crane's more complex intentions.

Edward Garnett, for instance, sees *George's Mother* as no more hospitable to the mother than to her drunkard son. In Crane's picture of the mother, writes Garnett, "all the mysterious craving of maternal love, its fierce pleasure in self-sacrifice, its self-regarding heroism, and self-denial based on its egotistic interests, is presented with an unerring truthfulness that leaves nothing further to be said."[5] Maxwell Geismar insists that in this work, in which "the alcoholic and oedipal worlds are interchangeable," Crane gives us in the mother an "aging, sick, ugly symbol of maternal love [that] combine[s] the offices of nursemaid and mistress."[6] Eric Solomon says that *George's Mother* shows "two characters as similar in their fantasies and their egos yet seriously in conflict in their views

2. Anonymous, *A Brief History of the Woman's Christian Temperance Union*, 2nd ed. (Evanston: Union Signal, 1907), 12.

3. Caroline A. Soule, "The Cry of the Women," in *Readings and Recitations, No. 1*, 12.

4. Frances E. Willard, *Woman and Temperance: or, The Work and Workers of the Woman's Christian Temperance Union* (Hartford: Park Publishing, 1883), 237.

5. Edward Garnett, "Two Americans," London *Speaker*, 30 (Aug. 6, 1904), 436–37. This review is reprinted in George Monteiro, "Stephen Crane: A New Appreciation by Edward Garnett," *American Literature*, 50 (Nov. 1978), 465–71.

6. Maxwell Geismar, *Rebels and Ancestors: The American Novel, 1890–1915* (Boston: Houghton Mifflin, 1953), 94, 95.

of the proper life." When the mother dies, concludes Solomon, "the conflict is over, and neither side has won. The dreams have failed, and love has died."[7]

Brenda Murphy offers the most detailed account of the pernicious, self-destructive war the little woman who is George's mother wages on the prodigality of her own self-destructive son. Detecting the irony implicit in Crane's original title for the story, *A Woman Without Weapons*, Murphy demonstrates convincingly that not only does the mother possess an arsenal of weapons but that she uses them skillfully enough to emerge in death (her death is the final weapon) as victor. "George's mother has succeeded in wresting her son from the forces of sin. It matters little to her 'moral victory' that she may have destroyed both of them in the process."[8]

One can only speculate why Crane changed the title of his book. If *George's Mother* gives the son and the mother close to equal billing, perhaps *A Woman Without Weapons* implies that the book is principally the mother's. Indeed, most readers see the novella, more or less, as the dramatization of the downward course traveled by an alcoholic son, greatly to the crushing disappointment of his earnest, well-meaning mother. In this, Crane's story recreates the paradigmatic story of a mother's defeat by her son's alcoholism, as it is told in "Stolen; or, the Mother's Lament," a temperance-reader poem voiced through the mother:

They have stolen my child!—they have stolen my child, I say!
My beautiful boy!—my precious one!—they have stolen away!
And the earth is a heap of ashes, the sun is no longer bright,
Since out of my home and my heart has vanished their chief
    delight.

. . . .

It was not done in a moment, with a sudden wrench or blow
As Death knows how to rob us of treasures we prize below,
But it came with the trail of a serpent—the soft, insidious thing!
And it spoke to my son like a siren, while it plunged in my heart
    its sting!

. . . .

I kept the old house cheerful with pictures and works of art,
With books, and a thousand nameless things that gladden the
    youthful heart;

---

7. Eric Solomon, *Stephen Crane: From Parody to Realism* (Cambridge, Mass.: Harvard University Press, 1966), 60, 66.

8. Brenda Murphy, "A Woman with Weapons: The Victor in Stephen Crane's *George's Mother*," *Modern Language Studies*, 11 (Spring 1981), 92.

And though I'd no daughters to aid me in this delightful task,
I tried to be sister, and mother, and all that a child could ask.

I noticed his anxious brow—for a mother's gaze is keen—
And I missed the honest look in his eyes I had always seen;
While into his voice came a harsher tone, and he seemed to avoid
      my sight,
For he knew that my heart was set on his doing exactly right.

O Love! is there any cross that can give thee such pain as this?
O Love! can aught else so embitter thy cup of bliss,
As to see the child thou hast nourished and cherished with tend'rest
      care,
Torn out of thy holy embrace by the tempter's snare?
 .   .   .   .
Who robbed me of this my joy, and took from my side the sire
Who wept o'er the empty chair that stood by the table or fire,
Until, grown weary with waiting for a change that never came,
He sickened, and under the daisies we buried his grief and shame?
 .   .   .   .
The serpent stole into my Eden—why not into yours?
Not even the bond of affection our treasure secures;
The child at your knee, full of prattle, whose future you can not
      divine,
May prove just as guilty a sinner, as wretched a wanderer as mine![9]

Continuing through several additional stanzas, each contributing to a generalized condemnation of the evils of drink, this poem laments the fate of a woman
not without weapons but with weapons that, save possibly for prayer, have
failed her. Notice that like George's mother, the mother in this poem follows
Frances Willard's domestic motto of "home protection" through cleaning and
decoration of her son's home—but to no avail. When Crane dropped his original title, there was some loss—perhaps a certain flair—but the logic of his dou-
ble-focus narrative—on both mother and son—dictated some sort of change.
George's mother is no stranger to a good fight. She has fought intemperance
as a member of the Woman's Christian Temperance Union. When Charley
Jones, the old acquaintance who will shepherd George along the primrose path
to better society and "improved" drinking, first encounters George, he starts
out by treating him to a drink. As natural as this moment might seem to today's

9. Josephine Pollard, "Stolen; or, the Mother's Lament," in *Readings and Recitations, No. 4*, ed. L[iz-
zie] Penny (New York: National Temperance Society and Publication House, 1882), 83–87.

reader, it had particular importance to Crane's contemporaries. The national meeting of the WCTU in 1874, in its "Plan of Work," provided for an "Anti-Treat Pledge," explaining: " 'Come, let's take something together,' has been to thousands the keynote of destruction. We are laboring for the organization of a league which shall enroll as members those, who, though not ready to sign the pledge, are willing to refrain from 'putting the bottle to their neighbor's lips,' by pledging their honor that they neither 'be treated' nor 'treat.' "[10] This ritual of treating, while seemingly promoting camaraderie, is deeply pernicious in that it vastly increases the amount of consumption, "since a man is expected to buy a round of drinks for every round he has received."[11] The thematic connection is then made perfectly clear when Jones asks George about his mother. " 'How is th' ol' lady, anyhow?' continued Jones. 'Th' last time I remember she was as spry as a little ol' cricket, an' was helpeltin' aroun' th' country lecturin' before W.C.T.U.'s an' one thing an' another.' "[12] These credentials serve, of course, to bolster the reader's respect for her skill in the war she conducts on behalf of her son's sobriety and Christian salvation. She herself seems to be aware, moreover, that she is far from being a helpless woman without weapons.

So common was the notion that each temperance fighter was engaged in nothing short of a war and that all methods and devices for carrying on that war were nothing less than weapons that the instruction manual published by the United Society of Christian Endeavor carried the title *Weapons for Temperance Warfare*. Presenting "Some Plans and Programmes for use in Young People's Societies, Sunday-schools and Christian Temperance Unions," this vade mecum carried an epigraph on its title page from John B. Gough (elsewhere called "the Cold-Water warrior"[13]), reading: "Fight the drink! Fight it, fight it wherever we find it, fight it in the social circle, fight it in the dram-shop, fight it at home, fight it abroad. I expect to my dying day to fight the drink with every lawful weapon." The book, dedicated to Frances E. Willard, whose message in 1896 to the Temperance Committees "suggested the preparation" of "This Little Volume," also reproduces Miss Willard's inspiring message, mixing Christianity with temperance:

10. Quoted in Helen E. Tyler, *Where Prayer and Purpose Meet: 1874—The WCTU Story—1949* (Evanston: Signal Press, 1949), 30.

11. John W. Crowley, *The White Logic: Alcoholism and Gender in American Modernist Fiction* (Amherst: University of Massachusetts Press, 1994), 30. Crowley makes his point in a chapter on Jack London's *John Barleycorn* (1913).

12. Stephen Crane, *George's Mother*, in *Bowery Tales*, Volume I of *The University of Virginia Edition of the Works of Stephen Crane*, ed. Fredson Bowers, intr. James B. Colvert (Charlottesville: University Press of Virginia, 1969), 113–78.

13. For John B. Gough pictured as "the Cold-Water warrior," see W. J. Rorabaugh, *The Alcoholic Republic: An American Tradition* (Oxford and New York: Oxford University Press, 1979), 98.

Only a clear brain can think God's thoughts after him.

Only a steady hand can glorify the divine Carpenter by faithful industry.

Only a heart unhurried by artificial stimulants can be loyal in its love toward Christ and humanity.

I beseech you to be incessant and ingenious in your efforts to teach total abstinence for the sake of Head, Hand, and Heart; and to take as your watchwords

HOME PROTECTION

and

THE LIQUOR TRAFFIC MUST BE DESTROYED

Yours in the purpose to glorify God in our bodies and our spirits, which are his.[14]

When the motto "home protection" was criticized as "organized mother love," Miss Willard countered by advocating proudly what she called the "politics of the mother heart,"[15] words that express the implicit creed by which George's mother lives and fights.

Weapons for Temperance Warfare, drawing on columns originally published in the *Sunday School Times*, offers practical advice on how to carry on war against the armies of intemperance. There are pieces on pledge signing, temperance budgets, and facts and figures. There are drawn-out plans and detailed sample programs for temperance meetings. There are suggestions for choosing the most useful biblical texts and the most appealing gospel hymns. In its list of hymns "especially adapted for use in temperance meetings" appear "Yield Not to Temptation," "Throw out the Life-Line," and "Where Is My Boy To-night?"—each dealing with the basic material of Crane's story of a boy and his mother. The hymn Crane has George's mother sing is by Isaac Watts:

Am I a soldier of the cross?
A follower of the Lamb!
And shall I fear to own his cause,
Or blush to speak his name?

Must I be carry'd to the skies,
On flow'ry beds of ease?

14. Belle M. Brain, *Weapons for Temperance Warfare* (Boston and Chicago: United Society of Christian Endeavor, 1897), [1], [3], [5].

15. Quoted in Mark Edward Lender and James Kirby Martin, *Drinking in America: A History* (New York: Free Press/London: Collier Macmillan, 1982), 107.

Whilst others fought to win the prize,
    And sail'd through bloody seas?

Are there no foes for me to face?
    Must I not stem the flood?
Is this vile world a friend to grace,
    To help me on to God?

Sure I must fight, if I would reign;
    Increase my courage Lord;
I'll bear the toil, endure the pain,
    Supported by thy word.

Thy saints, in all this glorious war,
    Shall conquer, though they die;
They view the triumph from afar,
    And seize it with their eye.

When that illustrious day shall rise,
    And all thy armies shine
In robes of victory through the skies—
    The glory shall be thine.[16]

Entitled "Holy Fortitude; or, The Christian Soldier" and listed as a hymn of warfare, it was a favorite among temperance workers as well as Methodists.[17]

Echoing the language of "Warfare," George's mother sees herself as truly a crusader. To fight against George's intemperance is to do the Christian God's work. Her opponent is the dragon of alcoholism that the ironically named George (recalling the saint) does not have the will to defeat.[18] This crusade will be fought in the home, the church, the saloon. This war will not be fought by George but over him.

16. *The Psalms, Hymns, and Spiritual Songs, of the Rev. Isaac Watts, D.D.*, ed. Samuel Worcester (Boston: Crocker and Brewster, 1838), 563.

17. John Julian, ed., *A Dictionary of Hymnology* (New York: Dover, 1957), 55; and Willard, *Woman and Temperance*, 312, 350. Interestingly, in chapter 5 of Mark Twain's *Adventures of Tom Sawyer* a minister reads this hymn in "a peculiar style which was much admired in that part of the country. His voice began on a medium key and climbed steadily up till it reached a certain point, where it bore with strong emphasis upon the topmost word and then plunged down as if from a spring-board" (Mark Twain, *Mississippi Writings*, ed. Guy Cardwell [New York: Library of America, 1982], 38).

18. Crane's obituary in *Publishers' Circular* actually listed him as the author of a book entitled *St. George's Mother* ("Mr. Stephen Crane," 72, June 9, 1900, 629). Curiously, there exists a later book by J[oseph] Johns entitled *St. George and the Dragon: England and the Drink Traffic* (London: S. W. Partridge [1907?]).

2

The *Illustrated London News* called *George's Mother* "a more than commonly able temperance tract." It allowed that Crane's novella rapidly, though convincingly, sketched "a very commonplace 'Rake's Progress'—the descent of a young New York working man, by means of friendly clubs and saloon-haunting, from dignity, self-respect, and the estate of the dutiful son to becoming a 'tough,' and breaking the heart of his old mother." "Mr. Crane's vein of bitter irony is to be seen in the maudlin friendship of the bar-loafers," continues the review, "but in the picture of the little brown old mother there is heart also."[19]

The promising suggestion that *George's Mother* recalls Hogarth's "Rake's Progress" has not been much explored by scholars.[20] What can be looked at here is the way George Kelcey's social progress (up and down) ties in, roughly, with his progress through drink (up and down). Just as George moves, in order, from the street to the saloon, the backroom, Bleecker's apartment, and the club's room above the saloon, he then reverses the procedure by returning, in order, to the saloon, the street, and, finally, the vacant lot where he becomes part of the street gang.

His is not the progress of a rake, exactly, but that of a drunkard. Initially, George accompanies an old acquaintance to "a little glass-fronted saloon that sat blinking jovially at the crowds." Charley Jones, ordering whiskey for himself while George drinks beer, exchanges a few words with the barkeep and then addresses his new friend: " 'This is th' hang-out fer a great gang,' said Jones, turning to Kelcey. 'They're a great crowd, I tell yeh. We own th' place when we get started. Come aroun' some night. Any night, almost. T'-night, b'jiminy. They'll almost all be here, an' I'd like t' interduce yeh. They're a great gang! Gre-e-at!' " That evening George returns to the saloon and is introduced to Bleecker. Shortly thereafter Bleecker and his crowd repair to the backroom to hold their private drinking party. Charley Jones drinks whiskey, but while George is also drinking, we are not told what he drinks. Bleecker works his spell over George, who not only "admired Bleecker immensely" but "developed a brotherly feeling for the others." Back home, in bed, George "had a pleasurable consciousness that he had made a good impression upon those fine fellows. He felt that he had spent the most delightful evening of his life." The next time he runs into Jones, he is told that Bleecker will host "a blow-out" the next night and that he "expressly" wants George to come.

19. Anonymous, [*George's Mother*]. *Illustrated London News*, 109 (Oct. 3, 1896), 439.

20. Alice Hall Petry argues for Hogarth's influence on *Maggie: A Girl of the Streets*, especially on Crane's portrait of the mother, in "*Gin Lane* in the Bowery: Crane's *Maggie* and William Hogarth," *American Literature*, 56 (Oct. 1984), 417–26. Gerard M. Sweeney extends her argument in "The Syphilitic World of Stephen Crane's *Maggie*," *American Literary Realism*, 24 (Fall 1991), 79–85.

George arrives at Bleecker's "apartments," is introduced to the other guests, and, along with them, is offered drink. "There were upon it [the table] a keg of beer, a long row of whiskey bottles, a little heap of corn-cob pipes, some bags of tobacco, a box of cigars, and a mighty collection of glasses, cups, and mugs." Kelcey takes a mug of beer. Later he switches to whiskey. When, still later, he trips over a pair of outstretched legs and strikes his head, he reacts by pouring himself "an extravagant portion of whiskey." Kelcey gets very drunk, wants to sing a song, but instead passes out.

He awakens the next morning to a scene of widespread destruction. "After the tumults of the previous night the interior of this room resembled a decaying battle-field. The air hung heavy and stifling with the odors of tobacco, men's breaths, and beer half filling forgotten glasses. There was ruck of broken tumblers, pipes, bottles, spilled tobacco, cigar stumps." It is of particular interest that Crane makes so much of pipes, tobacco, and smoke. During the earlier private party in the backroom of the saloon, the entrapped men have been described as garlanded by smoke: "the tobacco-smoke eddied about the forms of the men in ropes and wreaths. Near the ceiling there was a thick gray cloud."

As early as 1883 the WCTU had targeted tobacco as a grave danger to temperance, forming in that year a department called Effort to Overthrow the Tobacco Habit.[21] By 1895 the *Union Signal*, a WCTU publication, was arguing for everyone's "right to fresh air" and advocating that "smokers be permitted to smoke only in such places and ways as would not interfere 'with the rights and freedoms of any other individual.' "[22] One temperance piece attacks the widespread use of tobacco by pretending to extol its personal and social advantages:

How sweet it makes the breath! What a clean and wholesome odor lingers behind in the garments of those who use it! But one of the most conspicuous advantages accruing to mankind from smoking is its unselfishness; for, in this respect, it presents itself in striking contrast to the injurious habit of drinking. A man calls for a glass of ale, and there he sits, a selfish being, with perhaps a dozen or more around him, yet none but himself derive the least pleasure from the foaming beverage before him. Not so the smoker. He can purify and sweeten the air of the largest room; and, let it be ever so crowded, all present have a share of his smoke to enjoy. All present depart freshened and sweetened by the emanations from his pipe.[23]

---

21. *Brief History*, 39.

22. Ruth Bordin, *Woman and Temperance: The Quest for Power and Liberty, 1873–1900* (Philadelphia: Temple University Press, 1981), 109.

23. Anonymous, "The Logic of Smoking," in *Readings and Recitations, No. 5*, ed. L[izzie] Penney (New York: National Temperance Society and Book Publications, 1884), 73.

On the morning after the drunken celebrations at Bleecker's place, George awakens with a strong thirst. But when he finally manages to get himself a drink of water, it is "an intolerable disappointment. It was insipid and weak to his scorched throat and not at all cool." Bleecker invites him to go out for a cocktail. George makes "a movement of disdain for cocktails" but accompanies Bleecker to the street. Once outside, he goes his own way, parting company from his host of the night before, "the only man of them who knew much about cocktails."

It is not much later that George begins to wonder whether he still cares for beer. He recalls that "he had been obliged to cultivate a talent for imbibing it. . . . He was born with an abhorrence which he had steadily battled until it had come to pass that he could drink from ten to twenty glasses of beer without the act of swallowing causing him to shiver. He understood that drink was an essential to joy, to the coveted position of a man of the world and of the streets. The saloons contained the mystery of a street for him. When he knew its saloons he comprehended the street. Drink and its surroundings were the eyes of a superb green dragon to him. He followed a fascinating glitter, and the glitter required no explanation." Bleecker and the boys form a club with dues set at a dollar a week. The saloon keeper donates "half the rent of quite a large room over the saloon." On leaving one meeting of the club, Kelcey's legs are described as being "like whalebone when he tried to go up-stairs upon his return home, and the edge of each step was moved curiously forward."

In time George loses his job and, in need of money, approaches his friends Bleecker, Jones, and O'Connor for a loan. They do not lend him the money, and he discovers that now he is "below them in social position." But the seeds for new friendships and loyalties had already been sown when he helped the street tough Fidsey Corcoran beat up a man the latter had provoked into fighting. As George nears his home after being rebuffed by his erstwhile drinking friends, he encounters Fidsey and another member of the street gang. They invite George to partake of a "big can" of beer they have sneaked away from a "new barkeep." An argument breaks out, but it does not keep any one of them from his "smoke" at the can. Somehow Fidsey and the boys maneuver Kelcey into confronting one Blue Billie. But George avoids fighting when a little boy delivers the message that George's mother is sick. She dies shortly after George gets there. The reader last sees George, defeated and alone, as he sits staring at the wallpaper. "The pattern was clusters of brown roses. He felt them like hideous crabs crawling upon his brain."

Much of what George has done self-destructively, when not out of sheer fecklessness, he has done vindictively. When he thinks of getting drunk he relishes in anticipation the effect his actions will have, presumably, on his mother. Invited to Bleecker's party, he thinks of himself as "a very grim figure." "He was about to taste the delicious revenge of a partial self-destruction. The universe would regret its position when it saw him drunk."

The mother's arsenal of weapons will prove inadequate to the formidable task of wrenching George away from drink. Her boy is not amenable to "home protection," the bedrock of Miss Willard's temperance program.[24] Consequently, when all the cleaning and decorating and special cooking she can accomplish fails to reform George, this "poor, inadequate woman, of a commonplace religiosity" (as William Dean Howells called her)[25] turns to the church. By weeping at his truculent refusal to accompany her to prayer meeting, Mrs. Kelcey manages to get him there. But sadly for her, this one visit serves merely to confirm George's belief that he is damned. George is uncomfortable, angry, "wild with a rage in which his lips turned slightly livid." Yet his interest is piqued when "one by one people arose and told little tales of their religious faith. Some were tearful and others calm, emotionless, and convincing. Kelcey listened closely for a time. These people filled him with a great curiosity. He was not familiar with their types." At last, the clergyman, described as "a pale-faced, but plump young man in a black coat that buttoned to his chin"—reminiscent of the clergyman who, fearing for his respectability, spurns Maggie—speaks. "Kelcey was amazed, because, from the young man's appearance, he would not have suspected him of being so glib; but the speech had no effect on Kelcey, excepting to prove to him again that he was damned." The clergyman has spoken (though not to George), but he has not, as the temperance manuals preached, reached down to those young men who, going "down in evil ways," are "not riding a docile, well-broken steed" but "are on a monster, wild and blood-thirsty, going at a death rate."[26]

To his mother's bitter disappointment, George does not return to prayer meeting. It is only as his mother lays dying in the next room that standing before George is "the pale-faced but plump young clergyman."[27] " 'My poor lad—' began this latter." It is too late. Crane has had it both ways. The church has been ineffectual. And George, inadvertently in league with his mother's destructive impulses, has destroyed himself. Ironically, in the end the "woman without weapons" has apparently all the weapons she needs to vanquish her son.

24. She inscribed photographs of herself "Yours for Home Protection, Frances E. Willard"; see Bordin, *Woman and Temperance,* 44.

25. W. D. Howells, "New York Low Life in Fiction," *New York World* (July 26, 1896), 18.

26. Rev. T. De Witt Talmage, "True Help," in *Readings and Recitations, No. 3,* ed. L[izzie] Penney (New York: National Temperance Society and Publication House, 1879), 18.

27. In Crane's work the adjectives "pale-faced" and "plump" are usually denigrating.

5

Pale-Green Snowstorms

Let no Christian go to the play-house even once. . . . Why consent to act, even once, as decoy duck, to lure many, it may be, to their destruction?

—Rev. J. T. Crane, *Popular Amusements* (1870)

The theatre has, for the nonce, become a kind of post-graduate Sunday-school.

—William Cowper Brann, "Church and Stage" (1896)

1

Shortly before Stephen Crane was born, the Reverend Jonathan Townley Crane mounted an attack on "the theater." Crane's father would not live to see the clear evidence that his youngest child not only did not disdain the theater but would in the decade of his maturity make several attempts to write for it. It is bootless to speculate, but it is likely that had he lived beyond his twenty-ninth year, Crane would have seen some of his work produced in London or New York.

Crane moved to New York City after an academic year of indifferent attendance at Syracuse University. Precocious, energetic, the possessor of seemingly boundless writing talent, the young Crane came to the city to work in any literary medium that would provide him with a living and a chance at fame. He was ready to write news, feature stories, fiction, and even—it was once reported—"the libretto of *Dolores,* an opera" scheduled to "appear in New York during the holidays in 1892."[1] No such libretto has ever turned up, suggesting that somebody was needling the young Crane for his grandiosity, but Crane

---

1. Anonymous, "Ex-'94," undated, unsourced clipping, University Archives, Syracuse University Library, Syracuse, New York.

did take some interest in opera, as his piece on grand opera in New Orleans suggests.

The apocryphal "Dolores" notwithstanding, there is ample evidence that Crane's serious interest in drama and in the possibility of exploiting dramatic forms in his quest for literary prominence and a livelihood dated from his late teens. An early piece, unpublished in his lifetime but dating from 1890–91, reads like a scenario for a short dramatic interlude. "Greed Rampant" exists in manuscript with preliminary information presented in script form:

SCENE—Paradise, N.J.
Time—The end of it.
    Dramatis Personae.
    Mr. John P. St. Peter.
    Crowd of Gentiles.
    Mob of Jews.[2]

The piece is a juvenile, tasteless, satirical attack on the Jews for their proverbial cupidity. As such it is embarrassing for the broad prejudice that it displays. But as a document it tells us something about Crane's interest in the theater. There is no dialogue in the piece. In fact, it reads like a scenario for a drama of pure movement: a crowd scene at the Final Judgment, which is viewed by Crane as a circuslike meeting. The Jews have crowded the place, thereby keeping away the Gentiles, who are effectively prevented from nearing the turnstile to Paradise until one thoughtful Gentile comes up with a device for removing the Jews. He prepares a sign reading:

JOB LOTS. JOB LOTS
DOWN IN SHEOL, CAPE MAY COUNTY, NEW JERSEY.
Selling out at 2 per cent of cost.

When the Jews see this they rush from the place. Whereupon, as Crane tells us at the end, not exempting anyone from his satire, "the Gentiles had moved up to the front seats."

Two things here. There is Crane's interest in crowds and mobs, which would surface in his fiction—the armies, for example, of *The Red Badge of Courage* and the Bowery denizens of "The Men in the Storm." And mirroring in reverse the popular theater's interest in bringing the trappings and animals of the circus onto the stage as part of the dramatic productions of the day, the

2. Stephen Crane, "Greed Rampant," in *Tales, Sketches, and Reports*, Volume VIII of *The University of Virginia Edition of the Works of Stephen Crane*, ed. Fredson Bowers, intr. Edwin H. Cady (Charlottesville: University Press of Virginia, 1973), 7–10.

young Crane ingeniously adapts P. T. Barnum's famous "This Way to the Egress" ploy to his own satirical purposes.[3]

2

The young Crane knew almost intuitively that there were things the theater could do that had nothing to do with dialogue. William Gillette would later insist on the difference between a play and the directions for a play. "Incredible as it may seem," wrote Gillette in *The Illusion of the First Time in Acting*, "there are people in existence who imagine that they can read a play. . . . The feat is impossible. No one on earth can read a play. You may read the Directions for a Play and from these Directions imagine as best you can what the play would be like; but you could no more read the *Play* than you could read a Fire or an Automobile Accident or a Base-Ball Game. The Play—if it is Drama—does not even exist until it appeals in the form of Simulated Life. Reading a list of the things to be said and done in order to make this appeal is not reading the appeal itself."[4] Just how thoroughly Crane understood this crucial distinction is evident from a play he published in the *Roycroft Quarterly* in May 1896. Here is the entire play, called "A Prologue."[5]

> A GLOOMY STAGE. SLENDER CURTAINS AT A WINDOW, CENTRE. BEFORE THE WINDOW, A TABLE, AND UPON THE TABLE, A LARGE BOOK OPENED. A MOONBEAM, NO WIDER THAN A SWORD–BLADE, PIERCES THE CURTAINS AND FALLS UPON THE BOOK.
>
> A MOMENT OF SILENCE.
>
> FROM WITHOUT, THEN—AN ADJACENT ROOM IN INTENTION—COME SOUNDS OF CELEBRATION, OF RIOTOUS DRINKING AND LAUGHTER. FINALLY, A SWIFT QUARREL. THE DIN AND CRASH OF A FIGHT. A LITTLE STILLNESS. THEN A WOMAN'S SCREAM. "AH, MY SON, MY SON."
>
> A MOMENT OF SILENCE.
>
> CURTAIN.

Thus the shortest temperance play on record. The germ for Crane's own novel published in the same year, *George's Mother*, that neglected companion piece to

---

3. In the Western story, "The Five White Mice," when the Kid from New York attends a Mexican circus, Crane as narrator takes a swipe at Barnum: "In the United States [the circus] . . . is merely a matter of a number of rings, if possible, and a great professional agreement to lie to the public" (Crane, "The Five White Mice," in *Tales of Adventure*, Volume V of *The University of Virginia Edition of the Works of Stephen Crane*, ed. Fredson Bowers, intr. J. C. Levenson [Charlottesville: University Press of Virginia, 1970], 44).

4. William Gillette, *The Illusion of the First Time in Acting*, intr. George Arliss (New York: Dramatic Museum of Columbia University, 1915), 34.

5. Stephen Crane, "A Prologue," in *Tales, Sketches, and Reports*, 109.

the far more famous *Maggie: A Girl of the Streets*, "A Prologue" presents as succinctly as possible two of Crane's major themes: generational revolt within the family and the drama of the conflict between alcohol and religion.

Although Crane's major treatment of New York proletarian life remains the two novellas, *Maggie* and *George's Mother*, the young writer did try his hand at a comic treatment of the same material. In *Truth*, an illustrated humor magazine, he published, in 1893—the year in which *Maggie* was first published—a one-act, "At Clancy's Wake."[6] The play consists almost entirely of Clancy's widow's running account of her late husband's manly qualities. She is encouraged to do this by the presence of a reporter who has come to prepare an account of Clancy's life for the papers. Crane reproduces the speech of the Irish immigrant throughout. The commonplace notion that the Irish were uncommonly heavy drinkers fuels the slight dramatic machinery of the play, which is merely that as the widow talks she constantly feeds the reporter Clancy's finest alcohol, rapidly bringing him to the point of incoherence. This play reveals clearly that Crane saw his Bowery and Lower East Side materials not only with the somber eye of the author of *Maggie* but also with the amused eye of Edward Townsend's *Chimmie Fadden*. If others chose to exploit the Irish inebriate on the stage, there is evidence here to indicate that Crane, innovative as ever, had set his sights on exploiting the Irish mother and wife. There's more than a casual anticipation here of materials that would interest the later Eugene O'Neill.

It should come as no surprise that during these years Crane had easy accessibility to the theater. He not only hung around with actresses and actors but he lived for a while with some friends—artists—just around the corner from Daly's Theatre, near Twenty-ninth Street. We don't know how frequently he attended the theater, but we do know that he saw Gerhardt Hauptman's *Hannele*, about which he wrote: "I saw 'Hannele.' It's reason for being is back somewhere in the middle ages but as an irresponsible artistic achievement it's great. I sat and glowed and shivered."[7] And he recommended James Herne's *Shore Acres*, largely because "young Franklin Garland" (Hamlin's brother and Crane's friend) was in the cast and the fact, as he put it, that "Herne himself is a great admirer of my work, they say, so, really he must be a man of the most admirable perceptions, you know."[8] Unfortunately, there is no record of what Crane thought of the play.

What he thought of the New York theater overall can be determined from other published documents. Of the pernicious effect that the commonplace, hero-and-villain melodrama had on the inexperienced, impressionable theater-

6. Stephen Crane, "At Clancy's Wake," in *Tales, Sketches, and Reports*, 38–42.

7. *The Correspondence of Stephen Crane*, ed. Stanley Wertheim and Paul Sorrentino (New York: Columbia University Press, 1988), I, 69.

8. Crane, *Correspondence*, ed. Wertheim and Sorrentino, I, 63–64.

goer, one need only consult the generic description of plays such as those that Maggie and her like take to be examples of "transcendental realism." Maggie's lover, writes Crane, took her to see plays in which the hero rescues the beset heroine from her cruel guardian's home. The hero, of course, as we have read in *Maggie*, spends his time "out at soak in pale-green snow storms, busy with a nickel-plated revolver, rescuing aged strangers from villains." Inevitably, concludes Crane, "the last act was a triumph for the hero, poor and of the masses, the representative of the audience, over the villain and the rich man, his pockets stuffed with bonds, his heart packed with tyrannical purposes, imperturbable amid suffering."[9]

Crane also chose to attack the status quo of the New York theater by publishing a piece entitled "Some Hints for Play-Makers."[10] Still in 1893, and again in the humor magazine *Truth*, he set down what he called "a few valuable receipts for popular dramas." "It is needless to say," he continues, "that we have followed models which have received the sanction of tradition, and are upheld at the present day by a large and important portion of the public. We do not hesitate to claim a great excellence for our receipts, and if they withstand the ravages of time and the assaults of the press with the same fortitude that characterized their predecessors along the same lines, we have no doubt that our posterity far over the horizon of the future will turn their delighted eyes upon theatrical attractions identical with those which will here charm the senses of the enlightened public." But there is a caveat: "The plans given below are short, concise and direct; the literary essentials only are given. Play-makers using the receipts should fill in well with unimportant characters and specialty people. The dramas can be lengthened or shortened to suit the temper of the audience."

Crane offers four "receipts." The first is for "an Irish melodrama" to be called either "Acushla Mavourneen" or "Mavourneen Acushla." The cast? "HERO; HEROINE; VILLAIN." The second is the formula for a "society play" in two acts, in which it is decided first that "all men are odious pigs" (Act I) and then, by means of an extenuating letter, the discovery that the "Nice Man" is "really the pink of perfection, and not an odious pig" after all. For the scandal about the "Nice Man," as it turns out, has no foundation at all. "Dottie Hightights, at the Tinsel Theatre, is his own grandmamma, and not a bad, wicked woman," as was formerly thought. The third recipe is for an action play in which the hero, armed with "a Colt's revolver, 44 calibre," faces down the "Chief Villain." The fourth recipe calls for a kind of social romantic comedy musical replete with dancer, musicians, singers, acrobats, jugglers, and so on.

9. Stephen Crane, *Maggie: A Girl of the Streets (A Story of New York)* (1893), Norton Critical Edition, ed. Thomas A. Gullason (New York: Norton, 1979), 27–28.

10. Stephen Crane, "Some Hints for Play-Makers," in *Tales, Sketches, and Reports*, 42–47.

3

Crane's need to earn a livelihood, combined with his desire to find a place for himself in the New York theater, encouraged him to apply for the job of drama critic with the *Philadelphia Press*. Prematurely, from the office of the *Press*, he wrote to a friend on September 6, 1895, "It is dramatic criticism and nuttin else. I've taken it and am to go to work at once." But four days later, he wrote to the same friend, less jauntily, "Things fell ker-plunk. Stranded here in Phila. Dont you care! Nice town. Got lots of friends, though, and 23,842 invitations to dinner of which I have accepted 2. The Press wanted me bad enough but the business manager suddenly said: 'Nit.' "[11]

Nothing further came of Crane's efforts to land a job as a drama critic. The misfiring with the *Philadelphia Press* came only weeks before the publication in book form of the *Red Badge*, an event that encouraged him to turn almost completely to the writing of fiction. He would in the remaining years of his life publish more poetry and considerable reportage, but he would be identified in the main as a writer of novels and stories. Here the story of Stephen Crane's love-hate courtship of the theater might well have ended. But it did not, for Crane could never let go of the notion that he could and would write for the theater.

In England, in 1897, he thought he had convinced his new friend Joseph Conrad to collaborate on a play. "The Predecessor," as it was called, was never written, but the idea of the play, according to Conrad, writing in the early 1920s, "consisted in a man personating his 'predecessor' (who had died) in the hope of winning a girl's heart." The scenes were "to include a ranch at the foot of the Rocky Mountains," and "the action" would have been "frankly melodramatic." Crane's idea was "that one of the situations should present the man and the girl on a boundless plain standing by their dead ponies after a furious ride (a truly Crane touch)." Conrad objected that "a boundless plain in the light of a sunset could be got into a back-cloth," but he "doubted whether we could induce the management of any London theatre to deposit two stuffed horses on its stage."[12]

There is no record of Crane's reaction to Conrad's last objections. But elsewhere Crane did write obliquely about such actualism on the stage (or near actualism, in the case of stuffed horses). In "Manacled," a short story not published until two months after his death in 1900, Crane writes about the unexpected consequences of using real manacles on an actor to enhance the "realism" of a play. In a production of *Oliver Twist* David Belasco had once

11. Crane, *Correspondence*, ed. Wertheim and Sorrentino, I, 121, 122.

12. Joseph Conrad, Introduction, to *Stephen Crane: A Study in American Letters* by Thomas Beer (New York: Knopf, 1923), 29–30.

orchestrated Fagin's madness by wearing a special wig from which, "at the climax of his ravings," he would "tear great bunches of red hair out of his scalp," his audience, along with James Herne, "gasp[ing] with horror."[13] This example from Belasco may well be an extreme one in the movement toward actualization on the stage, but it is precisely this sort of thing that Crane has targeted in "Manacled." The story begins:

> In the First Act there had been a farm scene, wherein real horses had drunk real water out of real buckets, afterward dragging a real wagon off stage, L. The audience was consumed with admiration of this play, and the great Theatre Nouveau rang to its roof with the crowd's plaudits.
> The Second Act was now well advanced. The hero, cruelly victimized by his enemies, stood in prison garb, panting with rage while two brutal warders fastened real handcuffs on his wrists and real anklets on his ankles. And the hovering villain sneered.[14]

But in the midst of this playing out of what appears to be a conventional melodrama of the sort abhorrent to the author of *Maggie* and "Some Hints for Play-Makers," a fire breaks out in the theater. The theater quickly empties out, both audience and actors—with one exception: the hero, who has been manacled for the sake of authenticity. Deserted by everyone, he tries to make his way out of the burning building. Because of the handcuffs and anklets, his progress is not only tiring but too slow, ultimately, to enable him to escape the flames. At last he realizes that he cannot escape.

> A curiously calm thought came into his head. "What a fool I was not to foresee this! I shall have Rogers furnish manacles of papier-mâché to-morrow."
> The thunder of the fire-lions made the theatre have a palsy.
> Suddenly the hero beat his handcuffs against the wall, cursing them in a loud wail. Blood started from under his finger-nails. Soon he began to bite the hot steel, and blood fell from his blistered mouth. He raved like a wolf.
> Peace came to him again. There were charming effects amid the flames. . . . He felt very cool, delightfully cool. . . . "They've left me chained up."

Now, here is true authenticity. Real manacles, real fire, real victim—all of it played now, in a typically Cranean touch, to an empty house.

13. Herbert J. Edwards and Julie A. Herne, *James A. Herne: The Rise of Realism in the American Drama* (Orono: University of Maine Press, 1964), 28.
14. Stephen Crane, "Manacled," in *Tales, Sketches, and Reports*, 159–62.

Crane was an admirer of the work of William Gillette. Undoubtedly, he approved of Gillette's meticulous concern for realistic, if not "literalistic," details. He would have appreciated, for instance, Gillette's note for a scene in *Secret Service* in which a girl pins up her lover's uniform trousers to shorten them, insisting that she not actually use pins but merely go through the motions of putting pins in her mouth. It was because of his commonsensible concern for realism in the theater as well as the success of Gillette plays such as *Secret Service* that Crane was moved to search out Gillette as a potential collaborator for his own unfinished play about the Spanish-American War.

This untitled play survives in manuscript in the two acts that Crane actually wrote.[15] It is a war play in which shots are fired and men wounded. The setting is an Englishman's sugar plantation in Cuba. It is not a very compelling play. The American hero, Henry Patten, is a first lieutenant commanding a troop of U.S. cavalry. The villain is a Spanish colonel, Don Patricio de Mavida y Aguilar. The British plantation owner has two daughters. And so on. What Crane was hoping for, obviously, was to cash in on the popularity of America's "splendid little war" in a market that had for some time been receptive to plays about the Civil War, like Clyde Fitch's *Barbara Frietchie*, Augustus Thomas's *Alabama*, Belasco's *The Heart of Maryland*, and Herne's *Griffith Davenport*. Not surprisingly, given the affinities between the two writers, Crane's play, with its cool hero calmly in control and ever ready to command, anticipates Ernest Hemingway's Spanish Civil War play, *The Fifth Column*. Gillette turned down Crane's request that he finish the play and then star in it.[16]

Crane also tried to get an actor to dramatize his brilliant story "The Upturned Face." "I am sending a copy" of the story, wrote Crane, "to Forbes Robertson in an attempt to make him see that in a thirty minute sketch on the stage he could so curdle the blood of the British public that it would be the sensation of the year, of the time."[17] Sir Johnston Forbes-Robertson turned down Crane's proposal, unfortunately, for the story cries out for dramatization. Indeed, it is tempting to reprove Crane for not casting it as a one-act play in the first place. Sorely in need of money at the time (as he would be for the rest of his life), Crane, perhaps excusably, thought he could get double payment for selling "The Upturned Face" as a story to a magazine while at the same time getting it staged by a prominent actor, who would work out the details of dramatization to suit himself.

15. Stephen Crane, ["Spanish-American War Play"], in *Poems and Literary Remains*, Volume X of *The University of Virginia Edition of the Works of Stephen Crane*, ed. Fredson Bowers, intr. James B. Colvert (Charlottesville: University Press of Virginia, 1975), 139–58.

16. *Stephen Crane: Letters*, ed. R. W. Stallman and Lillian Gilkes (New York: New York University Press, 1960), 248 n. 201; Crane, *Correspondence*, ed. Wertheim and Sorrentino, II, 557 n.

17. Crane, *Correspondence*, ed. Wertheim and Sorrentino, II, 543.

4

Crane appears never to have written a full-length play. But he left three other texts, one finished and published, the other two unfinished and unpublished, that are relevant to this account of his interest in contributing to the drama and theater of his time. "The Blood of the Martyr," in three short acts, appeared in the *New York Press Magazine* on April 3, 1898.[18] It is a highly satirical piece with German imperialism in China as its target. The time is 1898, that is, Crane's own present. The central notion is that Prince Henry of Prussia, in his attempt "to accomplish my great civilizing task in the East" (as he puts it), works out a scam whereby he trades away the lives of missionaries for railway concessions. One wonders what Crane would have made of John Hay and Theodore Roosevelt's "Open Door Policy."

The second text, extant in a long beginning fragment, is a play set in "a little inn in old France."[19] It has to do with a bunch of wine-drinking guardsmen, a gentleman-stranger, and a sorcererlike figure. Again this play does not compel, but it is clear what Crane was hoping to achieve in it. Like *The O'Ruddy*, the "Irish" historical novel he also left unfinished at his death, the play was intended to cash in on the great wave of interest in the historical romance. Partly inspired, as was "The Ghost"—the Christmas play he concocted for his house guests and the townspeople of Brede in 1899—by the historicism awakened in him during his tenure at Brede Place, this "play" might have achieved some success in the theater. Whether or not that's so, however, it can be seen as still another of Crane's hasty attempts at constructing a play that would have wide popular appeal.

The third and last of these surviving texts is something else.[20] In this one, entitled "The Fire-Tribe and the Pale-Face," Crane was trying something new for him and something new, quite possibly, for the theater of his day. Also a historical play, this time one deriving from an encounter between white soldiers and American Indians, it opens in "the Council-hut of the Fire tribe." What we have of the play—some 130 lines—is largely the speech of Catorce, the Indian who has seen the white men who have defeated the warriors of Rostina and who will become the fire-tribe's new rulers. It is an effective fragment, presenting from the Indian point of view the theme of the impending death of one way of life before the advent of a different, if scarcely more palatable, way. We find this theme elsewhere in Crane's work, particularly in the Western stories, like "The Blue Hotel," "Moonlight on the Snow," and partic-

18. Stephen Crane, "The Blood of the Martyr," in *Tales, Sketches, and Reports*, 735–39.

19. Stephen Crane, ["Play Set in a French Tavern"], in *Poems and Literary Remains*, 129–38.

20. Stephen Crane, "The Fire-Tribe and the Pale-Face: Play," in *Poems and Literary Remains*, 160–64.

ularly "The Bride Comes to Yellow Sky." But elsewhere the conflict that interests Crane is the one between the Old White West and the New White
West. In this play, done sympathetically from the Indians' vantage but with no
attempt to turn them into heroes, it is the fall of Indian nations before the new
military that Crane dramatizes. Intriguingly, Crane's manuscript ends not only
in mid-act but in mid-sentence. That it does so fittingly symbolizes his frustrated career as a dramatist in the American theater. The Reverend Jonathan
Townley Crane could have drawn a pretty moral from that.

6

The Whilomville Head Count

Rumour is a pipe
Blown by surmises, jealousies, conjectures,
And of so easy and so plain a stop
That the blunt monster with uncounted heads,
The still-discordant wav'ring multitutde,
Can play upon it.

—Shakespeare, *2 Henry IV* (1600)

No face is homely that reflects a beautiful soul.

—Alice A. Crawford, *White Ribbon Birthday Book* (1887)

Fire! fire! fire! Shout it wild and loud. Startle the hot, lurid atmosphere about us, awake the very graves with the echo; rattle the horse-cart over the street; ring the bells, and let their brazen tongues swell the chorus of alarm. The whole land is on fire! Rum is burning the nation's hope to ashes. The conflagration is spreading, and the billows of its wrath beat remorselessly against what is fairest and dearest to our civilization. . . . Oh, the awful wreck of this night of Rum!

—Rev. H. A. Delano, "The World on Fire!" (1892)

The London *Academy*'s notice of the English edition of *The Monster and Other Stories* in 1901 quotes William Dean Howells on the book's title story: " 'The Monster' is the greatest short story ever written by an American, Henry Johnson was a real man—that is, he was burned horribly about the face; but he was a hero only as he was a horror. Out of the crêpe-bound face of a negro whom

Mr. Crane saw came the story of the 'Monster.' "[1] Howells's observation about the effect seeing the "crêpe-bound face" had on Crane (the incident is not corroborated in the scholarship) may have something to do with Howells's experience in reading Nathaniel Hawthorne's "The Minister's Black Veil," a tale the power of which has much to do not with any sight of the minister's face but with the veil that covers that face to his dying day and beyond. When "Droch" [Robert Bridges] read the story in *Harper's* magazine in 1898 he saw the point immediately: "In this tale he follows the admirable Hawthornesque plan of suggesting the horror by showing its effects upon various observers. The black veil over *Johnson's* disfigured face is far more terrible than any grewsome anatomical details."[2] Thomas Beer credits Arnold Bennett with a different insight. "He was for years," writes Beer, "troubled by a memory of the negro's shattered visage and, picking up the tale after Crane died, was surprised to find that all his horror had been excited by the simple statement, 'He had no face.' "[3] It is here that I would invoke the uplifting observation from the temperance worker's *White Ribbon Birthday Book* (1887), quoted as an epigraph to this chapter, that "no face is homely that reflects a beautiful soul."[4] Yet the bane for drinkers, as Frances E. Willard pointed out, is that "[your sin] advertises you by the trademark of the drink demon stamped upon your cheek, so that even little children know."[5] In Henry Johnson's case, substitute veil for face and consider the possibility that his sin is having no face or soul. As one of his customers says to the barber, "If losing faces became popular, you'd have to go out of business."[6]

2

"The Monster," set in "the little city" of Whilomville with its six or seven firefighting companies and no less than ten physicians, is not directed toward temperance movement matters. Yet below the surface of the action there exists what Kenneth Burke calls "a disguised ritual." Temperance workers were fond

1. Anonymous, "The Literary Week" [*The Monster and Other Stories*], *Academy*, 60 (Mar. 2, 1901), 177.

2. "Droch" [Robert Bridges], "Stephen Crane's 'The Monster,' " *Life*, 32 (Sept. 1, 1898), 166.

3. Thomas Beer, *Stephen Crane: A Study in American Letters*, intr. Joseph Conrad (New York: Knopf, 1923), 164.

4. Alice A. Crawford, quoted in *The White Ribbon Birthday Book*, ed. Anna A. Gordon (Chicago: Woman's Temperance Publishing Association, 1887), 232.

5. Frances E. Willard, *Woman and Temperance: or, The Work and Workers of the Woman's Christian Temperance Union* (Hartford: Park Publishing, 1883), 177.

6. Stephen Crane, "The Monster," in *Tales of Whilomville*, Volume VII of *The University of Virginia Edition of the Works of Stephen Crane*, ed. Fredson Bowers, intr. J. C. Levenson (Charlottesville: University Press of Virginia, 1969), 7–65.

of drawing a parallel between the slavery of blacks in the South and the enslavement of drinkers to alcohol. "The South, rejoicing to-day that the slavery of the negro race no longer blots her civilization, with earnest gladness unites with her friends of the North in helping to free the people from the slavery of the Liquor Traffic," wrote one temperance worker from Mississippi.[7] Indeed, temperance writings often refer to the abstention pledge those who would refrain from drinking King Alcohol signed as the "Declaration of Independence," making thereby the suggestive connection between political independence and spiritual and physiological independence. The temperance message is submerged in the description of the engraving at the Trescott home that falls to the floor during the fire: "In the hall a lick of flame had found the cord that supported 'Signing the Declaration.' The engraving slumped suddenly down at one end, and then dropped to the floor, where it burst with the sound of a bomb."

What falls here symbolically is the idea, as Owen Wister puts it in *Lin McLean* (1897), of "one man" being "as good as another"—"for one man has been as good as another in three places—Paradise before the Fall; the Rocky Mountains before the wire fence; and the Declaration of Independence."[8] The fire, as it turns out, takes no lives, thanks to the combination of luck and the courage of Henry Johnson, "the negro who cared for the doctor's horses," Doctor Trescott himself, and—to Henry's benefit—"a young man who was a brakeman on the railway, and lived in one of the rear streets near the Trescotts, [and who] had gone into the laboratory and brought forth a thing which he laid on the grass."

Blocked at first in his attempt to escape the flames while carrying the blanket-wrapped Jimmie, Henry seems about to give up:

When Johnson came to the top of the stairs with his burden, he took a quick step backward. Through the smoke that rolled to him he could see that the lower hall was all ablaze. He cried out then in a howl that resembled Jimmie's former achievement. His legs gained a frightful faculty of bending sideways. Swinging about precariously on these reedy legs, he made his way back slowly, back along the upper hall. From the way of him then, he had given up almost all idea of escaping from the burning house, and with it the desire. He was submitting, submitting because of his fathers, bending his mind in a most perfect slavery to this conflagration.

7. *The White Ribbon Birthday Book*, ed. Gordon, 42.
8. Owen Wister, *Lin McLean* (New York and London: Harper, 1908), 119. Crane's "bomb" "burst[ing]" may also recall Francis Scott Key's patriotic lyrics to "The Star Spangled Banner" in which the bombs bursting are those threatening the still relatively new nation as well as those defending it.

In short, the "negro" is victim (at least for the moment) to his heredity, even as it was a commonplace belief among temperance workers that sons of alcoholic fathers were inescapably determined to fall prey to intemperance. Suddenly, however, Henry remembers "a little private staircase," and in that instant his "submission to the blaze" departs. The staircase "led from a bedroom to an apartment which the doctor had fitted up as a laboratory and work-house, where he used some of his leisure, and also hours when he might have been sleeping, in devoting himself to experiments which came in the way of his study and interest."

Henry makes his way through the bedroom to the doctor's laboratory, where he confronts "a strange spectacle": the room is "like a garden in the region where might be burning flowers. Flames of violet, crimson, green, blue, orange, and purple were blooming everywhere." Henry halts on the threshold, crying out again in "the negro wail that had in it the sadness of the swamps." He rushes across the room. "An orange-colored flame leaped like a panther at the lavender trousers." There's an explosion, and then "suddenly before him there reared a delicate, trembling sapphire shape like a fairy lady." Quietly smiling, she "blocked his path," dooming him and the boy. "Johnson shrieked, and then ducked in the manner of his race in fights," aiming "to pass under the left guard of the sapphire lady. . . . But she was swifter than eagles, and her talons caught in him as he plunged past her." Henry falls "with his head at the base of an old-fashioned desk." On the desk is a row of jars. "For the most part, they were silent amid this rioting, but there was one which seemed to hold a scintillant and writhing serpent. . . . Suddenly the glass splintered, and a ruby-red snakelike thing poured its thick length out upon the top of the old desk. It coiled and hesitated, and then began to swim a languorous way down the mahogany slant. At the angle it waved its sizzling molten head to and fro over the closed eyes of the man beneath it. Then, in a moment, with mystic impulse, it moved again, and the red snake flowed directly down into Johnson's upturned face." There is no one there to protect the fallen Henry from the deeply destructive bite of the chemical red snake that will disfigure him. Figurally, these snakes, like those in "The Bride Comes to Yellow Sky" and "The Snake," are associated in Crane's imaginary with the snakes featured in depictions of the delirium tremens rendered so vividly by temperance workers before bringing out the "Declaration of Independence" for signing by those ready converts to the noble cause. This reading, in my view, does not necessarily conflict with Michael Fried's notion that at this point in "The Monster," as elsewhere in Crane, "the images of serpents and fire that turn up frequently in Crane's texts belong essentially to a metaphorics of writing."[9] For it is entirely possible that

9. Michael Fried, *Realism, Writing, Disfiguration: On Thomas Eakins and Stephen Crane* (Chicago and London: University of Chicago Press, 1987), 96.

in Crane's unconscious he did associate two activities seemingly proscribed by his father: alcohol (*Arts of Intoxication*) and the production of fiction (*Popular Amusements*). In this context, one might also see the image of the "sapphire lady" as suggestive, all too obviously, of the dangers posed by consorting with dangerous women. Such equations encourage seeing Doctor Trescott not only as young Jimmie's father but as Henry Johnson's "father" as well, one who can punish as well as protect and sustain.

Like Doctor Frankenstein, however, Doctor Trescott conducts scientific experiments. And of course, like Mary Shelley's doctor, Whilomville's Doctor Trescott will also provide the citizenry with a "monster." Doctor Trescott's monster will not be threateningly huge or exceedingly powerful. He will be a human being without a face. In this, Crane draws on the interest that the temperance workers had in faces, especially the faces of drunkards that gave away their situation as sinners. They saw those faces as an obstacle to their promotion of the notion of universal charity. The drunkard had his own incriminating badge. In *Woman and Temperance* (1883) Frances E. Willard describes those telltale signs as "that very inconvenient sort of sin that cannot be covered away out of sight," for it "advertises you by the breath which poisons all the air about you; it advertises you by the zig-zag steps you make along the street, so that he who runs may read; it advertises you by the trademark of the drink demon stamped upon your cheek, so that even little children know."

> But what if the demon of envy, malice, or pride; of ambition, greed, or appetite in other forms should set his mark upon the faces of us all— would any cheek be fair? Nay, verily; not one, except as Christ has lifted us above the level of the self that was, into the victory over sin. And so, because He has thus helped us, we have come to tell thee, brother. We have brought with us the Declaration of Independence—our total abstinence pledge—and we ask thy name. But we would not single thee out, like a specimen in a museum to be labeled and certified and set up to be gazed upon; we would not treat thee like a black sheep in this great, good-natured flock. No, not at all! You take the pledge—we'll take it too; you wear the badge of ribbon, blue or red—we'll wear it too, and we will make that pledge and badge, not on your part the confession of past degradation, but on the part of all of us the kindly bond of a present brotherhood and sisterhood.[10]

In "The Monster" Henry Johnson's badge is his facial disfigurement, not to be seen directly but seen darkly, through a veil. But the use of the veil will not palliate the discomfort of Whilomville's citizenry. Indeed, it seems to increase

10. Willard, *Woman and Temperance*, 177–78.

the general discomfort. For, as Bridges noted, "the black veil over *Johnson's* disfigured face is far more terrible than any grewsome anatomical details."[11] And worse, the very existence, after the fire, of this "village monster"[12]—every town or village, even in the days of my youth, had its "monster" just as it had its haunted abandoned house—promotes an ever-increasing ugliness in behavior all round, from that of Alek Williams, who not even for money will finally care for Henry, to that of Jake Winters, whose daughter's illness he blames on Henry, and of the Whilomville women who boycott the Trescott home on Mrs. Trescott's receiving day. If Henry Fleming is finally "licensed" by his red badge, Henry Johnson is branded by his black veil. No one cares for the color of his soul, not even, perhaps, the appreciative Doctor Trescott.

3

The Reverend T. De Witt Talmage addresses the problem of extending "True Help" to the sinful intemperate by invoking the image of "thousands of people in our midst who are on *fire* with evil habits, going down through the rapids in the awful night of temptation to the eternal plunge. O God! help us to save them." He recalls that he saw "a statue in Paris of Bacchus, the god of revelry," represented as "sitting on a *panther* riding at full leap." The memory provides him with his metaphor: "Those that go down in evil ways are not riding a docile, well-broken steed; but they are on a *monster*, wild and blood-thirsty, going at a death-rate."[13]

Consider the words that have been italicized: *fire* (temptation, evil habits), *panther* (ridden by the god of wine and intemperance), and *monster* (King Alcohol itself). The reason for italicizing the first and last terms is obvious, linking the conflagration that enables Crane's story and the title Crane has chosen. The reason for italicizing the second term, however, is less immediately evident. It lies in the sentence when Johnson, having hesitated on the threshold, rushes across the room Doctor Trescott uses as his laboratory: "An orange-colored flame leaped like a panther at the lavender trousers. This animal bit deeply into

---

11. "Droch" [Robert Bridges], "Stephen Crane's 'The Monster,' " 166.

12. Anonymous, "Another Crane Sensation" ["The Monster"], *Newburyport* (Mass.) *News* (July 28, 1898), 6.

13. Rev. T. De Witt Talmage, "True Help," in *Readings and Recitations, No. 3*, ed. L[izzie] Penney (New York: National Temperance Society and Publication House, 1879), 18. Interestingly enough, in *McTeague: A Story of San Francisco* (1899) Frank Norris employs the panther metaphor to characterize the brute nature of man that unchecked will turn him into a monster. Norris writes: "It was the old battle, old as the world, wide as the world—the sudden panther leap of the animal, lips drawn, fangs aflash, hideous, monstrous, not to be resisted, and the simultaneous arousing of the other man, the better self that cries, 'Down, down,' without knowing why; that grips the monster; that fights to strangle it, to thrust it down and back" (New York: Signet, 1981, 28).

Johnson."[14] When, later, Johnson is found alive, he is nevertheless brought out of the burning house as "a thing" to be "laid on the grass." Later that "thing," having survived its encounter with sure death, is further reified as the "monster," borrowing, ironically, the horrific force of intemperance as presented in T. S. Arthur's contemporaneous book-length homily aptly entitled *Grappling with the Monster; or, The Curse and the Cure of Strong Drink*.[15] Of course, the faceless monster of Whilomville will be no more succored or aided than, perhaps, are those other pariahs, the alcoholics who are "on fire," as Talmage says, "with evil habits." Just as the telltale evidence of the drunkard's serpentine intemperance lies in his face, so, too, does that of the monster, whose face has been eaten away by the "red snake" of Doctor Trescott's chemicals.[16] As Talmage implores, "we must get off our stilts as Christian ministers and Christian reformers, and walk side by side with men in the great and awful struggle of this life," whether the men, in this case, are drunkards or monsters in some other form.

In "The Monster" Doctor Edward Trescott's idealism is put fearsomely to

14. Cross-referencing similarities and duplications in Crane's work can lead to significant connections. For example, not only does Henry share a surname with the dysfunctional Bowery family in *Maggie: A Girl of the Streets*, but the son Jimmie in that work is described as crawling upstairs to a home in which both parents are drunkards "with the caution of an invader of a panther's den."

15. T. S. Arthur, *Grappling with the Monster; or, The Curse and the Cure of Strong Drink* (New York: John W. Lovell, *ca.* 1877).

16. Bill Brown argues that the chemicals in Doctor Trescott's laboratory behave like photographic developing chemicals, a fact, if established, that would link up "The Monster" to the general cultural interest in photography in Crane's day. "Alongside an illustration from the Kodak manual," he writes, "it is difficult not to read the scene [of Doctor Trescott's chemicals eating away at the flesh of Henry Johnson's face] as a 'mystic' version of a solution pouring itself and slowly flowing across the upturned plate, which here does not produce the figure of a face but is the face suffering disfigurement" (*The Material Unconscious: American Amusement, Stephen Crane, and the Economies of Play* [Cambridge, Mass.: Harvard University Press, 1996], 226).

The argument here is tricky in that it assumes the "reality" of a metaphor that is itself based on a metaphor. What is more likely, I think, is that Doctor Trescott would have been handling chemicals related to his work as a physician. In a time well before the establishment of laboratories to conduct tests, individual physicians were left pretty much to their own devices. It is not out of the question, of course, that Doctor Trescott is conducting chemical experiments in a spirit of pure science. David Halliburton suggests that Trescott "supplements his daily medical practice with scientific research, suggesting that he should also be numbered among those physicians who were delivering comparatively sophisticated medical care to American towns and smaller cities as well as to the main urban centers" (*The Color of the Sky: A Study of Stephen Crane* [Cambridge, Eng.: Cambridge University Press, 1989], 193). For the portrayal of such a physician working outside the main urban centers, see Harold Frederic's *The Damnation of Theron Ware*, a novel published in 1896, two years before the first publication of "The Monster." It may not be incidental that Crane's brother Wilbur was once interrogated by the police for storing a cadaver that he intended to render chemically so that he could learn enough anatomy to pass his course at the medical school. At the time Stephen Crane was twelve (Stanley Wertheim and Paul Sorrentino, *The Crane Log: A Documentary Life of Stephen Crane, 1871–1900* [New York: G. K. Hall, 1994], 28–29).

the extreme test. The moral question is not whether he will behave idealisti-
cally, of course, but what meaning, as a matter of fact, inheres in his personal
expression of "idealism." In other words, just how idealistic can the doctor be,
to what extent can he practice charity in the midst of Whilomville's righteous
fear? Now the idea begins to cut, for although the doctor saves the life of
Henry Johnson, whom he publicly credits with saving his young son from the
fire, the details of the story show that Johnson's actions were not in themselves
sufficient to save the child. Henry attempted to get the boy out, but he was not
able to get him all the way out. For Crane (as for the doctor) the difference
between the attempt and the achievement is crucial. So the doctor's efforts in
keeping the faceless man alive may not be entirely explained by his sense of
personal gratitude. Then are they motivated by charity? Perhaps he desires to
preserve the man's life because doing so will constitute an act of disinterested
benevolence. The paradoxical nature of the doctor's medically successful min-
istration to the "monster" is laid bare by Judge Hagenthorpe, Whilomville's
patriarch. He warns Trescott: "I am induced to say that you are performing a
questionable charity in preserving this negro's life. As near as I can understand,
he will hereafter be a monster, a perfect monster, and probably with an affected
brain. . . . I am afraid, my friend, that it is one of the blunders of virtue." Inevitably, the charitable preservation of Henry Johnson's life can be nothing but a
blunder of virtue, or so says the world's wisdom.

The life the doctor can provide for the impaired Henry is meager, at best.
Even the bare-bones solution of room and board with a poor family beyond
the margins of the little city proves abortive when Henry escapes to town and
frightens much of the community. The doctor comes to the decision that only
he can care for Henry. Why, then, has the doctor kept Henry alive? One possible answer is that he feels ultimately responsible for him as a result of his own
artful science: that Henry is indeed, with his brain damaged, the living upshot
of Doctor Trescott's experimental science. Human life may be precious beyond all things, but Doctor Trescott never says that this is so, and neither does
the author-narrator. Again Judge Hagenthorpe states the charges against Doctor Trescott: "He will be your creation, you understand. He is purely your creation. Nature has very evidently given him up. He is dead. You are restoring
him to life. You are making him, and he will be a monster, and with no mind."

What Crane manages, however, is to have it both ways: the doctor exercises
some form of charity in the case of Henry Johnson (though Crane makes it
clear that the doctor's motives are not entirely disinterested), while the populace fail to practice such charity (though their response, given Henry's fate, can
be interpreted, perversely, as more humane than the doctor's). With subtlety
and bite, Crane suspends both positions—the doctor's and the people's—
before the reader. Find a solution to this antinomy, he challenges, if you can.
The difficult truth, he implies, is that the man who would practice charity in

the Whilomvilles of this world is subject to social damnation that extends to his family and even his work.

The last sentences of "The Monster" are justly celebrated for their terrible power. "As he sat holding her head on his shoulder, Trescott found himself occasionally trying to count the cups. There were fifteen of them." The number fifteen for the unused cups set out for Mrs. Trescott's receiving day remains puzzling. But the major point is clear. The true Whilomville monster is Whilomville: Shakespeare's "blunt monster with uncounted heads."[17]

It is seldom noted that Henry Johnson makes a second appearance in Crane's Whilomville fiction. In "The Knife," written two years later, in 1899, and first published in 1900, Peter Washington, who has become Doctor Trescott's new "man," invites comparison with his predecessor: "His ideal had been the late gallant Henry Johnson whose conquests in Watermelon Alley as well as in the hill shanties had proved him the equal if not the superior of any Pullman-car porter in the country. Perhaps Peter had too much Virginia laziness and humor in him to be a wholly adequate successor to the fastidious Henry Johnson but at any rate he admired his memory so attentively as to be openly termed a dude by envious people."[18] Linking "The Knife" to "The Monster" tells us certain important things about the episode that is the substance of the latter. Discussing "The Knife" after discussing "The Monster" is to follow tragedy with comedy (in both senses of the word: comic and comedic [all turns out well in this tale of an abortive attempt at stealing a watermelon]), providing a dying fall to the Trescott family tragedy with which "The Monster" concludes. Putting the two stories together, in sequence, also provides a comedic ending to "The Monster" as a tale about the Trescott family fortunes. For we learn several important things: that Henry Johnson has died, that he has had a successor as Doctor Trescott's hostler, that the Trescotts have continued to live in Whilomville after Henry's death, that Doctor Trescott obviously can still afford to employ a "man." Evidently the ostracism of the Trescotts, so graphically indicated at the end of "The Monster" by the women's boycotting Mrs. Trescott on her receiving day, has not lasted beyond the disappearance of the faceless Henry Johnson from the scene. Far from being driven out of Whilomville, Doctor Trescott has continued to earn a living there. The social and economic hardships of the Trescotts, resulting from Doctor Trescott's ministering to and responsibility for the "monster," have been outlived. The long shadow cast by Henry Johnson's veil over the entire Trescott family

17. This view does not contradict Patrick K. Dooley's notion that Crane's "primary interest in *The Monster* is the story's impact upon the ethical sensibilities of his readers," if one considers the populace of Whilomville as representative of humankind (*The Pluralistic Philosophy of Stephen Crane* [Urbana and Chicago: University of Illinois Press, 1993], 98).

18. Stephen Crane, "The Knife," in *Tales of Whilomville*, 185–86.

has apparently been lifted by the death of the "monster." Even Henry John-son's biography has been freed of the aftermath of the fire in the Trescott house that disfigured the hostler, for he now lives in Peter Washington's memory not as a faceless inspiration for horror but as the model and standard for fastidious, elegant dress.

7

Red Blood, Black Passion

Ancient Greece made her sons a nation of heroes by holding up valor as the only true badge of earthly glory. She sought out every means of claiming for her heroes the admiration of the people, and taught courage by the force of example.

—General Horace Porter, "The Philosophy of Courage" (1888)

Thus the grand army of the consumers of alcohol is formed of many divisions, the rich and the poor, the high and the low, the wretches who rave in the drunkard's delirium or lie as dead men by the way-side.

—Rev. J. T. Crane, *Arts of Intoxication* (1870)

War is terrible, and many of our best men have gone to their graves through war; but strong drink has carried more victims to the grave, in America, than has war.

—D. L. Moody, "A Warning Against Wine" (1877)

1

Justly proud of his role in the publication of *The Red Badge of Courage,* Irving Bacheller was fond of telling the story of how Stephen Crane first brought him the manuscript of his war novel. He told it in *Coming Up the Road* in 1928 and repeated it in *From Stores of Memory* in 1933. Six years before his death in 1950, he was still telling the story. In less elaborate detail, he wrote: "I discovered Stephen Crane one day when he brought *The Red Badge* to me and asked me to read it. I took it home and read most of the vivid tale that night, bought it for the syndicate next day. He worked exclusively for me for a long time."[1]

1. MS letter, Irving Bacheller to Peggy Manley (Dec. 13?), 1944, Baker Library, Dartmouth College, Hanover, New Hampshire. Quoted with consent.

In December 1894, under the auspices of the Bacheller and Johnson Syndicate, Crane's novel was serialized, as a rule in six installments, sometimes in three, throughout the country. The newspapers that carried it ranged from the *Hartford Courant*, the *New York Press*, and the *Philadelphia Press*, to the *Nebraska State Journal*, the *Minneapolis Tribune*, and the *San Francisco Examiner*. Indeed, John Berryman estimates (improbably) that as many as 750 to 800 newspapers carried this shortened version of the *Red Badge*.[2]

This Bacheller version runs to less than 40 percent of the original text. While Crane himself seems to have done the cutting, much even of "the essential story disappeared," writes Berryman: "The youth's parting with his mother from Chapter I, continual speculation, the crucial irresolution of XI, and the final chapter—indeed all the last three chapters—are gone; and practically everything else that could be cut away: description, dialogue, narrative."[3] The loss of the mother's speech to her son on the eve of his departure for the war camp took away one of the essential clues to the way Crane's imagination worked. Henry Fleming is going off to war, perhaps to his death. But what his mother takes pains to warn him about is that he is in danger of falling in with a bad crowd.

An' allus be careful an' choose yer comp'ny. There's lots of bad men in the army, Henry. The army makes 'em wild and they like nothing better than the job of leading off a young feller like you—as ain't never been away from home much and has allus had a mother—and a-learning 'im to drink and swear. Keep clear of them folks, Henry. I don't want yeh to ever do anything, Henry, that yeh would be 'shamed to let me know about. Jest think as if I was a-watchin' yeh.[4]

Henry's mother's sentiments and concerns would not have been alien to the Woman's Christian Temperance Union worker that Crane's own mother was.[5] Nor would her statement to Henry about his father's own abstention: " 'Yeh must allus remember yer father, too, child, an' remember he never drunk a

---

2. John Berryman, *Stephen Crane* (New York: William Sloane, 1950), 94 n. Joseph Katz agrees with Berryman (Introduction, *"The Red Badge of Courage" by Stephen Crane: A Facsimile Reproduction of the New York Press Appearance of December 9, 1894* [Gainesville: Scholars' Facsimiles & Reprints, 1967], 26).

3. Berryman, *Stephen Crane*, 94–95.

4. Stephen Crane, *The Red Badge of Courage*, Volume II of *The University of Virginia Edition of the Works of Stephen Crane*, ed. Fredson Bowers, intr. J. C. Levenson (Charlottesville: University Press of Virginia, 1975), 1–135.

5. The WCTU was active among the nation's military. A department for "Work Among Soldiers and Sailors" was adopted in 1882 because "of the terrible temptations to which the men are subjected" (Anonymous, *A Brief History of the Woman's Christian Temperance Union*, 2nd ed. [Evanston: Union Signal, 1907], 38).

drop of licker in his life and seldom swore a cross oath.' "[6] Mary J. Safford, a physician quoted in *The White Ribbon Birthday Book*, published by the Woman's Temperance Publishing Association in 1887, would have agreed with Henry's mother. "The wide range of experience that we have had on the battle field and in the hospitals, during our war," she wrote, "taught us that frequently a man's most deadly enemy was his own bad habits."[7]

Truncated product that it was, serialization of the *Red Badge* had an immediately salutary effect on Crane's professional career. By mid-December 1894, as the *Philadelphia Press* announced, "The editorial approval of the story of Stephen Crane which recently ran as a serial in *The Press* has been confirmed by the judgment of one of our greater publishers. Mr. Crane has received a very flattering offer from one of the largest publishing houses in this city for a contract for the publication of that story in book form, and has accepted it. He will revise it somewhat, not materially."[8] But Crane did not then have the time to revise his manuscript, for in early 1895, at Bacheller's behest, he was off "to Mexico for some color."[9] By the time he returned east in May 1895, *The Black Riders and Other Lines*, his first trade book, was about to appear under the aegis of Copeland and Day of Boston, and he was no longer dealing with a Philadelphia publisher for the *Red Badge* but with Appleton of New York. The complete, though revised, *Red Badge* did not hit the bookstores until autumn 1895.

2

Despite its critical success overall, Appleton's *Red Badge* had its vociferous detractors. For them, the major issue was that the book had pretensions at realistic representation. They did not find credible Crane's portrayal of the young soldier (a question of rendering) or creditable (a question of social and historical mimesis). They judged the detailed incidents of war and the anatomized emotions of the soldiers to be inauthentic. One comment stands for many: "As Mr. Crane is too young a man to write from experience, the frightful details of his book must be the outcome of a very feverish imagination."[10] To many readers, the book's narrative language and its mixture of styles were problematic. "Pic-

6. Drunken fathers are legion in temperance literature. For the dire results of the excesses emanating from a "kindly father's drunken rage," see "Oh, Let Me In," in *Temperance Battle Songs*, comp. S. W. Straub (Chicago: S. W. Straub, 1883), 56–58.

7. *The White Ribbon Birthday Book*, ed. Anna A. Gordon (Chicago: Woman's Temperance Publishing Association, 1887), 40.

8. "Holland" [E. J. Edwards], Editorial, *Philadelphia Press* (Dec. 19, 1894), 8.

9. MS letter, Bacheller to Manley.

10. Anonymous, "Book Notes" [*The Red Badge of Courage*], *Peterson Magazine*, n.s. 6 (June 1896), 654.

turesqueness of description allied to a grim realism of dialogue and frequent imaginative strokes of a somber sort make this story striking. But the immaturity of the writer is exhibited in many sins of diction, in a self-conscious forcing of metaphors, and in not a few untruths to human nature in the situations delineated."[11]

To complaints about Crane's narrative style were added the questions raised by the behavior of the young soldier Henry Fleming. It was not always what readers saw as Henry's improbable behavior that vexed them and sparked heated controversy but what that implied about the overall battlefield behavior of the typical American soldier. Some readers applauded Crane's acuity in discerning the type, consciously ignoring the fact that the author of the *Red Badge* was no veteran of the war he had written about and therefore could not write out of personal, "realistic" observation. Other readers, including a general officer, focused on that fact in order to undermine Crane's authority by denying validity to his portrayal of Americans in battle. Writing in the *Dial*, General A. C. McClurg called the book "a vicious satire upon American soldiers and American armies" and a "work of diseased imagination."[12] McClurg's attack released a flow of negative criticism. Throughout that spring of 1896, the *Red Badge*'s popularity had increased steadily, but the general's words gave Crane's detractors something more tangible to throw at him than their annoyance at what they perceived to be his idiosyncratic use of primary colors and seemingly bizarre similes. That a war-experienced soldier of the highest rank had spoken against a twenty-four-year-old born six years after the war's end lent credibility to McClurg's otherwise shrill and bombastic attack.

Even before McClurg's attack, however, there were readers who had privately impugned Crane's creditability, among them the younger Oliver Wendell Holmes's friend Sir Frederick Pollock. The Englishman put the matter succinctly shortly after the book appeared in England. "I have read *The Red Badge of Courage*—the psychology seems to me artificial and forced," he wrote to Holmes as early as February 1, 1896. "If a recruit did go through all those complex emotions he would never remember them. For the general picture you can bear witness—but I guess the discipline must have been better in your regiment."[13] Holmes's reaction to Pollock's statement at this time has gone un-

---

11. Anonymous, "Recent Fiction" [*The Red Badge of Courage*], *Sunday-School Times*, 38 (June 6, 1896), 367–68.

12. A. C. McClurg, "The Red Badge of Hysteria," *Dial*, 20 (Apr. 16, 1896), 227–28. For an analysis of issues surrounding McClurg's charges against Crane, see Donald Pease, "Fear, Rage, and the Mistrials of Representation in *The Red Badge of Courage*," in *American Realism: New Essays*, ed. Eric J. Sundquist (Baltimore and London: Johns Hopkins University Press, 1982), 155–75.

13. *Holmes-Pollock Letters: The Correspondence of Mr Justice Holmes and Sir Frederick Pollock, 1874–1932*, ed. Mark De Wolfe Howe, intr. John Gorham Palfrey (Cambridge, Mass.: Harvard University Press, 1941), I, 68.

recorded, but there does exist Holmes's battlefield diary in which he, an officer seriously wounded in his first battle and later rewounded, recorded his changing emotions—of well-being as well as letdown. Holmes's changes of mood, however, do not occur in periods of nervous disquiet followed by fear, of panic succeeded by bravado, as they do for Crane's Henry Fleming. Yet it is not unimaginable that Henry might have written to reassure his mother, as Holmes did, shortly after his first wounding:

> I can't write an account now but I felt and acted very cool and did my duty I am sure—I was out in front of our men encouraging 'em on when a spent shot knocked the wind out of me & I fell—then I crawled to the rear a few paces & rose by help of the 1st Ser^{gt}; & the Colonel who was passing said "That's right Mr Holmes—Go to the rear" but I felt that I couldn't without more excuse so up Ī got and rushed to the front where hearing the Col. cheering the men on I waved my sword and asked if none would follow me when down I went again by the Colonel's side— The first shot (the spent ball) struck me on the belly below where the ribs separate & bruised & knocked the wind out of me—The second time I hope only one ball struck me entering the left & coming out behind the right breast in wh. case I shall probably recover and this view is seconded by finding a ball in my clothes by the right hand wound—I may be hit twice in which case the chance is not so good—But I am now so well that I have good hopes . . . I am very happy in the conviction I did my duty handsomely.[14]

Clearly Holmes wishes to assuage his family's fears, and there is only a trace of bravado in his words. Nowhere in Holmes's diary or in his letters home does he sound the more grandiosely heroic note sounded by other soldiers. Only in the early days of the war did this soldier see "the greatness of the crisis, the Homeric grandeur of the contest" that "surrounds and elevates us all," as did E. C. Stedman, the stockbroker poet, writing to his mother.[15] Thomas Wentworth Higginson, another wounded officer, later recalled the "emotions of that period of early war enlistments": "It was as if one had learned to swim in air, and were striking out for some new planet. All the methods, standards, habits, and aims of ordinary life were reversed, and the intrinsic and traditional charm

14. *Touched with Fire: Civil War Letters and Diary of Oliver Wendell Holmes, Jr., 1861–1864*, ed. Mark De Wolfe Howe (Cambridge, Mass.: Harvard University Press, 1946), 13, 18.

15. *Life and Letters of Edmund Clarence Stedman*, ed. Laura Stedman and George M. Gould (New York: Moffat, Yard, 1910), I, 242. It will be recalled that Henry Fleming's early desire is to engage in "Greek-like struggles" (Crane, *The Red Badge of Courage*, 8).

of the soldier's life was mingled in my own case with the firm faith that the death-knell of slavery itself was being sounded."[16]

Yet in his review of the *Red Badge* in 1896, Higginson explains how right from the start time effaces the real-life recruit's immediate sense of "the breathlessness, the hurry, the confusion, the seeming aimlessness, as of a whole family of disturbed ants, running to and fro." The "result of too much perspective" is that everything is changed. "Afterward, perhaps, when the affair is discussed at the campfire, and his view compared with what others say," he writes shrewdly, "it begins to take shape, often mixed with all sorts of errors; and when it has reached the Grand Army Post and been talked over afterward for thirty years, the narrator has not a doubt of it all. It is now a perfectly ordered affair, a neat and well arranged game of chess, often with himself as a leading figure."[17]

So too, in its time, there had emerged the formalized talk of high motives and the strife for glory. Holmes himself participated in that revisionary discourse. In a Memorial Day Address in 1884, he insisted that "the generation that carried on the war has been set apart by its experience." As one of that war generation, he could boast: "Through our great good fortune, in our youth our hearts were touched with fire."[18] It had been their portion to strive for "glory," in fact, for that "bit of red ribbon that a man would die to win."[19]

In Holmes and Higginson—two officers obviously more conversant with the larger issues of the war than the typical recruit would be—can be discerned the same volunteer's euphoria that motivates Crane's recruit to go to war. What we no longer have in their later writings is the sense of what battle itself was like, something that at the time Holmes had conveyed rather well. To his father he confided that courage was not always the order of the day: "Once when *entre nous* the right of Lowell's Co begun to waver a little and fall back our left stood and didn't give an inch—But really as much or rather more is due to the file closers than anything else[—]I told 'em to shoot any men who ran and they lustily buffeted every hesitating brother—I gave one (who was

16. Thomas Wentworth Higginson, *Cheerful Yesterdays* (Boston and New York: Houghton Mifflin, 1898), 248–49.

17. T. W. Higginson, "A Bit of War Photography," *Philistine*, 3 (July 1896), 34, 35.

18. Oliver Wendell Holmes, "Memorial Day, An Address Delivered May 30, 1884," in *Speeches by Oliver Wendell Holmes* (Boston: Little, Brown, 1913), 11. Holmes's reinterpretation of his overall Civil War experience is discussed by Amy Kaplan, "The Spectacle of War in Crane's Revision of History," in *New Essays on The Red Badge of Courage*, ed. Lee Clark Mitchell (Cambridge, Eng.: Cambridge University Press, 1986), 77–108. See also Giorgio Mariani, *Spectacular Narratives: Representations of Class and War in Stephen Crane and the American 1890s* (New York: Peter Lang, 1992), 156.

19. Oliver Wendell Holmes, "Harvard College in the War," in *Speeches*, 14. A decade later, however, he was ready to admit that "war, when you are at it, is horrible and dull" ("The Soldier's Faith, An Address Delivered on Memorial Day, May 30, 1895, at a Meeting Called by the Graduating Class of Harvard University," ibid., 62).

cowering) a smart rap over the backsides with the edge of my sword—and stood with my revolver & swore I'd shoot the first who ran or fired against orders."[20] Even Henry Adams, who did not go to the war, thought he understood the psychology of the raw recruit under fire. In the days after his wife's suicide in 1885, Adams describes his plight in the very terms that would guide Crane's own understanding of battlefield behavior: "I feel like a volunteer in his first battle. If I don't run ahead at full speed, I shall run away. If I could but keep in violent action all the time, I could manage to master myself; but this wretched bundle of nerves, which we call mind, gives me no let up."[21]

Crane's fictional problem was both similar to and different from Adams's. Since he wished to write about war experiences he had not had, he, too, resorted to imagining them. Yet as a writer he saw himself as committed, as he put it, to "the beautiful war between those who say that art is man's substitute for nature and we are the most successful in art when we approach the nearest to nature and truth, and those who say—well, I don't know what they say."[22] His task was to discover within himself the experiences that would release the emotions and language he needed to imagine the fictional world of the novel he subtitled *An Episode of the American Civil War.*

Crane attempted to explain away this seeming anomaly in theory and practice. The "big reviews" in England praised the *Red Badge* for its "psychological portrayal of fear," he noted, but they insisted that he was "a veteran of the civil war, whereas the fact is, as you know, I never smelled even the powder of a sham battle." Yet he knew what battle must feel like. "I know what the psychologists say, that a fellow can't comprehend a condition that he has never experienced, and I argued that many times with the Professor. Of course, I have never been in a battle, but I believe that I got my sense of the rage of conflict on the football field, or else fighting is a hereditary instinct, and I wrote intuitively; for the Cranes were a family of fighters in the old days, and in the Revolution every member did his duty."[23]

Crane's claim to instinctive knowledge of warfare does not carry him far, but his notion that he learned about "the rage of conflict" from the football field offers an oblique clue to the source for his indirect "knowledge" of the

---

20. Holmes, *Touched with Fire*, 51.

21. Letter, Henry Adams to John Hay, December 17, 1885, in *The Letters of Henry Adams, Volume II: 1868–1885*, ed. J. C. Levenson, Ernest Samuels, Charles Vandersee, and Viola Hopkins Winner (Cambridge, Mass., and London: Harvard University Press, 1982), 643. General Horace Porter's experience was different: "The question is often asked whether men in battle, when they break, run to the rear very fast. Usually they do not; they often do not run at all; the most provoking part of it is that they deliberately walk away" ("The Philosophy of Courage," *Century*, 36 [June 1888], 250).

22. *The Correspondence of Stephen Crane*, ed. Stanley Wertheim and Paul Sorrentino (New York: Columbia University Press, 1988), I, 63.

23. Ibid., 322.

psychological truth of a recruit's battlefield behavior. First, however, we should be reminded that even this explanation that his knowledge was indirect and that he was able to transfer it to another "theater"—his strategy for discovering what would suffice—was itself seemingly in violation of his stated creed. "I understand that a man is born into the world with his own pair of eyes and he is not at all responsible for his quality of personal honesty," he had earlier written. Yet "there is a sublime egotism in talking of honesty," he added. "This aim in life struck me as being the only thing worth while."[24]

Crane's statement bears on what would otherwise seem to be his transgressions against his own principles as a realist. It points to his working assumption that for him knowledge derived essentially from vision, though not limited to what could be seen, literally, with the natural eye. A writer's "honesty"—Crane's, at least—had as much to do with "seeing" the emotional reality of those thoughts emanating from "seeing" things as it did with directly and accurately registering the visual image. Thinking this way enabled Crane the young writer to take on those subjects and situations beyond his direct and unmediated experience, as in *Maggie, George's Mother,* or the *Red Badge,* without seemingly compromising his principle of personal honesty to what one sees with one's own pair of eyes.

The problem after the appearance of the 1893 *Maggie* was simply that Crane now wanted to write a book about the American Civil War though he had not yet witnessed a battle, let alone fought in one. If his first knowledge of the Civil War came through tales told by his teachers and veterans he encountered, he fortified that knowledge by a reading of writers such as J. W. DeForest, Ambrose Bierce, Zola, and Tolstoy, personal war narratives (some of which were then running in the New York newspapers), and old issues of *Century* magazine containing installments of its series on Civil War battles and leaders.[25] Of the personal narratives in the *Century* he complained specifically: "I wonder that *some* of these fellows don't tell how they *felt* in those scraps! They spout eter-

---

24. Ibid., 195–96.

25. See George Wyndham, "A Remarkable Book," *New Review* (London), 14 (Jan. 1896), 30–40; Sydney Brooks, "In the School of Battle: The Making of a Soldier," *Saturday Review* (London), 81 (Jan. 11, 1896), 44–45; Lyndon Upson Pratt, "A Possible Source of *The Red Badge of Courage,*" *American Literature,* 11 (Mar. 1939), 1–10; H. T. Webster, "Wilbur F. Hinman's *Corporal Si Klegg* and Stephen Crane's *The Red Badge of Courage,*" *American Literature,* 11 (Nov. 1939), 285–93; Gordon S. Haight, Introduction to *Miss Ravenel's Conversion from Secession to Loyalty* by John William De Forest (New York and London: Harper, 1939), xi; James B. Colvert, "*The Red Badge of Courage* and a Review of Zola's *La Débâcle,*" *Modern Language Notes,* 71 (Feb. 1956), 98–100; and Stanley Wertheim, "*The Red Badge of Courage* and Personal Narratives of the Civil War," *American Literary Realism,* 6 (Winter 1973), 61–65. For the argument that Crane's indebtedness in the *Red Badge* was to a subgenre of Civil War fiction, not to a single work, see Donald Gibson, "Crane's Own Red Badge: The Origins of That Species," paper presented at "One Hundred Years After the Publication of *The Red Badge of Courage,*" a conference held at the United States Air Force Academy, Colorado Springs, Colorado, Nov. 30-Dec. 1, 1995.

nally of what they *did*, but they are as emotionless as rocks!"[26] Importantly, for the depiction of the commonplace daily activities of the soldier, Crane had access to Winslow Homer's war engravings for *Harper's Weekly*, work that resembled his oil paintings of the time, such as *Soldiers Pitching Quoits*. Exaggerating the claim (but not by much), the novelist Wright Morris, echoing Ernest Hemingway, ventures that "Brady & Co. photographs of the Civil War, reproduced in books, provided the imagination of Stephen Crane with all the war he needed to write *The Red Badge of Courage*."[27]

Encouraged by his knowledge of such sources, Crane was not to be deterred by his own notion that one had to have witnessed war to write about it. He plunged into a narrative that seemed to reflect an infantryman's direct impressions of soldiering in and out of battle. His decision to focus on the private foot soldier (rather than an officer of cavalry, say) was daring enough, but he also decided on a style that was both innovative and highly idiosyncratic. That style he employed everywhere in the *Red Badge* with the exception of the New York scenes and some of the early camp scenes.

Crane's first biographer, Thomas Beer, addressed the problem of Crane's "imagined" *Red Badge* and came up with what is now known to be a novelist's answer, rather than a biographer's:

> He could stand through nights in a blizzard of late March to write "Men in the Storm" or sleep in a Bowery shelter to get at the truth of "An Experiment in Misery" but the emotions of a boy in battle he must find for himself, in himself, and the birth of the book was travail incomprehensible to men who have never hunted in themselves passions and the flood of acts to which they are alien. However, there had been a boy who went confidently off to make war on a world and a city. He had been beaten to shelter and had lurched up a lane in darkness on the arm of some stranger. He had been praised for his daring while his novel, like a retreating army, lay in unsold heaps and the maker of images was sure of his own clay.[28]

26. Corwin K. Linson, *My Stephen Crane*, ed. Edwin H. Cady (Syracuse: Syracuse University Press, 1958), 37.

27. Wright Morris, "Some by That Master, Anon," *New York Times Book Review* (Jan. 20, 1980), 33. Hemingway's assertion that Crane had seen "Matthew Brady's wonderful photographs" appears in his Introduction to *Men at War: The Best War Stories of All Time*, ed. Ernest Hemingway (New York: Crown, 1942), xvii.

28. Thomas Beer, *Stephen Crane: A Study in American Letters*, intr. Joseph Conrad (New York: Knopf, 1923), 98–99. Stanley Wertheim offers a plausible overall explanation for the way Crane's family heritage infused *The Red Badge of Courage*. Following John Berryman, who had built much of his interpretation of Crane's life and work around the notion that the boy's "mistress" was "fear," Wertheim proposes that "into his parable of the Civil War," Crane, who was "thoroughly familiar with the anatomy of fear, . . . projected the same religious conflicts found in *The Black Riders*. The sinful boy

Impersonating the biographer, Beer forges his facts through a kind of back-formation as if to honor Crane's imagination without impugning his notions about personal honesty. Without documentation, Beer posits the transfer or transformation of emotional experience from one set of circumstances to another—from life to fiction. Crane knew what it would be like for a wounded soldier to be led by the arm in darkness by a stranger because he had undergone a similar experience in some street in a New Jersey town, and he knew what it would be like to be praised undeservedly for being daring and courageous when the truth was that he was neither. Beer's answer is appealing, but the hard fact is that we simply do not know.

We do know that after Crane himself had been to war and had professed the *Red Badge*'s realism confirmed by his experience, he never again wrote about war quite so spectacularly as he had in his earlier fiction.[29] He no longer had to "imagine" war in the same way. Memory encouraged him to stick largely to the actual facts of direct experience, to what he literally saw. Crane's depiction of battle in *Wounds in the Rain*, coming after he had participated in the Cuban and Puerto Rican campaigns as a correspondent, bears only sporadic resemblance to his depiction of warfare in the *Red Badge*. And although there is irony aplenty in the later book, there is precious little to deflate or diminish those Crane sees as heroes. Rather than the (by turns) panic-stricken and intermittently self-aggrandizing Henry of the *Red Badge*, the volunteers and veterans who appear in *Wounds in the Rain* are more the likes of the heroic Henry Fleming of the short story "The Veteran."

The second major difference between the *Red Badge* and *Wounds in the Rain* is stylistic. Crane's highly imagistic, symbolic, naturalistic style in the *Red Badge* has largely disappeared from Crane's later war fiction. Crane's imagination served a different purpose. He could now forge his fictional reality out of the recalled details of his actual experience. Within this context can be proposed (apart from watching football or working out of inherited instinct) some sources for Crane's early imaginings of battle in the *Red Badge*.

3

There are two singularly dramatic instances in which Crane's young soldier encounters the death of others: he comes upon the corpse in the glen, and he

---

who had rebelled against the Unjust Father and in so doing had separated himself from the community of the faithful became the youth who in panic fled from the protection of the tribe and who was, therefore, forced to wander in a fearful hinterland in order to redefine his identity and to learn his relationship to nature and to society" ("Stephen Crane and the Wrath of Jehovah," *Literary Review*, 7 [Summer 1964], 505).

29. In *The Double Life of Stephen Crane* (New York: Knopf, 1992), Christopher Benfey argues for the thesis that Crane strangely often lived out many of his experiences after having first imagined them.

witnesses the death of the tall soldier. In the first of these scenes, the youth, going "into the deep thickets,"

> reached a place where the high, arching boughs made a chapel. He softly pushed the green doors aside and entered. Pine-needles were a gentle brown carpet. There was a religious half-light.
>
> Near the threshold, he stopped horror-stricken at the sight of a thing.
>
> He was being looked at by a dead man who was seated with his back against a column-like tree. The corpse was dressed in a uniform that once had been blue but was now faded to a melancholy shade of green. The eyes, staring at the youth, had changed to the dull hue to be seen on the side of a dead fish. The mouth was open. Its red had changed to an appalling yellow. Over the grey skin of the face ran little ants. One was trundling some sort of a bundle along the upper lip.

It is worth noting at the outset that at this point Crane is not working in a literary vacuum. This scene recalls other scenes drawing on what was already a literary topos, what the French called "the corpse amid the flowers" ("cadavre aux fleurs").[30] The topos appears, for example, in Rimbaud's widely acclaimed poem "The Sleeper in the Valley." It takes place in "a green hollow":

> A young soldier, his mouth open, his head bare,
> And the nape of his neck bathing in the cool blue watercress,
> Sleeps; he is stretched out on the grass, under clouds,
> Pale on his green bed where the light rains down.
>
> His feet in the gladiolas, he sleeps. Smiling as
> A sick child would smile, he is taking a nap:
> Nature, cradle him warmly: he is cold.
> Odors do not make his nostrils quiver.
> He sleeps in the sun, his hand on his breast,
> Quieted. There are two red holes in his right side.[31]

Rimbaud's soldier is stretched out, mouth open, as if asleep. In the last line the poem reveals its secret. The sleeper is dead.

Before Rimbaud, Victor Hugo, Léon Dierx, George Sand, and Leconte de Lisle had employed the "corpse" trope. But Edgar Quinet's use in his autobi-

---

30. See Claude Duchet, "Autour du 'Dormeur du Val' de Rimbaud," *Revue d'Histoire Littéraire de la France*, 62 (July–Sept. 1962), 371, and Sergio Cigada, "Una questione di fonti: George Sand, Leconte de Lisle, Arthur Rimbaud," *Letterature moderne*, 9 (July–Aug. 1959), 486–97.

31. *Rimbaud: Complete Works, Selected Letters*, ed. and trans. Wallace Fowlie (Chicago and London: University of Chicago Press, 1966), 57.

ography anticipates Crane's use most closely. Like Crane's young soldier, the young Quinet stumbles on a body, arms stretched out, a bullet hole in its side: "In a small glen, on ground dotted with violets and cowslips, I came upon a corpse. It was that of a soldier. There was in his right side a large bullet hole. His already congealed blood had spilled out at length along the ground. Its mouth was wide open and its two arms, tattooed with flowers and eagles, were extended. There was no one near the dead man. Later I learned that he had been killed as he tried to desert by going through the brush."[32] Desertion, of course, is an important matter in the *Red Badge*.[33]

But Crane's most direct source for "the corpse amid the flowers" topos was Caroline Norton's "Bingen on the Rhine." Widely reprinted in schoolbooks and anthologies, Caroline Norton's poem focuses on a wounded soldier dying in Algiers. It will be recalled that in "The Open Boat" lines from this very poem worry the correspondent. Significantly, the correspondent dwells not on words uttered by Caroline Norton's dying soldier but on the "look" of his body: "The correspondent plainly saw the soldier. He lay on the sand with his feet out straight and still. While his pale left hand was upon his chest in an attempt to thwart the going of his life, the blood came between his fingers. In the far Algerian distance, a city of low square forms was set against a sky that was faint with the last sunset hues."[34] Still, adducing Caroline Norton, Quinet, or Rimbaud will not finally account for what is most telling in Crane's han-

---

32. *Œuvres complètes de Edgar Quinet* (Paris: Pangerre, 1858), X, 170.

33. It is interesting, too, that none of the more clearly literary texts—Crane's, Quinet's, or Rimbaud's—gives any hint that a decaying body gives off odor. Contrast their literary use of "the corpse amid the flowers" with, for instance, Oliver Wendell Holmes's more naturalistic observations of what one might encounter in the aftermath of battle: "Today is pleasant and hot—It is singular with what indifference one gets to look on the dead bodies in gray clothes wh. lie all around—(or rather did—We are burying them today as fast as we can—) As you go through the woods you stumble constantly, and, if after dark, as last night on picket, perhaps tread on swollen bodies already fly blown and decaying, of men shot in the head back or bowels—Many of the wounds are terrible to look at—especially those fr. fragments of shell" (*Touched with Fire*, 50–51). Holmes's account seems to follow no "literary" example. It has none of the expressionistic quality that Crane resorts to when dealing with corpses in the *Red Badge*.

Michael Fried reads Crane's death scenes as coded accounts of his necessary preoccupation with the related acts of "writing" and "writhing." This provocative reading, serving as a sort of postmodern all-explaining monomyth, denies Crane those aesthetic dimensions, moral interests, and authorial qualities that earlier readers found in his work (*Realism, Writing, Disfiguration: On Thomas Eakins and Stephen Crane* [Chicago and London: University of Chicago Press, 1987], 93–161).

34. Stephen Crane, "The Open Boat," in *Tales of Adventure*, Volume V of *The University of Virginia Edition of the Works of Stephen Crane*, ed. Fredson Bowers, intr. J. C. Levenson (Charlottesville: University Press of Virginia, 1970), 86. For the link between "The Open Boat" and specific pictorial treatments of the text of Caroline Norton's poem, see "Blue Skies," chapter 11, below. In "Crane's 'Soldier of the Legion' " (*American Literature*, 30 [May 1958], 242–44), Edward Stone draws parallels between Caroline Norton's poem and the *Red Badge* but does not link the "corpse in the glen" episode with the poem.

dling of the "corpse" in the *Red Badge*. Nowhere in the works so far mentioned is there full precedent for the details in Crane's description of the corpse. For those he went elsewhere. It is not out of whole cloth that Crane imagined his deserter's horror at the unexpected inhabitant of that green chapel.

Consider two excerpts, which, together, suggest a stylized description that proved eminently useful to an inexperienced novelist. The first one reads: "We walked down to the foot of the lawn, and I remember looking over the fence, whilst the boy peeped through the bars, and there lay a man bloated and offensive to every sense, his face purple and blistering in the hot summer sunlight, his mouth wide open, and the summer flies buzzing about and crawling in and out upon the dry tongue." The second excerpt reads: "His gray eyes dim and blood-shot, his lips dry and covered, as it seemed, almost with fish scales; sensuality seated upon those cracked, broken lips of his—the whole man was revolting . . . blear-eyed, bloated, sensual."[35] To these passages can be added a third, taken from Crane's 1893 novella *Maggie*, describing the corpselike "fat man in torn and greasy garments" who follows the young prostitute to the river: "His grey hair straggled down over his forehead. His small, bleared eyes, sparkling from amidst great rolls of red fat, swept eagerly over the girl's upturned face. He laughed, his brown, disordered teeth gleaming under a grey, grizzled moustache from which beer-drops dripped. His whole body gently quivered and shook like that of a dead jelly fish. Chuckling and leering, he followed the girl of the crimson legions."[36]

Not one of these passages describes a corpse. The first two excerpts, which come from temperance readers used at "drawing-room meetings" held by the WCTU,[37] describe in unsettling detail the corpselike drunkards lying by the side of the road—fish-scaly, bloated, and blistering, with cracked, broken lips crawling with insects. Crane's own parlor might have been the setting for young Stephen's first experience of the lurid poems and millennial homilies collected in the temperance reader. There the incipient writer could experience at first hand the theatrical presentation of the horrors attributed to drink and the portentous, melodramatic language used to describe those horrific experiences. The impressed memories of the vividly lurid description of drunks

---

35. John B. Gough, "Who Did It?" in *Readings and Recitations, No. 3*, ed. Miss L[izzie] Penney (New York: National Temperance Society and Publication House, 1879), 73, 74.

36. Stephen Crane, *Maggie: A Girl of the Streets (A Story of New York)* (1893), Norton Critical Edition, ed. Thomas A. Gullason (New York: Norton, 1979), 53.

37. "Drawing-room Meetings became a distinct feature of our work at the Boston convention [in 1880], Mrs. Mary C. Johnson of Brooklyn, N.Y., being appointed superintendent" (*Brief History*, 34–35). Mary Johnson was a well-known leader of the WCTU from its very start. She was described as "mild but firm" (Rev. J. B. Wakeley, *The American Temperance Cyclopædia of History, Biography, Anecdote, and Illustration* [New York: National Temperance Society and Publication House, 1875], 217). It will be recalled that in *Maggie: A Girl of the Streets* Crane assigns the name "Mary Johnson" to the dissipated mother.

lying beside the road, dead to the world, were undoubtedly the closest thing to the description of the dead in war that the young author knew when he set about writing the *Red Badge*.

Beyond the corpse in the glen, there is a second major "corpse" in the *Red Badge*. Henry and the "tattered soldier" watch as the "tall soldier," Jim Conklin, turns and lurches and finally dies. "There was something rite-like in these movements of the doomed soldier," reads the third-person narrative. "And there was a resemblance in him to a devotee of a mad religion, blood-sucking, muscle-wrenching, bone-crushing." At last the two recruits, when they see him "stop and stand motionless," perceive that his face wears "an expression telling that he had at last found the place for which he had struggled." He was "at the rendezvous." In the throes of death, he does not die simply or quickly.

> Finally, the chest of the doomed soldier began to heave with a strained motion. It increased in violence until it was as if an animal was within and was kicking and tumbling furiously to be free. . . .
>
> Suddenly, his form stiffened and straightened. Then it was shaken by a prolonged ague. He stared into space. . . . He was invaded by a creeping strangeness that slowly enveloped him. For a moment, the tremor of his legs caused him to dance a sort of hideous horn-pipe. His arms beat wildly about his head in expression of imp-like enthusiasm.
>
> His tall figure stretched itself to its full height. There was a slight rending sound. Then it began to swing forward, slow and straight, in the manner of a falling tree. A swift muscular contortion made the left shoulder strike the ground first.[38]

38. The Conklin death is "reprised"—but more closely done from the "wounded" man's point of view—when Crane describes Henry's behavior when a fellow soldier strikes him in the head with his rifle:

> The youth's fingers had turned to paste upon the other's arm. The energy was smitten from his muscles. He saw the flaming wings of lightning flash before his vision. There was a deafening rumble of thunder within his head.
>
> Suddenly his legs seemed to die. He sank writhing to the ground. He tried to arise. In his efforts against the numbing pain he was like a man wrestling with a creature of the air.
>
> There was a sinister struggle.
>
> Sometimes, he would achieve a position half erect, battle with the air for a moment, and then fall again, grabbing at the grass. His face was of a clammy pallor. Deep groans were wrenched from him.
>
> At last, with a twisting movement, he got upon his hands and knees and from thence, like a babe trying to walk, to his feet. Pressing his hands to his temples, he went lurching over the grass.
>
> He found an intense battle with his body. His dulled senses wished him to swoon and he opposed them stubbornly, his mind portraying unknown dangers and mutilations if he should fall upon the field. He went, tall soldier-fashion. He imagined secluded spots where he could fall and be unmolested. To search for one, he strove against the tide of his pain.

Readers have often marveled at the peculiar manner of Jim Conklin's strange and contortive death—his bizarre, ritelike dance of death—without suspecting that the artistic rendering of that death also has its source in the young author's exposure to the texts of the temperance reader. The death of this "devotee of a mad religion" (the phrase echoes Crane's father's references to "the devotees of alcohol"[39]) exemplifies less Crane's innate sense of the bizarre than his creative use of the temperance worker's description of drunkards suffering through delirium tremens. Generalized, the DTs were typically described: "The ruin that it [drink] brings into the nervous system often culminates in *delirium tremens.* Have you ever seen a man under its influence? Have you heard him mutter, and jabber, and leer, and rave like an idiot? Have you heard him moan, cry, shriek, curse, and rave, as he tried to skulk under the bedclothes? Have you looked into his eyes, and seen the horrors of the damned there? . . . Have you seen him heave on his bed, as though his body was undulating upon the rolling waves like a fire?"[40] In Jim Conklin's case it is as if a bursting shell has brought on the deadliest case imaginable of the DTs. Moreover, such an "alcoholic" death in battle is not limited to the "tall soldier." The death of the enemy's standard-bearer, in this context, takes on a new look.

> The youth, in his leapings, saw as through a mist, a picture of four or five men stretched upon the ground or writhing upon their knees with bowed heads as if they had been stricken by bolts from the sky. Tottering among them was the rival color-bearer whom the youth saw had been bitten vitally by the bullets of the last formidable volley. He perceived this man fighting a last struggle, the struggle of one whose legs are grasped by demons. It was a ghastly battle. Over his face was the bleach of death but set upon it was the dark and hard lines of desperate purpose. With this terrible grin of resolution, he hugged his precious flag to him and was stumbling and staggering in his design to go the way that led to safety from it.
>
> But his wounds always made it seem that his feet were retarded, held, and he fought a grim fight as with invisible ghouls, fastened greedily upon his limbs.

It is not surprising that the young realist who describes such battlefield ghouls greedy for flesh but has never seen a wartime army, either at rest or on the march, under the midday sun or in the dark of night, would think of a

---

39. Rev. J. T. Crane, *Arts of Intoxication: The Aim, and the Results* (New York: Carlton & Lanahan/ San Francisco: E. Thomas/Cincinnati: Hitchcock & Walden, 1870), 171.

40. Rev. H. M. Scudder, "The Destroyer," in *Readings and Recitations, No. 1,* ed. Miss L[izzie] Penney (New York: National Temperance Society and Publication House, 1877), 52.

moving army, by turns, as an undulating monster and a stationary horde, its campfires over a hillside as the myriad eyes of a dark beast. Like an actor reaching back for the experience that will potentiate the rendering of a fictional moment—a form of what J. C. Levenson calls "metonymic inference"[41]—Crane might have drawn, in such cases, on his response to temperance-reader descriptions such as that of the lurid and terrifying "serpent of the still."[42]

> The bowels of this mountain are a nest of millions of flying, hissing, stinging serpents, commissioned of hell to fly through all this world, to touch only to sting, and stop only to kill. . . . They lie in wait in our paths; they coil in our gates and doorways; they crawl over our thresholds, hide under our pillows, creep into our purses and money-drawers. They would charm every youth, and breathe their poisonous breath into the nostrils of children; strike their deadly fangs for life-blood, and wind their cold folds around the neck and suck your breath. Serpents that poison the sunniest nooks of society, trail their hellish slime over the loveliest flowers of social joy, and swathe the earth in the winding-sheet of woe.[43]

This evil mountain of intemperance, a teeming, threatening "red dragon,"[44] looms behind the war-inexperienced Crane's imagined account of Henry Fleming's vision of the enemy, as does his father's description of the drunkard who "sees the gliding serpent noiselessly approaching his fellow victims, and throwing around them fold after fold":[45]

> The youth could occasionally see dark shadows that moved like monsters. . . . Staring, once, at the red eyes across the river, he conceived them to be growing larger, as the orbs of a row of dragons, advancing. . . . A moment later the regiment went swinging off into the darkness. It was now like one of those moving monsters wending with many feet. . . . There was an occasional flash and glimmer of steel from the backs of all these huge crawling reptiles. . . . The youth saw that the landscape was streaked with two long, thin, black columns which disappeared on the

41. J. C. Levenson, "*The Red Badge of Courage* and *McTeague*: Passage to Modernity," in *Cambridge Companion to American Realism and Naturalism: Howells to London*, ed. Donald Pizer (Cambridge, Eng., and New York: Cambridge University Press, 1995), 162.

42. M. Florence Mosher, "It Is Coming," in *Readings and Recitations, No. 5*, ed. L[izzie] Penney (New York: National Temperance Society and Publication House, 1884), 7.

43. Rev. Duncan McGregor, "What is Intemperance?" in *Readings and Recitations, No. 4*, ed. L[izzie] Penney (New York: National Temperance Society and Publication House, 1882), 12–13.

44. George W. Bungay, "The Battle of the Rain," in *Readings and Recitations, No. 3*, 41.

45. Crane, *Arts of Intoxication*, 213. He also writes of "the lair where the alcoholic monster waits for his prey," from which "great hosts, uncounted myriads, have never returned" (207).

brow of a hill in front and rearward vanished in a wood. They were like two serpents crawling from the cavern of the night. . . . But the long serpents crawled slowly from hill to hill without bluster of smoke.

The temperance reader sheds its influence over Crane's handling of the flag-saving episode, though the emotion involved is not fear or terror but joy, pride, and ecstasy. At the end of chapter 4, for the first time, Henry is suffused with emotion over the flags he sees sticking up over the battlefield. "The youth felt the old thrill at the sight of the emblems. They were like beautiful birds strangely undaunted in a storm." It is not until chapter 19, however, that Henry has the opportunity to take direct action based on those feelings. Within him, "as he hurled himself forward, was born a love, a despairing fondness for this flag which was near him": "It was a creation of beauty and invulnerability. It was a goddess, radiant, that bended its form with an imperious gesture to him. It was a woman, red and white, hating and loving, that called him with the voice of his hopes. Because no harm could come to it, he endowed it with power. He kept near as if it could be a saver of lives and an imploring cry went from his mind."

To gather up an appropriate image for the virtues of the temperance army, one writer for the cause linked its fight to the Civil War, turning to the glories of patriotism and the flag, and quoting along the way Keats ("a thing of beauty is a joy for ever") and Tennyson's most patriotic poem:

The flag is the emblem of a nation's glory and a nation's power. There is a spirit of inspiration in its very folds. . . . Are not the "stars and stripes" to us Americans "a thing of beauty and a joy forever?"

Our Fathers loved their brilliant folds, but do not we love them even more since they came back through the dense death-smoke of the cruel war lately closed?
> "Came through the jaws of death,
> Back from the mouth of hell,"
rent and torn, to be sure, and leaving many a brave standard bearer behind on the field, dead, but victory-crowned, and showing to our gladdened eyes not one star plucked from its glorious constellation! Oh, yes, that grand old flag is a magnetic battery sending thrilling power and enthusiasm through and through every hand that touches the pole of its standard.

The late war has filled the world with the romantic stories—stories whose truth is stranger than fiction—of valiant deeds done under the inspiration of our national flag and for its protection. What's a nation without a flag? What's an army without a banner? In the holy wars of the Jews, the peculiar people of God carried their ensign, and every tribe knew and followed its own banner. And we must have a flag, an ensign, for the tribes of that "peculiar people" that the Lord God has raised up among us, the tribes of the *total abstinence nation.*[46]

Incorporating lines quoted from Tennyson's poetic celebration of patriotic obedience and personal courage at Balaclava, the temperance writer singles out the brave standard-bearer, dead on the field but victorious in death. To Crane the flag episode offers still another opportunity to describe death in battle. When the color-serjeant is struck, Henry springs to the pole.

> At the same instant, his friend grabbed it from the other side. They jerked at it, stout and furious, but the color-serjeant was dead and the corpse would not relinquish its trust. For a moment, there was a grim encounter. The dead man, swinging with bended back, seemed to be obstinately tugging, in ludicrous and awful ways, for the possession of the flag.
>
> It was past in an instant of time. They wrenched the flag furiously from the dead man, and, as they turned again, the corpse swayed forward with bowed head. One arm swung high and the curved hand fell with heavy protest on the friend's unheeding shoulder.

Only later, after he had himself gone to report his first war, would Crane dispense with what he had learned from the temperance reader about the drunkards who experience the delirium tremens.

4

This chapter on *The Red Badge of Courage* has a curious postscript. In 1902 Colonel Henry H. Hadley, the "leading spirit" of the Christian Abstainers' Union, published his memoirs, calling the book *The Blue Badge of Courage.* Hadley was once a "notorious" drunkard and gambler but was "converted," as one reviewer put it, to "a peripatetic campaign for the enlistment of recruits in the ranks of abstainers."[47] Having served during the Civil War as a private in Company H, 90th Ohio Volunteer Infantry, Hadley was able, years later, to put that military experience to use in what he believed to be a much greater war—the cause of "total abstinence and rescue work." Now he drew great crowds to his "Blue Button Temperance and Rescue Meetings" ("the blue button signifying total abstinence from a Christian standpoint") and brought into being, as a re-

---

46. Rev. W. H. Boole, "Run Up the Flag—Nail It to the Staff!" in *Readings and Recitations, No. 2,* ed. L[izzie] Penney (New York: National Temperance Society and Publication House, 1878), 65.

47. Anonymous, "Among the Books: Recent Publications" [*The Blue Badge of Courage*], *Watchman,* 84 (Nov. 20, 1902), 15.

sult of the many conversions he effected, "several local Unions and Blue Button Brigades and Clubs."[48] Blue was the color of temperance and those unions and brigades made up the cold-water army whose wagonloads of abstainers wearing blue buttons paraded everywhere. They, too, were soldiers fighting the skirmishes and battles of what they saw as a war over the future of society itself. "This imperial temperance army," rallying "under a common standard, with one motto and one heart," warned one temperance writer, "must not fight in independent divisions without unity of purpose; but in whatever part of the field a corps or a brigade may be engaged, its blows must fall upon the foe at that point where it can push through the enemy's thinned ranks, to the Capitol of the Rebellion as the objective point of operations, *the legalized traffic in liquid poison!*"[49] How fitting, then, for Crane's quite different purposes in the *Red Badge*, that this large-scale struggle against alcohol should itself be seen, historically and metaphorically, as a second War of Rebellion. Since the movement against alcohol and for temperance was conceived by those involved to be a series of battles in a great and bitter war, it was ingenious of Crane to turn the equation around by enlisting for his dramatization of war itself the very terms used in the fight for temperance.

With this in mind, it is appropriate to acknowledge, by way of conclusion, Christopher Benfey's suggestion that Crane might have taken his title from Shakespeare. In *2 Henry IV*, Sir John Falstaff, extolling the virtues of drink, holds forth on the source of what is sometimes called Dutch courage:

> The second property of your excellent sherris is the warming of the blood, which, before cold and settled, left the liver white and pale, which is the *badge of pusillanimity and cowardice*. But the sherris warms it and makes it course from the inwards to the parts extremes. It illumineth the face, which as a beacon gives warning to all the rest of this little kingdom, man, to arm, and then the vital commoners and inland petty spirits muster me all to their captain, the heart, who, great and puffed up with this retinue, doth any deed of *courage*, and this valor comes of sherris. So that skill in the weapon is nothing without sack. . . . Herof comes it that prince Harry is valiant. . . . (IV, iii) [Benfey's emphasis][50]

That drink is here associated with badges of courage makes Benfey's suggestion especially appealing.

48. Henry H. Hadley, *The Blue Badge of Courage* (Akron, New York, and Chicago: Saalfield Publishing, 1902), vii–ix.

49. Boole, "Run Up the Flag," 66.

50. Christopher Benfey, "Badges of Courage and Cowardice: A Source for Crane's Title," *Stephen Crane Studies*, 6 (Fall 1997), 2.

The Drunkard's Progress
Original in Fruitlands Museums, Harvard, Massachusetts.
Copy from the Collection of George Monteiro

WEAPONS

FOR

TEMPERANCE WARFARE

SOME PLANS AND PROGRAMMES

FOR USE IN

YOUNG PEOPLE'S SOCIETIES, SUNDAY-SCHOOLS,
AND CHRISTIAN TEMPERANCE UNIONS.

BY

BELLE M. BRAIN,

AUTHOR OF "FUEL FOR MISSIONARY FIRES."

" Fight the drink! Fight it, fight it wherever we find it, fight it in the social circle, fight it in the dram-shop, fight it at home, fight it abroad. I expect to my dying day to fight the drink with every lawful weapon."— JOHN B. GOUGH.

PUBLISHING DEPARTMENT
UNITED SOCIETY OF CHRISTIAN ENDEAVOR.
BOSTON AND CHICAGO.

The title page of *Weapons for Temperance Warfare*, by Belle M. Brain, issued by the United Society of Christian Endeavor, copyright 1897
Courtesy of the Homer Babbidge Library, University of Connecticut, Storrs, Connecticut

TEMPERANCE HOUSE.

No. 17, Church Street,
New Haven, Ct.

THE subscriber would inform the friends of Temperance, and the public generally, that he has
enlarged his building on the corner of Church and
Crown Streets, opposite the Franklin Building, by
building a commodious Brick front, which is finished
into rooms calculated to please the traveler. His object is to furnish a comfortable HOME for strangers
visiting the city, where they need not be disgusted
with the fumes of any Intoxicating Beverage. His
TABLE will be furnished with the best the Market
affords; good STABLING for Horses by the day,
week, or otherwise. The countenance and patronage
of that portion of the public who desire to promote
the cause of Temperance, is respectfully solicited.
Feb. 4—11℃.   H. P. JONES.

Advertisement for a Temperance House, from *The Fountain*, organ of the Connecticut Washington Total Abstinence Society, New Haven, June 26, 1846
From the Collection of George Monteiro

THE FIRST DROP.   THE LAST DROP.
"Come in and take a drop." The first drop led to other drops. He dropped his position, he dropped his respectability, he dropped his fortune, he dropped his friends, he dropped finally all his prospects in this life, and his hopes for eternity; and then came the last drop on the gallows. BEWARE OF THE FIRST DROP.—*The Watchman.*

"The First Drop. The Last Drop," from *World Book of Temperance*, compiled by Dr. and Mrs. Wilbur F. Crafts (Abridged edition, 1909)
From the Collection of George Monteiro

Illustrations by W. T. Smedley for *Bingen on the Rhine*, by Caroline E. S. Norton (Philadelphia: Porter & Coates, 1883)
From the Collection of George Monteiro

Stephen Crane in Tampa, Florida, in 1898
From the Illustrated American, *June 24, 1898.*
Courtesy Brown University Libraries, Providence, Rhode Island

8

The New Blue Battalions

Do you hear the nation tremble as an earthquake shakes the ground?
'Tis the waking of a people—'tis a mighty battle sound.

> —M. Florence Mosher, "It Is Coming" (1884)

From the Hills of Maine to the Everglades,
From the Great Old Atlantic to the Western Plains,
You will hear the march of the New Crusade,
'Till we conquer the Foe and raise our banner.

> —Mrs. Claude H. Mayo, "The New Crusade March"

The fire is out, and spent the warmth thereof,
(This is the end of every song man sings!)
The golden wine is drunk, the dregs remain,
Bitter as wormwood and as salt as pain;
And health and hope have gone the way of love
Into the drear oblivion of lost things.
Ghosts go along with us until the end;
This was a mistress, this, perhaps, a friend.
With pale, indifferent eyes, we sit and wait
For the dropt curtain and the closing gate:
This is the end of all the songs man sings.

> —Ernest Dowson, "Dregs" (1899)

The attempt here will be to link up Crane's puzzling " 'Intrigue' " poems with his so-called "Blue Battalions" poem to demonstrate that their true meaning emerges only when they are read within the literary and cultural contexts characterized, on the one hand, by fin de siècle poetry of love shaped by an aesthetics of religion, and, on the other, by the moral dictates of middle-class religion, exemplified, specifically in Crane's case, by the imperatives of the American temperance movement. Thus Eros, Dionysus, and Salvation.

Though his specific targets differ in " 'Intrigue' " and "The Blue Battalions," Crane argues his somewhat sardonic point of view through parody, questioning the sincerity of the peoples and the poets by mocking excessive expressions of what otherwise might be considered reasonable and acceptable sentiment.

1

A clipping in the Syracuse University Archives celebrates three "facts" about Stephen Crane. He is identified as "Ex-'94," his story "A Tent in Agony" will appear in the holiday number of *Cosmopolitan* magazine, and "the libretto of *Dolores*, an opera which will appear in New York during the holidays, has brought Mr. Crane many complimentary notices."[1] Crane was in fact a dropout from the class of 1894, and his story appeared, as announced, in the December 1892 *Cosmopolitan*, but no one has ever seen a trace of his libretto for *Dolores*. The "Dolores" that does exist is neither opera nor libretto but the well-known poem by Algernon Charles Swinburne. Credit some Syracuse University wag with an insider's joke about Crane as would-be fin de siècle decadent.

Published in 1866 in *Poems and Ballads*—an immediately controversial book—"Dolores" scandalized the mainstream readers of its day and continued to stand for contemporary scandal with many such readers into the early twentieth century. "While older people were denouncing publicly the book they were reading secretly," writes Swinburne's biographer, "the younger generation received it with enthusiasm. Especially at the two universities were there eager neophytes. Professor Saintsbury has told of the band of students, of whom he was one, who marched in lock step around the courts and cloisters of Oxford, chanting 'Dolores.' "[2] In the fall of 1892, when the Syracuse University item appeared, Swinburne's name was again in the news. Arguments had broken out in the press, even on the American side of the Atlantic, over whether he would be a suitable successor to the late Poet Laureate Alfred Lord Tennyson. An unnamed contributor to the *Atlantic Monthly* said flatly: "If the laureateship is not given to Mr. Swinburne, so much the worse for the laureateship."[3] Others thought that circumstances in his private life rendered him

1. Anonymous, "Ex-'94," undated, unsourced clipping, University Archives, Syracuse University Library, Syracuse, New York.

2. Samuel C. Chew, *Swinburne* (Boston: Little, Brown, 1929), 72.

3. Anonymous, "Who Will Be Poet Laureate?" *Atlantic Monthly*, 70 (Dec. 1892), 856.

unfit for the post and the honor that went with it. The *Critic* in New York thought that the strongest objection to Swinburne's candidacy for the laureateship was "the moral tone of his poetry."[4] It is more than a good bet that the anonymous writer in Syracuse could count on his readers to recognize immediately that he was playing the ancient game of linking the name of Syracuse University's own incipient *poète maudit* with that of the notorious and controversial British poet Swinburne. After all, the Syracuse University writer probably knew the young Crane's interests well enough, long before Elbert Hubbard and the Philistines first heard of him, to poke fun at some of Crane's more "decadent" impulses.

Its subject identified by Swinburne as "Notre-Dame des Sept Douleurs," "Dolores" runs to fifty-five eight-line stanzas in anapestic trimeter (with a truncated last line—Swinburne's innovation).[5] Writing to William Michael Rossetti in 1866, Swinburne claimed that he had "proved Dolores to be little less than a second Sermon on the Mount."[6] And W. H. Mallock reported that the poem "expressed the passion with which he [Swinburne] had sought relief, in the madnesses of the fleshly Venus, from his ruined dreams of the heavenly."[7] A more extreme way of putting the matter is that "Dolores" (as do several other works by Swinburne) records its author's pathological interest in erotic masochism and its pleasures, having found them to be most characteristic of historical Christianity.[8]

4. Anonymous, [Swinburne and the Laureateship], *Critic* (New York), 21 (Oct. 15, 1892), 213; see also Anonymous, "The Laureateship," *Critic* (New York), 21 (Nov. 5, 1892), 255–56.

5. Chew traces the form to John Gay's *Beggar's Opera* by way of Byron's "Stanzas to Augusta" (*Swinburne*, 92).

6. *The Swinburne Letters, Volume I: 1854–1869*, ed. Cecil Y. Lang (New Haven: Yale University Press, 1959), 186.

7. Quoted in Clyde Kenneth Hyder, *Swinburne's Literary Career and Fame* (Durham, N.C.: Duke University Press, 1933), 58.

8. To Cardinal Newman's observation that Swinburne's poems, like Rossetti's, "are soaked in an ethical quality, whatever it is to be called, which would have made it impossible in the last generation for a brother to read them to a sister," Swinburne responded (in a letter to Edmund Gosse):

I was interested by the extracts you sent me from Newman's letter, which you once mentioned to me before: and amused beyond measure at a Catholic leader finding "amorousness" and "religion" "such irreconcilable elements" (well, at any rate *I* can hardly be accused of trying to reconcile Venus and Mary or Jesus and Priapus): but has he never heard of the last goddess of his Church, Marie Alacoque, the type and incarnation of *furor uterinus*? It may be convenient, but it is at least cool, for a priest of that faith to forget that his Church has always naturally and necessarily been the nursing mother of "pale religious lechery" (as Blake with such grand scorn labels the special quality of celibate sanctity "that wishes but acts not"), of holy priapism and virginal nymphomania. Not to speak of the filthy visions of the rampant and rabid nun who founded "the worship of the Sacred Heart" (she called it heart—in the phallic processions they called it by a more—and less—proper name), he might have found passages from St. Theresa which certainly justify from a carnal point of view her surname of the Christian Sappho. There is as much detail, if I mistake not (judging by extracts), in her invocations of her Phaon—Jesus

This "perverse litany to his Lady of Pain"[9] stands at the head of similar but even more secularized poetry of the period, particularly some of the verse dedicated by masochistic lovers to their partners—actual, would-be, or, even, imagined—in the poems of, say, Lionel Johnson ("The Dark Angel"), William Butler Yeats ("When You Are Old"), Arthur Symons ("To One in Alienation"), Ernest Dowson ("In Tempore Senectutis"—which echoes Yeats's "When You Are Old"), and again Dowson ("Non Sum Qualis Eram Bonae Sub Regno Cynarae," which translates as "I am not what I once was under the rule, or spell, of kind Cynara").[10]

Daniel Hoffman concludes that while sharing certain traits with the British Decadents of his time, Crane was divided "decisively from the Decadence in his conviction, everywhere implicit, that art, like life, is moral. What makes him seem to resemble the Decadents is, surprisingly, a certain likeness between their original aesthetic ideal and his own." Despite emphasizing the divisions between Crane and the Decadents, Hoffman does acknowledge that "such books as Rossetti's *Poetical Works*, Swinburne's *Poems and Ballads*, or Shelley's *Poems*"—all of which were in Crane's library—"might have been partly responsible for the lushness of his 'Intrigue.' "[11]

The lushness that Hoffman refers to is apparent in "Dolores," right from the start:

> Cold eyelids that hide like a jewel
> Hard eyes that grow soft for an hour:
> The heavy white limbs, and the cruel
> Red mouth like a venomous flower;
> When these are gone by with their glories,
> What shall rest of thee then, what remain,

Christ—as in the Ode to Anactoria itself—which, as Byron justly observes, is *not* "a good example." As for my poor paraphrase, it (with Dolores and the rest) is too mild and maidenly for mention in the same year (*The Swinburne Letters, Volume III: 1875–1877*, ed. Cecil Y. Lang [New Haven: Yale University Press, 1960], 116 n. 2, 116–17).

The pathology of Swinburne's masochism is taken up by Dr. William B. Ober in "Swinburne's Masochism: Neuropathology and Psychopathology," in his *Boswell's Clap and Other Essays: Medical Analyses of Literary Men's Afflictions* (New York: Harper & Row, 1988), 43–88.

9. Chew, *Swinburne*, 93 n.

10. It has been suggested that Crane did meet William Butler Yeats (*The Correspondence of Stephen Crane*, ed. Stanley Wertheim and Paul Sorrentino [New York: Columbia University Press, 1988], II, 674) and on one occasion took tea with Swinburne (John Berryman, *Stephen Crane* [New York: William Sloane, 1950], 198). In "List of Books/Brede Place" appear copies of Swinburne's poetry and Yeats's *The Secret Rose* (R. W. Stallman, *Stephen Crane: A Biography* [New York: Braziller, 1968], 554–55).

11. Daniel Hoffman, *The Poetry of Stephen Crane* (New York and London: Columbia University Press, 1957), 230, 31.

O mystic and sombre Dolores
Our Lady of Pain?[12]

While Swinburne addresses his poem to an allegorizing "Notre Dame des
Sept Douleurs" (though Swinburne's "mistress," Adah Isaacs Menken, the
"tawdrily picturesque actress"—the description is Samuel Chew's—"often
called herself 'Dolores' "[13]), it has been argued that Crane's poem addresses
more directly a more mundane lover (or, perhaps, his conflict over lovers—
Cora Howarth Stewart and Lily Brandon Munroe).[14] Consider the Swinburnean atmosphere of "Intrigue" (Part I, stanza 9):

> Thou art my love
> And thou art a priestess
> And in thy hand is a bloody dagger
> And my doom comes to me surely
> Woe is me.[15]

Crane's notion of a "priestess" of love/pain and his employment of a truncated refrain recall Swinburne's notion of "Our Lady of Pain," as she is referred
to in the refrain. Yet it is as true of Crane's " 'Intrigue' " poems as has been written about Swinburne's "Dolores" that "the reader of to-day is not likely to be
attracted by this reverie upon the sensualities of a man foiled in love and weary
of loving who 'decorated with the name of goddess, crowns anew . . . some
woman, real or ideal, in whom the pride of life with its companion lusts is in-
carnate.' "[16] And this, of course, is Crane's point. His " 'Intrigue' " is a parody,

12. Algernon Charles Swinburne, "Dolores," in *Poems*, intr. Ernest Rhys (New York: Boni and
Liveright, 1919), 103.

13. Chew, *Swinburne*, 79. Here are Chew's speculations at greater length: "It is likely that there is
a faint glimmering of autobiography in 'Dolores.' The tawdrily picturesque actress, Adah Isaacs Menken, who is the only woman to whom Swinburne is known to have referred as his mistress, often called
herself 'Dolores', and in a copy of her little volume of poems, 'Infelicia', Swinburne wrote the line
from his poem: 'Lo, this is she that was the world's delight.' It is possible that she may have inspired the
poem which Swinburne described as a reverie upon 'the transmigrations of a single soul . . . clad always
in the same type of fleshly beauty' " (79–80).

On the other hand, see Jean Overton Fuller, who writes: "*Dolorida* was the verse Swinburne had
written in Adah Menken's notebook, and [Edmund] Gosse, apparently oblivious that Swinburne had
not met her when *Dolores* was composed, was obviously going to make this identification, which was
erroneous, central to his book. He was going to say that Adah Menken was Dolores" (*Swinburne: A
Critical Biography* [London: Chatto & Windus, 1968], 297).

14. Stallman, *Stephen Crane*, 426.

15. Stephen Crane, " 'Intrigue,' " in *Poems and Literary Remains*, Volume X of *The University of Virginia Edition of the Works of Stephen Crane*, ed. Fredson Bowers, intr. James B. Colvert (Charlottesville:
University Press of Virginia, 1975), 62–69.

16. Chew, *Swinburne*, 91.

not solely of Swinburne's poem but of the spate of decadent, less transcendent, and clearly more profane love poems spawned by Swinburne's "Dolores." It sends up the Swinburne who announced to one of the Rossettis that "Dolores" was "little less than a second Sermon on the Mount."[17]

Crane's point becomes clear when one turns to Ernest Dowson's poem to Cynara. A century after it was first published in the April 1891 issue of the *Century Guild Hobby Horse*, "Non Sum Qualis Eram Bonae Sub Regno Cynarae," described extravagantly as "a poem of sin" and a "parable of the Decadent soul,"[18] remains Dowson's best known and most widely quoted work. Writing after the poet's death, Arthur Symons, the author of *The Symbolist Movement in Literature* (1899), called it "one of the greatest lyrical poems of our time; in it he [Dowson] has for once said everything, and he has said it to an intoxicating and perhaps immortal music." Dowson's favorite English poet was Swinburne, of course, and "Dolores" was "to Dowson at the time one of the finest poems in the language." A friend remembered that Dowson's copy of "Dolores" was "heavily scored."[19] There is no doubt that Swinburne's poem lies behind Dowson's paean to Cynara, a poem in which, to quote Swinburne, "Venus rose red out of wine":[20]

> Last night, ah, yesternight, betwixt her lips and mine
> There fell thy shadow, Cynara! thy breath was shed
> Upon my soul between the kisses and the wine;
> And I was desolate and sick of an old passion,
>   Yea, I was desolate and bowed my head:
> I have been faithful to thee, Cynara! in my fashion.
>
> All night upon mine heart I felt her warm heart beat,
> Night-long within mine arms in love and sleep she lay;
> Surely the kisses of her bought red mouth were sweet;
> But I was desolate and sick of an old passion,
>   When I awoke and found the dawn was gray:
> I have been faithful to thee, Cynara! in my fashion.
>
> I have forgot much, Cynara! gone with the wind,
> Flung roses, roses riotously with the throng,
> Dancing, to put thy pale, lost lilies out of mind;
> But I was desolate and sick of an old passion,

17. *The Swinburne Letters*, ed. Lang, I, 186.

18. Thomas Burnett Swann, *Ernest Dowson* (New York: Twayne, 1964), 25, 23.

19. Quoted in Mark Longaker, *Ernest Dowson* (Philadelphia: University of Pennsylvania Press, 1944), 81, 35.

20. Swinburne, "Dolores," 112.

Yea, all the time, because the dance was long:
I have been faithful to thee, Cynara! in my fashion.

I cried for madder music and for stronger wine,
But when the feast is finished and the lamps expire,
Then falls thy shadow, Cynara! the night is thine;
And I am desolate and sick of an old passion,
    Yea hungry for the lips of my desire:
I have been faithful to thee, Cynara! in my fashion.[21]

Dowson's own immediate debt to Swinburne in his poem on Cynara may be suggested in the way his refrain "I have been faithful to thee, Cynara! in my fashion" echoes ironically the line in "Dolores": "Thou wert fair in the fearless old fashion."[22] But there are many other images and phrases in Dowson's famous poem that echo "Dolores"; among them are "bought red mouth" ("cruel red mouth"), "pale, lost lilies" ("the lilies and languors of virtue"), "desolate and sick of an old passion" ("what new passions for daytime or night?"), "gone with the wind" ("lives are as leaves overblown"), "flung roses, roses riotously with the throng" ("mystical rose of the fire"), "stronger wine . . . hungry for the lips of my desire" ("the new wine of desire, / The fruit of four lips as they clung," "lips full of lust and of laughter"), "between the kisses and the wine" ("orgies with kisses and wine"), and "cried for madder music" ("music that scares the profane").[23]

The speakers of both Swinburne's "Dolores" and Dowson's "Cynara" complain of lost loves or, at least, unavailable ones. But Crane's late love poems wallow in the pain caused in the speaker of the poem by his exquisite entertainment of thoughts about his lover's previous lover. While it is Cynara whose "shadow" falls "betwixt her [his bought companion's] lips and mine," it is, in Crane's " 'Intrigue' " poems, "The shadow of another lover" who "intrude[s] his shade / Always between me and my peace." Moreover, in the first poem of Crane's sequence the speaker's lover is "the ashes of other men's love." And to what conclusion does this knowledge bring him? Only that he will "bury" his "face in these ashes," and he will "love them." The silliness of it all is apparent as he repeats through eleven stanzas the refrain "Woe is me," capping off each time some exaggerated expression of obeisance and abasement (and ending with an expanded version of the refrain in the twelfth and final stanza):

21. Ernest Dowson, "Non Sum Qualis Eram Bonae Sub Regno Cynarae," in *Verses* (1896): in *The Poetical Works of Ernest Christopher Dowson,* ed. Desmond Flower (London: Cassell and John Lane the Bodley Head, 1934), 22.

22. Swinburne, "Dolores," 111.

23. Algernon Charles Swinburne, *Poems,* intr. Ernest Rhys (New York: Boni and Liveright, 1919), 103, 105, 105, 103, 107, 103, 112, 105.

Thou art my love
And thou art the peace of sundown
When the blue shadows soothe
And the grasses and the leaves sleep
To the song of the little brooks
Woe is me.

Thou art my love
And thou art a storm
That breaks black in the sky
And, sweeping headlong,
Drenches and cowers each tree
And at the panting end
There is no sound
Save the melancholy cry of a single owl
Woe is me!

Thou art my love
And thou art a tinsel thing
And I in my play
Broke thee easily
And from the little fragments
Arose my long sorrow
Woe is me.

Thou art my love
And thou art a weary violet
Drooping from sun-caresses.
Answering mine carelessly
Woe is me.

Thou art my love
And thou art the ashes of other men's love
And I bury my face in these ashes
And I love them
Woe is me.

Thou art my love
And thou art the beard
On another man's face
Woe is me.

Thou art my love
And thou art a temple
And in this temple is an altar
And on this altar is my heart
Woe is me.

Thou art my love
And thou art a wretch.
Let these sacred love-lies choke thee
For I am come to where I know your lies as truth
And your truth as lies
Woe is me.

Thou art my love
And thou art a priestess
And in thy hand is a bloody dagger
And my doom comes to me surely
Woe is me.

Thou art my love
And thou art a skull with ruby eyes
And I love thee
Woe is me.

Thou art my love
And I doubt thee
And if peace came with thy murder
Then would I murder.
Woe is me.

Thou art my love
And thou art death
Aye, thou art death
Black and yet black
But I love thee
I love thee
Woe, welcome woe, to me.[24]

24. Crane, " 'Intrigue,' " in *Poems and Literary Remains*, 62–69. It is possible though unlikely that Crane knew the poem, for it was still unpublished at the time of Dowson's death in 1900, but Dowson's other poem "To Cynara" concludes: "Thou lovedst me once and I am still thy lover / Fain of thee as of old / Fain of thy lips and thy locks that did ever hover / Twixt brown and gold / Ay woe is me" (Dowson, *Poetical Works*, ed. Flower, 115).

In *Degeneration* (1893) Max Nordau had criticized Dante Gabriel Rossetti's "predilection for refrains" as being indicative of the "brain-work" of "weak degenerate minds." Yet Nordau does acknowledge that "the refrain is an excellent artistic medium for the purpose of unveiling the state of a soul under the influence of a strong emotion. It is natural that, to the lover yearning for his beloved, the recurring idea of her should be ever thrusting itself among all the other thoughts in which he temporarily indulges."[25] It is precisely the obsessive, banal quality of the Decadent poet's refrain that is the target of Crane's truncated "Swinburnean" refrain.

John Berryman saw it differently. To him " 'Intrigue' " was "a set of harsh, awkward, jealous, impassioned, guilty, despairing love poems . . . some of which seem to have his wife in mind and others some vanished love."[26] R. W. Stallman speculated that the "vanished love" was Lily Brandon Munroe, whose image "possessed" Crane when he wrote the " 'Intrigue' " poems.[27] Perhaps. But it is of interest that Crane instructed his agent to send the " 'Intrigue' " poems to Heinemann, an English publisher, who did not publish them.[28] Stallman thinks that Heinemann might have found the "poems not in good taste." He himself finds the poems "mainly interesting as biography"—"as poetic documents of personal feeling."[29] When the " 'Intrigue' " poems are read against the background provided by the seemingly straightforward love poetry being written at the time by Ernest Dowson, as well as other English poets such as Lionel Johnson, Arthur Symons, and John Gray, there seems to be merit in the suggestion that Crane was parodying the standard poems on the theme of masochistic, cloying love that were then being produced hand over fist by the younger English Decadents.

Take their sentimental insistence upon mirror-imaging sex and death. Here is Crane, in a poem unpublished at the time of his death:

> Bottles and bottles and bottles
> In a merry den
> And the wan smiles of women
> Untruthing license and joy.
> Countless lights
> Making oblique and confusing multiplication
> In mirrors
> And the light returns again to the faces.

25. Max Nordau, *Degeneration* (New York: D. Appleton, 1895), 91–92.
26. Berryman, *Stephen Crane*, 228.
27. Stallman, *Stephen Crane*, 62.
28. Crane, *Correspondence*, ed. Wertheim and Sorrentino, II, 380.
29. Stallman, *Stephen Crane*, 430.

★ ★ ★ ★

A cellar, and a death-pale child.
A woman
Ministering commonly, degradedly,
Without manners.
A murmur and a silence
Or silence and a murmur
And then a finished silence.
The moon beams practically upon the cheap bed.

An hour, with its million trinkets of joy or pain,
Matters little in cellar or merry den
Since all is death.[30]

It may well be, as is charged by Hoffman (the first one to publish this poem), that "the final three lines" show that Crane "did not know when to stop," that the two juxtaposed scenes are enough to make Crane's point.[31] But that is to take the final three lines at face value. It is their satirical thrust as an exaggeration of the Decadents' own overstated sense of the death that permeates all the human experiences they valued—for example, Dowson's Omarian wine, women, and song, as well as his pedophilia. (It was widely believed that the Cynara of his poem was the twelve-year-old Adelaide Foltinowicz, a waitress in a restaurant when, in 1891, Dowson, aged twenty-four, met her. Dowson's editor calls her "the best-known object of Dowson's unhappy affections."[32] It was to Adelaide that he dedicated *Verses,* his first book. Crane's sexual proclivities took him toward more experienced, often older, women.)

Writing in 1913, Holbrook Jackson saw Dowson's cry "for 'Madder music and for stronger wine' " as "nothing less than a demand for that uniting ecstasy which is the essence of human and every other phase of life." The Crane who was the son of fervid temperance workers saw it differently. The educated Dowson, like Swinburne, Beardsley, Wilde, and Lionel Johnson, was playing at alcoholic degradation. He was no less deluded in his own way than were the excessive drinkers Crane found in the beer gardens and saloons of the Bowery. It is possible to read " 'Intrigue' " as his prime parody of their privileged delusions about the spirituality of art for art's sake and sickly passion of illicit love. Crane, who abhorred artificiality, saw through the Decadent poetry of his day. "The eroticism which became so prevalent in the verse of the younger poets

---

30. Stephen Crane, "Bottles and bottles and bottles," in *Poems and Literary Remains,* 89.
31. Hoffman, *Poetry,* 185.
32. Desmond Flower, "Notes," to Dowson, *Poetical Works,* 244. See also Longaker, *Ernest Dowson,* 73–79.

was minor because it was little more than a pose; not because it was erotic," decided Holbrook Jackson. "It did not ring true: for one reason because it was an affectation, and for another because it was perhaps a little too much like the life the decadents were trying to live."[33] The words are Jackson's a dozen years after Crane's death, but they convey a truth that Crane had addressed, as he did so many other matters of importance to him, in his "lines." Crane had little patience with the minor poets of the nineties. "Perhaps it is because I lived on borrowed money and ate in lunch-wagons when I was trying to be someone," he explained dismissively, "that these magnified sinners in good duds bore me so."[34]

2

Crane did not have uppermost in mind the sentimental excesses of the Decadent poets when he came to write "The Blue Battalions." As will be seen, he had other targets in mind.

Usually read as a millennial Christian poem with an optimistic message,[35] "The Blue Battalions" can be read differently when it is located within its appropriate historical and biographical context.

> When a people reach the top of a hill
> Then does God lean toward them,
> Shortens tongues, lengthens arms.
> A vision of their dead comes to the weak.
> The moon shall not be too old
> Before the new battalions rise
> —Blue battalions—
> The moon shall not be too old
> When the children of change shall fall
> Before the new battalions
> —The blue battalions—

33. Holbrook Jackson, *The Eighteen Nineties: A Review of Art and Ideas at the Close of the Nineteenth Century*, intr. Karl Beckson (New York: Capricorn Books, 1966), 70, 162.

34. Crane, *Correspondence*, ed. Wertheim and Sorrentino, II, 507.

35. See Hoffman, *Poetry*, 163–74; Pietro Spinucci, "La Poesia di Stephen Crane," *Studi Americani* (Rome), 17 (1971), 111–13; John Blair, "The Posture of a Bohemian in the Poetry of Stephen Crane," *American Literature*, 61 (May 1989), 228; David Halliburton, *The Color of the Sky: A Study of Stephen Crane* (Cambridge, Eng.: Cambridge University Press, 1989), 313–21; and Patrick K. Dooley, *The Pluralistic Philosophy of Stephen Crane* (Urbana and Chicago: University of Illinois Press, 1993), 122. Even those who do not much care for the poem read it as one of Christian affirmation. See Harland S. Nelson, "Stephen Crane's Achievement as a Poet," *Texas Studies in Literature and Language*, 4 (Winter 1963), 574–77; Marston LaFrance, *A Reading of Stephen Crane* (Oxford: Clarendon Press, 1971), 148–49 n. 16.

Mistakes and virtues will be trampled deep
A church and a thief shall fall together
A sword will come at the bidding of the eyeless,
The God-led, turning only to beckon.
    Swinging a creed like a censer
    At the head of the new battalions
        —Blue battalions—
    March the tools of nature's impulse
    Men born of wrong, men born of right
    Men of the new battalions
        —The blue battalions—

The clang of swords is Thy wisdom
The wounded make gestures like Thy Son's
The feet of mad horses is one part,
—Aye, another is the hand of a mother on the brow of a son.
    Then swift as they charge through a shadow,
    The men of the new battalions
        —Blue battalions—
    God lead them high. God lead them far
    Lead them far, lead them high
    These new battalions
        —The blue battalions—.[36]

The poem's battalions are "blue" because at some level of his consciousness the poet is thinking of temperance movement colors, and the battalions are "new" because Crane is mocking the 1890s fin de siècle craze for the "nouveau," an honorific nomination that carried everything before it, sweeping away the "old," by adding the word "new" to the titles of reviews, essays, ideas, and movements. "Like *fin de siècle*, it hailed from France," wrote Holbrook Jackson, "and, after its original application in the *phrase l'art nouveau* had done considerable service in this country [England] as a prefix to modern pictures, dresses and designs, our publicists discovered that other things were equally worthy of the useful adjective. Grant Allen wrote of 'The New Hedonism'; H. D. Traill, of 'The New Fiction,' opening his essay with the words: 'Not to be *new* is, in these days, to be nothing.' " There was, Jackson continues, the "New Paganism," the "New Voluptuousness," the "New Remorse," the "New Spirit," the "New Humour," the "New Realism," the "New Drama," the "New Unionism," the "New Woman."[37]

36. Stephen Crane, ["The Blue Battalions"], in *Poems and Literary Remains*, 82.
37. Jackson, *The Eighteen Nineties*, 21, 22.

Yet it was the gadfly Elbert Hubbard who first published Crane's poem in the *Philistine*, a journal inaugurated in 1895 out of East Aurora, New York, that carried as its subtitle *A Periodical of Protest*. And in this instance the facts of first publication, including Crane's decision to send his work to the *Philistine*, might be usefully factored into an interpretation of the poem.

In the first issue of the *Philistine*, dated June 1895, Hubbard had included a note on the publication of *The Black Riders and Other Lines*.[38] By the third issue, dated August 1895, Hubbard was able to include a contribution from Crane himself: the poem beginning "The chatter of a death-demon from a tree-top."[39] Crane would publish rather regularly in the *Philistine* during the next two years. Indeed, in February 1898 Hubbard boasted, in "lines" deployed on the page as if they were by Crane:

> Arrangements have been
> Made with
> Stephen Crane
> (There's only one)
> To supply "Lines"
> For the back of every
> Philistine for a decade.
> Stevie has sent me enuff
> Of the Choice Stuff
> To last several lustrums
> (As he may be shipwreckt any time)
> And the matter will be
> Duly printed
> Regardless of
> Cancellations.[40]

Hubbard was true to his word, printing "Lines" on the back cover of the April issue:

> You tell me this is God?
> I tell you it is a printed list,
> A burning candle and an ass.[41]

38. [Elbert Hubbard], [*The Black Riders*], *Philistine*, 1 (June 1895), 27.
39. Stephen Crane, ["The chatter of a death-demon from a tree-top"], *Philistine*, 1 (Aug. 1895), 93.
40. [Elbert Hubbard], ["Arrangements have been made"], *Philistine*, 6 (Feb. 1898), 77.
41. Stephen Crane, "Lines," *Philistine*, 6 (Apr. 1898), back cover.

In May he printed the longer poem beginning "On the desert."[42] In June he followed up with more "Lines," beginning "When people reach the top of a hill," the poem now known as "The Blue Battalions."[43] Timing made it appear to some that an opportunistic editor had rushed into print a timely war poem. Not so. First of all, Hubbard usually prepared copy for the *Philistine* at least a couple of months before publication.[44] In the second place, the war with Spain was not even mentioned in the *Philistine* that entire summer. Only in retrospect was Crane's poem seen as being about the war when it was included (mistakenly) in an anthology titled *Spanish-American War Songs: A Complete Collection of Newspaper Verse During the Recent War with Spain*, published in late 1898. There Crane's poem was called, for the first time in print, "The Blue Battalions," a title that Crane himself employed in an undated list of his poems.[45] It is not clear when the poem was written. If not by April 1896, as Daniel Hoffman suggests, it was written at least no later than 1897, as Joseph Katz argues, after Crane's arrival in London.[46] Drawing parallels with Crane's dispatches from the Greek-Turkish war, Katz decides that the poem draws on Crane's first war experience, especially at Velestino. Crane was attentive, he notes, to the fact that the Turks wore black uniforms, but the Greeks, whom he favored, wore blue uniforms, as did the Union soldiers during the Civil War (and as would the Americans in the Cuban war).

Despite Hubbard, Sidney Witherbee, and Katz, however, it can be argued that "The Blue Battalions" is not a war poem even though it does describe an army, or at least part of an army, on the move. And it does not make a positive Christian statement. If it "abounds in the imagery of war," as Hoffman argues, "The Blue Battalions" is not commensurate with either an "apocalyptic ethical vision" or a "militant vision of a New Jerusalem."[47] Adopting Hoffman's reading of the poem as a straightforwardly Christian statement, David Halliburton writes that it approximates a "prophetic oracle," "predicting the apocalyptic

42. Stephen Crane, "On the desert," *Philistine*, 6 (May 1898), 166–67.

43. Stephen Crane, "When a people reach the top of a hill," *Philistine*, 7 (June 1898), 9–10.

44. For evidence of this, see Hubbard's obituary for Crane, which he wrote a week after Crane's death on June 5, 1900, but which did not appear until the September issue of the *Philistine* (11 [Sept. 1900], 123–28). For an account of Crane's presence in Hubbard's magazine (1895–1900), see David H. Dickason, "Stephen Crane and the *Philistine*," *American Literature*, 15 (Nov. 1943), 279–87.

45. Stephen Crane, "The Blue Battalions," in *Spanish-American War Songs: A Complete Collection of Newspaper Verse During the Recent War with Spain*, comp. by Sidney A. Witherbee (Detroit: Sidney A. Witherbee, 1898), 182–83. Crane's list of poems containing the reference to the "Blue Battalions" is transcribed in *Poems and Literary Remains*, 220–21.

46. Hoffman, *Poetry*, 162–63, 163 n. 17; Joseph Katz, " 'The Blue Battalions' and the Uses of Experience," *Studia Neophilologica*, 38, No. 1 (1966), 107–16; Katz, Introduction to *The Portable Stephen Crane*, ed. Katz (New York: Viking, 1969), xiii–xiv. In *Poems and Literary Remains*, Fredson Bowers opts for 1897 (232).

47. Hoffman, *Poetry*, 162, 165.

appearance of the blue battalions." In this poem, continues Halliburton, Crane gives "poetic form to impulses that elsewhere lead to the military sublime, an uplifted and uplifting form that transfigures secular militarism into militant spirituality."[48] What Hoffman's and Halliburton's readings ignore is that in mode the poem is parodic and that the thrust of the parody is satiric. If it transfigures secular militarism into militant spirituality, it does so for satiric purposes. Not Union army blue or Greek blue is the principal source for the blue of "The Blue Battalions."

As Crane was well aware, blue was one of the two colors (the other being white) universally associated with the members of the "cold-water army."[49] Blue was chosen by most of the American temperance forces in the fight for a "cold-water society."[50] The readers prepared for use at temperance meetings are replete with references to blue things: blue inns advertising temperance, blue ribbon clubs, blue badges worn by those eligible to ride on temperance parade wagons, even, in rousing parody of Tennyson's poem about Balaclava, a "Blue Brigade" that charges against the forces of intemperance. Such blue brigades add up to an "imperial temperance army" whose flag should be, as one writer instructs, "a field of pure white, emblematic of the stainless sincerity of our soldiers' *total abstinence*," its border "blue, betokening the imperial power of the omnipotent God," and its folds "covered with golden stars, the bright and precious promises of God's holy Book."[51]

There is more in these temperance readers to support the suggestion that Crane's millennial army has its experiential basis—if not its spiritual and aesthetic roots—in the vigorous and fierce wars the "blue brigades" wage on the gin palace and the rum shop. "There is war about it [liquor traffic] in America, the pledge of total abstinence is its muster roll; the gospel hymns are its rallying songs, the *badge of blue its uniform*"; "we must enlist them [men of business], or get them to fall into line and keep step to the company's music, or *our battalions*

48. Halliburton, *Color of the Sky*, 319, 320.

49. Anonymous, "The Cold-Water Army," in *The National Temperance Orator*, ed. L[izzie] Penney (New York: National Temperance Society and Publication House, 1879), 136.

50. Frances E. Willard, "The Great Evil," in *Readings and Recitations, No. 5*, ed. L[izzie] Penney (New York: National Temperance Society and Publication House, 1884), 69. If Thomas Beer is to be trusted for once, we can point to Crane's awareness of Frances E. Willard on at least two occasions: first, Crane "seriously shocked the wife of another [Syracuse University] authority by declining to meet Miss Frances Willard at her house for the reason that he thought Miss Willard a fool;" second, " 'Frances Willard,' he told Miss Harris, 'is one of those wonderful people who can tell right from wrong for everybody from the polar cap to the equator. Perhaps it never struck her that people differ from her. I have loved myself passionately now and then but Miss Willard's affair with Miss Willard should be stopped by the police' " (*Stephen Crane: A Study in American Letters*, intr. Joseph Conrad [New York: Knopf, 1923], 57–58, 205).

51. W. H. Boole, "Run Up the Flag—Nail It to the Staff!" in *Readings and Recitations, No. 2*, ed. Miss L. Penney (New York: National Temperance Society and Publication House, 1878), 66.

shall never march to victory"; and "the side will win that has most votes, and in spite of church and woman's union, *blue ribbon* clubs and Y.M.C.A., the side will go to the wall, in utter defeat and rout, that has the fewest votes" (emphases added).[52] Moreover, the battle for souls is to be fought between the two educators of the young, the grogshop and the church and Sabbath school. "Between the two there is the old 'irrepressible conflict' over again. It is war to the knife, and the knife to the hilt, and only one can win. And in the warfare, we of Christ's army are outnumbered."[53] All the quotations so far given come from Frances E. Willard, the longtime president of the WCTU.

Descriptions of an ultimate victory over the forces of drink and intemperance were almost always constructed in unmistakably apocalyptic terms. "The race is climbing upwards; not in a straight line is it going . . . by the winding path we are ascending. The temperance cause is growing. There is the winding path of light; there is the zig-zag path of glory. The time will come when the temperance standard, the flag of total abstinence, shall be planted on the very mountain-top of vision and of victory. God hasten the day!"[54] Recall that Crane's mock-hymn begins, "When a people reach the top of a hill / Then does God lean toward them"—"God lead them high. God lead them far. / Lead them far, lead them high / These new battalions / —The blue battalions." The march of the militant temperance warriors is described similarly in another piece, "Is There No Hope?" This piece focuses not merely on waging war on intemperance but on the salvation of souls through militant Christianity; and, as such, it epitomizes Christianity's promise that through the Church of Jesus the weak and the docile can win through to "the hour of God."

Ordinary warfare will make no impression upon this mail-clad diabolus; the lance and spear have failed to penetrate to his vitals. A sad spectacle presents itself, when, in the face of the Church of Jesus, this Philistine defies the armies of the living God, and triumphantly enters family, altar, and pulpit, to grasp and destroy the fairest and best.

. . . .

Christianity is the only vital force that claims any power to overthrow this evil. Can it do it? Will it do it? Jesus waits the answer, "from henceforth expecting until His enemies be made His footstool." A heathen world looks for the answer; and upon that answer depends the extension of Christ's kingdom! . . . Now, "upon the side of the oppressor there is

52. Frances E. Willard, "Everybody's War," in *Readings and Recitations, No. 4*, ed. L[izzie] Penney (New York: National Temperance Society and Publication House, 1882), 54–56.

53. Frances E. Willard, "Which Shall Win?" in *Readings and Recitations, No. 1*, ed. L[izzie] Penney (New York: National Temperance Society and Publication House, 1877), 9.

54. Bishop Samuel Fallows, "We Have Not Begun to Fight Yet," in *Readings and Recitations, No. 3*, ed. L[izzie] Penney (New York: National Temperance Society and Publication House, 1879), 13.

power," but does not the time hasten when He will "judge the fatherless
and the oppressed?"

"When wealth and power have had their hour,
Comes for the weak the hour of God."[55]

Recall, incidentally, that in "The Blue Battalions" it is "a vision of their dead
[that] comes to the weak." And who are the weakest of the weak? In another
temperance poem lies the answer to the question. It begins:

> Bring out your dead, bring out your dead!
> A great bell tolled and tolled,
> And over sea and over land
> The dread commandment rolled.
> Bring out your dead, bring out your dead,
> One funeral let there be;
> Come, pile them on this mountain-top,
> That all the world may see.

The "dead" are those killed by drink and now to be carried to the mountaintop
(Crane's "the top of a hill"). Mothers carry their sons, wives bear their hus-
bands, and, in the temperance poem,

> Fair children staggered 'neath the weight
> Of fathers—shame that you,
> O little ones, so pure and weak,
> Should have such work to do![56]

Such are the apocalyptic wars waged between the two armies of temperance
and intemperance. Temperance poets versified these encounters as battles between hosts of the temperate waving banners of "blue" and armies of the intemperate raising flags of "black":

> Do you see the temperance banners
> Waving clearly now in view?
> Do you hear the loud hosannas?
> Do you see the badge of blue?
> 'Tis the temperance host advancing
> With a firm and martial tread;
> With the sunlight 'round them dancing,
> And the "red cross" overhead!

55. Rev. H. W. Conant, "Is There No Hope?" in *Readings and Recitations, No. 2,* 39–40.
56. Ellen M. H. Gates, " 'Bring Out Your Dead,' " in *Readings and Recitations, No. 1,* 89–90.

And against whom is the "temperance host" with its banners, its "badge of blue," marching? The enemy ultimately speaks for itself:

> The Rum Fiend sees, and affrighted
> Goes back to his native hell,
> To the place where souls benighted
> With devils incarnate dwell;
> And he summons his friends together
> In council many an hour,
> And asks of his subjects, whether
> They'll help him to keep his power.
>
> Then a thousand grog-shops answer,
> And tavern, and bar, and still,
> And they shout aloud, "We can, sir;
> We'll help you, of course we will."
> "Up with our black flag," they shout now,
> "Maddened with rum be each brain,
> The temperance band we will rout now
> And their children shall be slain!"[57]

It will be recalled that when Crane arrived in Greece in 1897, he seems to have immediately favored Greeks in blue over Turks in black.[58] Set aside Crane's political and historical allegiances and look at his earliest poems for evidence of his use of colors such as red and black. His first book of poems opens with the title poem:

> BLACK RIDERS CAME FROM THE SEA.
> THERE WAS CLANG AND CLANG OF SPEAR AND SHIELD,
> AND CLASH AND CLASH OF HOOF AND HEEL,
> WILD SHOUTS AND THE WAVE OF HAIR
> IN THE RUSH UPON THE WIND:
> THUS THE RIDE OF SIN.[59]

57. Rev. W. R. Fitch, " 'My People Shall Be Free!' " in *Readings and Recitations, No. 2*, 33–34. See also E. Wentworth, "The 'Blue Ribbon,' " in *Readings and Recitations, No. 2*, 14–15.

58. See "The Blue Badge of Cowardice," Crane's report from Athens on May 11, 1897, in which he is critical not of the blue-clad Greeks but of the Crown Prince Constantine, who ordered the victorious Greek army to "retreat before the enemy it had defeated." On May 12, 1897, it appeared in the *New York Journal, Chicago Tribune,* and several other newspapers. It is reprinted in *Reports of War: War Dispatches: Great Battles of the World,* Volume IX of *The University of Virginia Edition of the Works of Stephen Crane,* ed. Fredson Bowers, intr. James B. Colvert (Charlottesville: University Press of Virginia, 1971), 44–48.

59. Stephen Crane, *The Black Riders and Other Lines* (Boston: Copeland and Day, 1895), 1.

And poem XLVI of *The Black Riders and Other Lines* reads:

> MANY RED DEVILS RAN FROM MY HEART
> AND OUT UPON THE PAGE,
> THEY WERE SO TINY
> THE PEN COULD MASH THEM.
> AND MANY STRUGGLED IN THE INK.
> IT WAS STRANGE
> TO WRITE IN THIS RED MUCK
> OF THINGS FROM MY HEART.[60]

The red muck from the poet's heart shares its redness with the standard—the "red banner of death"—carried by the enemies of temperance.[61] It might even be instructive some time to read the whole of *The Black Riders and Other Lines* as if it were visionary, somewhat akin to the subversive parts of William Blake's *The Marriage of Heaven and Hell*, especially the "Proverbs of Hell."

Just as subversive, however, is the "The Blue Battalions." Its apocalyptics derive from those of the American temperance movement. The war against rum is waged by cold-water, blue-battalion warriors fully confident that their cause is favored by heaven and the gods. That Crane targets the temperance movement explains why he sent the poem to Hubbard's *Philistine* to begin with. After all, when Crane makes the anatomical observation that God can "shorten . . . tongues, lengthen . . . arms," he is merely pointing to the omnipotence of a God who can even in bizarre ways rectify whatever physical deficiencies one might find in his chosen militant warriors.[62]

So, maybe critics hostile to the poem, like Marston LaFrance, have to be taken into account after all. The line " 'When a people reach the top of a hill' is suspect," he warns, "because this image in the poems always implies the literal truth which Crane rejects; the image of 'the eyeless, / The God-led, turning only to beckon. / Swinging a creed like a censer' presents the quick stream of undiscriminating lemmings in huddled procession; and Crane elsewhere never calls human beings 'the tools of nature's impulse.' " To this point there is no problem with LaFrance's reading. But then he concludes that in "The Blue Battalions" Crane deliberately abandoned "irony to produce commercially acceptable goods for a sentimental market."[63] For once, and perhaps at

---

60. Ibid., 49.

61. G., "For What Are We Battling?" in *Readings and Recitations, No. 2*, 95.

62. That "God . . . lengthens arms" (lines 2–3) appears to be Crane's extension of a common notion. See William Holmes and John W. Barber's entry under "Passion and Patience" in *Religious Allegories: Being a Series of Emblematic Engravings*, their highly popular nineteenth-century emblem book: "If he finds his own arm too short, he is intimate with *One* who is mighty to save, and who is a very present help in times of trouble" (Boston: L. P. Crown, 1854, 73–74).

63. LaFrance, *Reading*, 148 n. 16.

the wrong time, he abandons his thesis that Crane is primarily and essentially an ironist to read "The Blue Battalions" as a straightforwardly presented Christian poem, misreading it because he fails to recognize that in mode it is parodic and in intention ironic. This typical Crane performance was certain to appeal to the *Philistine*'s readers. It could not have escaped them that when Crane refers to the "children of change" who are the target of the temperance movement's "blue battalions," he has in mind precisely those beings who will "change breath," those "children" well accustomed to taking drink, those "black riders" of sin.[64] After all, it was drink that made them—the armies on both sides of the temperance question—kith and kin. As Crane put it in poem IX of *The Black Riders and Other Lines* (echoing Psalms 18: "He maketh my feet like hind's feet, and setteth me in high places"),

> I STOOD UPON A HIGH PLACE,
> AND SAW, BELOW, MANY DEVILS
> RUNNING, LEAPING,
> AND CAROUSING IN SIN.
> ONE LOOKED UP, GRINNING,
> AND SAID, "COMRADE! BROTHER!"[65]

Crane had not only absorbed the moralistic sentiments, attitudes, and slogans expressed by the temperance workers but, as we have seen, he had taken over the very symbols, images, and words that did their work for them.

3

Thomas Beer is the source for the story that while a student at the Hudson River Institute at Claverack, New York, in the spring of 1888, Crane got into a fight over Tennyson's poetry. "The fight began with Stephen's assertion that Lord Tennyson's poems were 'swill.' He lost a bit of a front tooth in making good his opinion."[66] On the basis of Beer's brief reference, Berryman speculates that "this was less a critical estimate, presumably, than residue of an agony earlier in having to memorize and recite 'The Charge of the Light Brigade'—an experience so acute that he devoted long afterward a whole small

---

64. See Harold Wentworth and Stuart Berg Flexner, *Dictionary of American Slang*, 2nd Supplemented ed. (New York: Crowell, 1975), 93. It is intriguing that Swinburne's "Dolores" also refers to "the children of change." These, however, are punished in a "city" that "lay red" from the "rods" of "Our Lady of Pain" (110).

65. Crane, *Black Riders*, 10.

66. Beer, *Stephen Crane*, 53.

story to it ('Makin' an Orator')."[67] R. W. Stallman builds on Berryman, adding that one of Crane's fellow students at Claverack remembered that Crane could "quote from Tennyson's 'In Memoriam.' "[68] Whether Crane recited the poem in jest or satirically he does not say. Whatever his attitude toward Tennyson's poetry, there is no gainsaying that "The Charge of the Light Brigade" served Crane the writer well (if not the quarreling student) on more than one occasion.

Recent discoveries have impugned Beer's work. His facts and his sources are suspect at best. With a single exception, originals for the many letters he quotes have never surfaced, and his working drafts reveal that the very text of the letters he "quotes" is subject to change from version to version.[69] "It seems most likely that he did not alter or destroy Crane's letters," concludes John Clendenning, "he wrote them."[70] That the letters appear to be forgeries calls into doubt much of the undocumented information contained in Beer's book. So, the strongest piece of evidence to indicate that Crane disliked at least some of Tennyson's poetry comes not from Beer's report of a schoolboy's fistfight but from Crane's late story, "Making an Orator."

Immediately on publication in 1854 Tennyson's literary ballad "The Charge of the Light Brigade" was such a popular success that when officially asked to do so, the poet readily agreed to send copies of his poem to the Crimea for distribution to British troops in the field.[71] With such an auspicious start, it is no wonder that this poem on the Victorian principles of valor and obedience quickly made its way into textbooks, school readers, and recitation collections on both sides of the Atlantic and insinuated its way into the schools of Crane's fictional small town, Whilomville. It is Tennyson's notorious poem, of course, that the terrified Jimmie Trescott fails to recite in the Whilomville story "Making an Orator."[72]

Tennyson's durable poem was also adapted for hard use by the temperance workers. Parodies of "The Charge of the Light Brigade" found their way into temperance readers intended for the "Drawing-room Meeting," a ritualized

---

67. Berryman, *Stephen Crane*, 15.

68. Stallman, *Stephen Crane*, 19.

69. Stanley Wertheim and Paul Sorrentino, "Thomas Beer: The Clay Feet of Stephen Crane Biography," *American Literary Realism*, 22 (Spring 1990), 2–16. In their edition of the *Correspondence*, Wertheim and Sorrentino relegate those letters whose source is solely Thomas Beer to an appendix (II, 661–92).

70. John Clendenning, "Thomas Beer's *Stephen Crane*: The Eye of His Imagination," *Prose Studies*, 14 (May 1991), 69.

71. *The Letters of Alfred Lord Tennyson, Volume II: 1851–1870*, ed. Cecil Y. Lang and Edgar F. Shannon, Jr. (Cambridge, Mass.: Harvard University Press, 1987), 118 n., 132–33.

72. Stephen Crane, "Making an Orator," in *Tales of Whilomville*, Volume VII of *The University of Virginia Edition of the Works of Stephen Crane*, ed. Fredson Bowers, intr. J. C. Levenson (Charlottesville: University Press of Virginia, 1969), 158–63.

occasion for proselytizing by the WCTU. It would not be surprising to learn that such meetings were held by Crane's mother, who served as national superintendent for the WCTU's Committee on Juvenile Work.[73] The temperance workers also had considerable success in incorporating temperance lessons in the public school curriculum. "Thanks to the Woman's Christian Temperance Union, temperance teaching in the public schools is compulsory in almost all States of the Union," it was reported in 1897.[74] As early as 1877, encouraged by the "advance during the past year in the Sabbath schools and Public schools," Frances Willard had called for the preparation of "a manual of temperance instruction for use in public schools, embodying readings, recitations, illustrations from natural science and experiments."[75] In the same year appeared *Readings and Recitations, No. 1*, fulsomely subtitled *A New and Choice Collection of Articles in Prose and Verse, embracing argument and appeal, pathos and humor, by the foremost temperance advocates and writers. Suitable for use in schools, all temperance organizations, reform clubs, lodges, divisions, etc., and also adapted for public and private readings.* This volume launched the series edited by Lizzie Penney that by 1886 ran to five volumes.

Miss Penney's volumes contained numerous parodies, among them the two given below showing how Tennyson's poem on the English blunder at Balaclava could be appropriated for use in the temperance cause. The first one sees the destructive charge as being made by a brigade of drunkards, men destroyed by those tradesmen who have sold them drink. "The Charge of the Rum Brigade" reads in part:

> All in league, all in league,
> All in league onward,
> All in the Valley of Death,
> Walked the Six Hundred.

> "Forward the Rum Brigade!
> Cheers for the Whisky Raid!"
> Into the Valley of Death
> Walked the Six Hundred.

> "Forward the Rum Brigade!"
> Were all their friends dismayed?
> Yes; and the soldiers knew
> Each one had blundered.

73. Anonymous, *A Brief History of the Woman's Christian Temperance Union*, 2nd ed. (Evanston: Union Signal, 1907), 14, 29.

74. Belle M. Brain, *Weapons for Temperance Warfare* (Boston and Chicago: United Society of Christian Endeavor, 1897), 10.

75. *Brief History*, 33.

Theirs not to make reply,
Theirs not to reason why,
Theirs but to *drink and die.*
Into the Valley of Death
    Walked the Six Hundred.

Drunkards to right of them,
Drunkards to left of them,
Drunkards in front of them,
    One million numbered.
Oaths fell like shot and shell,
Rum did its work so well.
Into the jaws of Death,
Into the mouth of Hell
    Walked the Six Hundred.

. . . .

Curses to right of them,
Curses to left of them,
Curses behind them
    Volleyed and thundered.
Stormed at by those who sell,
They, who had paid so well,
    Well had been plundered.
Clenched teeth and livid brow,
Delirium tremens now.
Thus young and old men fell
Into the jaws of Death
Into the mouth of Hell.
Not one was left of them,
    Left of Six Hundred.[76]

The second parody of Tennyson's poem celebrates a triumphant charge by
temperance troops into the ranks of the intemperate and all those who aid and
abet their alcoholism.

The Charge of the Blue Brigade
After Tennyson

Now a league, then a league,
    Many leagues onward—

76. Mary S. Wheeler, "The Charge of the Rum Brigade," in *Readings and Recitations, No. 1,*
27–29.

Into the forts of rum,
   Rode the six hundred.
"Forward, the Blue Brigade!
Charge for the guns!" he said;
Up to the forts of rum,
   Rode the six hundred.

"Forward, the Blue Brigade!"
Never a heart dismayed,
Though ev'ry woman knew
   Lawyers had blundered.
Useless to reason why,
Useless to make reply;
"Better to do or die,"
   Thought the six hundred.

Wine to the right of them,
Cider to left of them,
Whisky in front of them,
   Branded and numbered;
These are the shot and shell,
Guns that have "carried" well;
   These are the jaws of death,
These are the mouths of hell,
   More than six hundred.

Their sword, the mighty pen,
Their flag, a ribbon blue,
   Dauntless six hundred.
Forward, through north and south
Into the demon's mouth,
Onward from East to West,
Blue ribbons on their breast,
   Rode the six hundred.

Flashed all their foreheads bare,
Flashed all their hands in air;
Bowed were their hearts in prayer,
Guarding the penmen there,
   More than six hundred.
Ah, this was not a joke,
Never their ranks they broke,

Saved one at every stroke,
  While the world wondered.

"Schnapps" to the right of them,
Beer to the left of them,
Doctors in front of them,
  Sputtered and grumbled.
Oh, the grand charge they made!
How can their glory fade?
Honor the Blue Brigade,
  Now many hundred.[77]

The closest Crane came to writing a true parody of "The Charge of the Light Brigade" was "The Blue Battalions." But in his 1899 poem "War Is Kind" he not only presents attitudes toward war that were "the complete antithesis" of Tennyson's, it has been argued, but he "even imitates the incremental repetitions used so effectively by Tennyson," achieving, however, "a completely different emotional tone."[78] Between Tennyson's poem and Crane's there is a mediating text.

Echoing the Twenty-third Psalm just as Tennyson did, Frances E. Willard gives "voice to the motherhood of the nation" that, like the brigade at Balaclava, "has gone down into the valley of unutterable pain and in the shadow of death, with the dews of eternity upon the mother's brow."[79] "Mother whose heart hung humble as a button / On the bright splendid shroud of your son," writes Crane toward the end of "War Is Kind," echoing Willard's phrase "mother's brow" in his "mother . . . shroud."[80]

There is no gainsaying that Tennyson's poem was, early on, part and parcel of Crane's cultural baggage and, as such, readily available to him for creative purposes. The "Charge" appears, significantly, in two fictional texts—*The Red Badge of Courage* and "Making an Orator." In the Whilomville story Crane quotes directly from Tennyson's poem, while in the *Red Badge* he uses "The Charge of the Light Brigade" less explicitly. In the novel Tennyson's poem hovers over the incidents leading to the 304th's mad charge against an entrenched enemy and the mad charge itself.

77. Anonymous, "The Charge of the Blue Brigade," in *Readings and Recitations, No. 2*, 27–28.

78. Thomas Arthur Gullason, "Tennyson's Influence on Stephen Crane," *Notes and Queries*, n.s. 5 (Apr. 1958), 164–65.

79. Frances E. Willard, "The Widening Horizon," in *Frances E. Willard Recitation Book, Werner's Readings and Recitations, No. 18* (New York: Edgar S. Werner, 1898), 91.

80. It is of more than passing interest that Crane's "War Is Kind" also echoes Swinburne's "Dolores." For example, Swinburne's use of "splendid" in the image "splendid with swords" emerges in Crane in his description of the "splendid shroud" of the fallen soldier (110).

In chapter 6 of the *Red Badge*, as Henry Fleming flees from battle, he looks down at moving troops: "He saw a brigade going to the relief of its pestered fellows. He scrambled upon a wee hill and watched it sweeping finely, keeping formation in difficult places. The blue of the line was crusted with steel-color and the brilliant flags projected. Officers were shouting. This sight, also, filled him with wonder. The brigade was hurrying briskly to be gulped into the infernal mouth of the war-god. What manner of men were they, anyhow. Ah, it was some wondrous breed. Or else they didn't comprehend—the fools."[81] Henry slips away but later comes upon officers talking about how the "force" in "the fix" had somehow held, that the brigade had resisted and—to his surprise surely—had not been "gulped into the infernal mouth of the war-god." What no one knows at the moment is that the next time he will overhear talk about a "foolish" charge he will learn that it is his own unit—the 304th—that will be sent in.

Chapter 18 begins with a momentary lull in the fighting, during which, as Henry and his companions soon become aware, there emerges a disconcerting continuous sound from a man shot through the body. He is one of their comrades. But they will not go near him. "When their eyes first encountered him there was a sudden halt as if they feared to go near." He may be dying. "He was thrashing about in the grass, twisting his shuddering body into many strange postures." His agonized writhing recalls the movements of Jim Conklin, the tall soldier, who "was invaded by a creeping strangeness that slowly enveloped him." Confronted by this wounded man, the "youth's friend" Wilson suddenly has a notion, based on what the narrator calls "a geographical illusion concerning a stream," to run off to look for water. Hurriedly, the two of them search for the stream but do not find it.[82] Their quest has led them to high ground where they can look down on the slow movements of their fellow soldiers. "Looking over their own troops, they saw mixed masses slowly getting into regular form." Into their vicinity ride "a jangling general and his staff." The officers are directly in front of the two young soldiers when another officer rides up with a report. Unnoticed by the officers, the two privates then become privy to a startling and deeply disturbing exchange. The general orders a charge. Can the reporting officer "spare" any troops? No, he can't—"but there's th' 304th. They fight like a lot 'a mule-drivers," he says, "I can spare them best of any." The general tells him to get them ready; and then he adds, "I don't believe many of your mule-drivers will get back."

81. Stephen Crane, *The Red Badge of Courage*, Volume II of *The University of Virginia Edition of the Works of Stephen Crane*, ed. Fredson Bowers, intr. by J. C. Levenson (Charlottesville: University Press of Virginia, 1975), 1–135.

82. This quest for water reappears as a desperate run for water in Crane's story "A Mystery of Heroism."

The two privates are astounded. "New eyes" were given to Henry. "And the most startling thing was to learn suddenly that he was very insignificant." When they arrive at camp, their lieutenant berates them for returning empty-handed but brightens up at their news that the unit has been chosen to make the next charge. " 'Charge?' said the lieutenant. 'Charge? Well, b'Gawd! Now, this is real fightin'.' Over his soiled countenance there went a boastful smile. 'Charge? Well, b'Gawd!' " Others, however, are skeptical, and they question Wilson and Fleming intensely. But when their story holds up, it is as if the regiment "seemed to draw itself up and heave a deep breath. None of the men's faces were mirrors of large thoughts. The soldiers were bended and stooped like sprinters before a signal."

Significantly, the two inadvertent messengers do not reveal the rest of their information. They keep to themselves the general's prediction that not many of the 304th's mule-drivers will survive their suicidal charge. Their shared secret—"an inner knowledge"—emboldens them. They turn, with the others, to await the order to charge. The order comes and these expendable "mule-drivers" make their charge. The result, surprisingly, is not a disaster but a success, especially for Henry and Wilson.

Crane's handling of the charge of the 304th can be likened to (and contrasted with) Tennyson's immediate memorializing of the historical charge of the British brigade against the standing and secure Russians and Cossacks. Tennyson's inspiration for his ode to military virtue and unquestioning duty came in newspaper accounts of the ill-fated charge at Balaclava on October 25, 1854. He read in the London *Times* that the order given to charge was ill-advised. "Even accident would have made it more tolerable," wrote the *Times* on November 13, 1854, "but it was a mere mistake—evidently a mistake, and perceived to be such when it was too late to correct it." The next day the *Times* called the charge "a noble but disastrous deed—a fatal display of courage which all must admire while they lament"—"a spectacle so strange, so terrific, so disastrous, and yet so grand."[83] It is important to remember that although the charge accomplished nothing of military value and casualties were high, an appreciable number of survivors were able to ride back safely out of that "valley of Death."

Under orders the "six hundred" members of the light brigade rode into "the valley of Death" because "some one had blunder'd." They did so, not because they did not know that a blunder had been committed or because they trusted unquestioningly the sagacity of their officers or in the Providence of a protecting God but because they knew their duty. "Their's not to make reply, /

---

83. Quoted in Edgar Shannon and Christopher Ricks, " 'The Charge of the Light Brigade': The Creation of a Poem," *Studies in Bibliography*, 38 (Charlottesville: University Press of Virginia, 1985), 29, 32.

Their's not to reason why, / Their's but to do and die."[84] As the *Times* had put it, "The British soldier will do his duty, even to certain death, and is not paralyzed by feeling that he is the victim of some hideous blunder." In Tennyson's poem, "the word 'duty,' unuttered, becomes not what the poem says but what it breathes."[85]

In calling this place in Balaclava "the valley of Death" Tennyson follows the *Times* of November 13.[86] In both instances the phrase is obviously intended to invoke the similar phrase in the Twenty-third Psalm:

> The Lord is my shepherd: I shall not want.
> He maketh me to lie down in green pastures: he leadeth me beside
>   the still waters. . . .
> Yea, though I walk through the valley of the shadow of death, I
>   will fear no evil. . . .

Interestingly enough, the Twenty-third Psalm, hovering as it does over the charges of the 304th in chapters 18–23, also surfaces in some of the imagery Crane employs in Henry's reverie in the book's final chapter. The images of water and pastures borrowed from the Psalmist, countering those thoughts of "the valley of the shadow of death" that have plagued the young recruit's consciousness throughout, not only appear ironically in Wilson and Fleming's unsuccessful search through the countryside for the "supposed" waters but also in Henry's thoughts after he has decided that he is now "a man," who having "touch[ed] the great death," has "found that, after all, it was but the great death." Resting in "soft and eternal peace," and acting as if death has no dominion over him, Henry "turned now with a lover's thirst, to images of tranquil skies, fresh meadows, cool brooks." His "sultry night-mare" over, he has emerged from the valley of death and is again safe—for the moment, anyway.[87]

Interestingly, this feeling of escape parallels that of young Jimmie Trescott in "Making an Orator." Unable to recite beyond the poem's first five lines, Jimmie, too, has been led to the altar of sacrifice. Like that of Henry Fleming (and the mule-drivers of the 304th), Jimmie's story is one of botched initiation. In the schools of Whilomville, training in elocution and declamation is an up-

---

84. "The Charge of the Light Brigade," in *The Poems of Tennyson*, ed. Christopher Ricks (London and Harlow: Longmans, 1969), 1034. In an early version Tennyson named the officer who ordered the Charge: " 'Forward, the Light Brigade! / Take the guns,' Nolan said" (1035). Oddly enough, in the Puerto Rican—Cuban campaign stories, "Regulars Get No Glory" and "The Price of the Harness," Crane also writes about a soldier named Nolan.

85. Quoted in Shannon and Ricks, " 'Charge,' " 30.

86. Quoted ibid., 20.

87. Crane also echoes the Twenty-third Psalm in "The Blue Battalions"—"swift as they charge through a shadow" (*Poems and Literary Remains*, 82).

dated manifestation of an ancient ritual. Friday afternoon, an apt time for ordeals of all sorts, has become the setting for harrowing "ceremonies," with those children fortunate enough to have "already passed over the mountain of distress" now looking down at the latest victim of education as "another lamb brought to butchery." Their ceremony is a "great crisis" and a "spectacle" of "torture" that transforms audiences of peers and earlier victims into modern descendants of the vicious "Roman populace in Nero's time." What Crane's diction insists upon is that this educational practice is itself a barbarous rite of passage. In an age that too easily assumed man's evolution beyond rituals of cruelty and sadism, Crane notes that the modern equivalents of such rites occur in the suffering of children forced to "pass through the flames" in the questionable ways and manner of their formal education.

The full story of Jimmie's ordeal is instructive, especially for the language— images and symbols—Crane employs. The child long fears being promoted to that class where it was the habit to "devote" Friday afternoons to "what was called elocution." His worst fears are about to be realized. He now lives terrified of the Friday when, his number called, he must take his turn at reciting. The first time he is scheduled to perform Jimmie feigns an illness that deceives his mother, and he is kept home from school. But the next Friday rolls around soon enough. Surprisingly, on that day everything rushes along—"geography, arithmetic, and spelling—usually great tasks—quite roll off" Jimmie until the time set aside for elocution. In wild discomfort Jimmie sits through three exercises, "going half blind with fear of his approaching doom." Even the sun's progress that afternoon, with the "minutes march[ing] on towards his great crisis," intimates sacrifice and contest, as the maple trees "defeat . . . the weakening rays of the afternoon sun." Then he is summoned, and Jimmie stands terrified before peers and teacher, called upon to recite "The Charge of the Light Brigade." Several false starts and continuous promptings from his teacher enable Jimmie to stumble his way to the fifth line of the poem, but he can go no further. His angry teacher orders "the miserable wretch before her" to stay after school, warning him that by no stretch of the imagination should he think that he has avoided his fate. In a week he will again be put to the test. But the teacher's threat means little to Jimmie, who feels nothing but total relief. Had his persecutor "suddenly and magically made a spirit of him and left him free to soar high above all the travail of our earthly lives[,] she could not have overjoyed him more," for "no thought to the terrors of the next Friday" did he give. "The evils of the day had been sufficient, and to a childish mind a week is a great space of time."

One possible moral emerges from "Making an Orator" when it is read against the *Red Badge*. Wordsworth's child is father to the man. "Making an Orator" offers a gloss on Private Henry's moments of calm acquiescence and fancied well-being in the final paragraphs of the *Red Badge*. After all, even a short interval between battles can be perceived as "a great space of time."

9

A Blue Inn

The subscriber would inform the friends of Temperance [that] . . . his object is to furnish a comfortable HOME for strangers visiting the city, where they need not be disgusted with the fumes of any Intoxicating Beverage.

—H. P. Jones, Advertisement (1846)

Where does "Old Nick" erect his throne
Of kegs and bottles, blood and bone,
And rule in power all his own?
. . . .
Where do we find the liquid fire,
Where hope, and joy, and life expire,
Where bloody, hellish deeds transpire?

—Anonymous, "The Saloon" (1877)

1

In early 1895, on the basis of the successful newspaper publication of *The Red Badge of Courage,* Crane was sent to parts west on behalf of the Bacheller and Johnson Syndicate. He traveled light, as he made his way out to Nebraska and down to Mexico, always testing the popular and literary views of the West he carried around in his head, such as his mother's views on the evils of the saloon and Mark Twain's notions of a lawless West defined by whiskey. In *Life on the Mississippi,* the latter rhapsodizes:

How solemn and beautiful is the thought, that the earliest pioneer of civilization, the van-leader of civilization, is never the steamboat, never the railroad, never the newspaper, never the Sabbath-school, never the missionary—but always whiskey! Such is the case. Look history over; you will see. The missionary comes after the whiskey[;] . . . next comes the poor immigrant, with axe and hoe and rifle; next, the trader; next, the miscellaneous rush; next, the gambler, the desperado, the highwayman, and all their kindred sin of both sexes; and next, the smart chap who has bought up an old grant that covers all the land. . . . All these interests bring the newspaper; the newspaper starts up politics and a railroad; all hands turn to and build a church and a jail,—and behold, civilization is established forever in the land. But whiskey, you see, was the van-leader in this beneficent work. It always is.[1]

Not only was whiskey the van-leader, it was a perdurable factor in the evolution of Western values, as Crane's fiction would argue time and again.

Mark Twain's view of the West and Crane's mother's notions of the dire effects of intemperance are hardly complementary. Taken together, they offer a broad context for Crane's conflicted view of the American West. It repelled him even as it fascinated him, and those two responses were the engine that drove his fictional image of the West in stories such as "The Bride Comes to Yellow Sky," "Moonlight on the Snow," "Twelve O'Clock," "The Wise Men," "The Five White Mice," and "The Blue Hotel."

2

In his journey westward Crane was ultimately able to outride and outwalk the reaches of the organized temperance movement. Yet the antiliquor sentiment had already had an effect on the real Nebraska, he found out when he got there, and would no doubt soon rear its head aggressively in his fictional Yellow Sky even if, for the moment, the equally fictional War Post and unnamed town of "Twelve O'Clock" remained untainted by the WCTU or any other organized temperance group. Yet it is the temperance worker's attitude toward whiskey that haunts Crane's major Western fiction. His mature imagination continued to be potentiated by the language and incidents the temperance worker devised in hordes of stories, poems, and homilies he had internalized at an early age. In nearly all of Crane's Western stories, King Whiskey has its way. More than the "van-leader of civilization," it simply would not go away.

One of the temperance readers reports on an American gentleman who, when asked "how it was that he never by any chance took a single glass of spirits, but always two or three or more," answered that "whenever he had

1. Mark Twain, *Life on the Mississippi*, in *Mississippi Writings*, ed. Guy Cardwell (New York: Library of America, 1982), 581.

taken one glass of spirits he felt himself to be another man, and then he felt himself bound to treat that other man."[2] In Crane's work there are two major "Swedes." In each of them there is the Swede sober and there is the Swede drunk. Both of them—the Swede in "The Veteran" and the Swede in "The Blue Hotel"—are the agents of grave misfortune. Alcohol directs their behavior. In the nineteenth century the Swedes (as a nation) were reputed to be the Western world's "heaviest consumers of distilled spirits"[3] (hence the Swede, never given a name—not in "The Veteran" or "The Blue Hotel"—becomes on this level the stereotypical, rubricized, and depersonalized "Swede"), followed only by the Irish (hence the Irish hotel keeper, Patrick Scully, who in "The Blue Hotel" keeps his whiskey bottle hidden). Swedes abound in American temperance literature. They feature prominently in the social scientist's statistics. The alcoholic predilections of the Swedes were given special prominence in the *Arena*, published in Boston, just after Crane's own work had begun to appear in its pages.[4] In "The Blue Hotel" the Swede's sense of reality derives, in the words of the "little silent man from the East" (who stands for Crane), from impressions culled from Western "dime-novels."[5] Indeed, the Swede—possessed—thinks that in Fort Romper "he's right out in the middle" of his dime-novel West, with "shootin' and stabbin' and all." "He thinks," concludes the Easterner, "he's right in the middle of hell." The Swede "knows" that Fort Romper equals the West and that the West is synonymous with violence. He is a "Stranger," as the cowboy types him after he has vanquished Scully's son (to give him this name, by which the cowboy and the Irish mean "invader," is to banish him) and that as a "Stranger" he is marked to suffer violent pain. When the sources of the Swede's fears become known, the hotel keeper tries to rout them by denying that Fort Romper is the wild West. "Why, man, we're goin' to have a line of ilictric street-cars in this town next spring," he boasts; "there's a new railroad goin' to be built down from Broken Arm to here. Not to mintion the four churches and the smashin' big brick school-house. Then there's the big factory, too. Why, in two years Romper'll be a met-tro-*pol*-is." These are the signs of civilization.

Scully's Palace Hotel offers evidence that even before the arrival of electric

2. Canon F. W. Farrar, "The Serpent and the Tiger," in *Readings and Recitations, No. 2*, ed. L[izzie] Penney (New York: National Temperance Society and Publication House, 1878), 10.

3. John Koren, "The Liquor Traffic Without Private Profits," *Arena*, 9 (Apr. 1894), 561.

4. See ibid., 561–70, and B. O. Flower, "The Corrupting Influence of the Liquor Power in Politics, and Outlines of Two Practical Methods for Dealing with the Saloon Evil," in "How to Deal with the Liquor Traffic: A Symposium," *Arena*, 9 (May 1894), 840–41. Crane's story "An Ominous Baby" appeared in the *Arena*, 9 (May 1894), 819–21.

5. Stephen Crane, "The Blue Hotel," in *Tales of Adventure*, Volume V of *The University of Virginia Edition of the Works of Stephen Crane*, ed. Fredson Bowers, intr. J. C. Levenson (Charlottesville: University Press of Virginia, 1970), 142–70.

cars and factories, Fort Romper is already a civilized place. It is a refuge for visitors and strangers in which, as Scully maintains, every guest is safe. Collaring potential customers at the railroad station, Scully offers to every one of them, including the "shaky and quick-eyed Swede," the sacred privileges to be enjoyed under his roof. The classical virtue of hospitality having surfaced in Fort Romper, Scully would set up as an avatar of the model hotel keeper, circa 1895: "The proprietor [of a hotel] has 'all sorts and conditions of men' to deal with; he must know human nature in its varied phases; and he must solve race and class problems with delicate tact. He must have a fair knowledge and conception of trade, and of everything that meets and supplements the wants and desires of mankind."[6] Scully, who thinks he knows human nature, has an entrepreneur's eye for color:

> The Palace Hotel at Fort Romper was painted a light blue, a shade that is on the legs of a kind of heron, causing the bird to declare its position against any background. The Palace Hotel, then, was always screaming and howling in a way that made the dazzling winter landscape of Nebraska seem only a gray swampish hush. It stood alone on the prairies, and when the snow was falling the town two hundred yards away was not visible. But when the traveler alighted at the railway station he was obliged to pass the Palace Hotel before he could come upon the company of low clap-board houses which composed Fort Romper, and it was not to be thought that any traveler could pass the Palace Hotel without looking at it.

That thematically there is more to this "blue" than mere color is suggested by the Nebraska saying, "She's all painted up like a new saloon."[7] It is doubtful that readers in Crane's day could have failed to see, at least in retrospect, the irony of Scully's choosing to paint his hotel in one of the two colors favored by the temperance movement. The cold-water army riding the temperance wagon sported blue tags, and the day's temperance tracts and readings are laced with references to the brandishing of the blue. As one writer warned, "There is war about it [the liquor traffic] in America, the pledge of total abstinence is its muster roll, the gospel hymns are its rallying songs, the badge of blue its uniform."[8]

6. Hiram Hitchcock, "The Hotels of America," in *1795–1895: One Hundred Years of American Commerce*, ed. Chauncey M. Depew (New York: Haynes, 1895), I, 155.

7. Ruth Odell, "Nebraska Smart Sayings," *Southern Folklore Quarterly*, 12 (Sept. 1948), 187.

8. Frances E. Willard, "Everybody's War," in *Readings and Recitations, No. 4*, ed. L[izzie] Penney (New York: National Temperance Society and Publication House, 1882), 54. See also E. Wentworth, "The 'Blue Ribbon,'" in *Readings and Recitations, No. 2*, ed. L[izzie] Penney (New York: National Temperance Society and Publication House, 1878), 14–15.

Although the Swede requires considerable urging, Scully's presentation of his family credentials—"the picter of my little gal that died. . . . And then here's the picter of my oldest boy . . . a lawyer in Lincoln an' doin' well"—and a stiff shot of whiskey, he finally accepts Scully's overtures of hospitality. He does more. The "tenderfoot,"[9] who knows only fear and compensatory hatred, is transformed, almost instantaneously, into a screaming counterpart of the hotel itself. "Other time he was scared," complains the hotel keeper's son, "now he's too fresh." Indeed, by suppertime, "the Swede fizzed like a fire-wheel. He sometimes seemed on the point of bursting into riotous song. . . . The Swede domineered the whole feast, and he gave it the appearance of a cruel bacchanal." This new perception of his counterparts and of his situation among them seems to have changed him wonderfully. "He seemed to have grown suddenly taller; he gazed, brutally disdainful, into every face." There is even a moment of imagistic foreshadowing of his fate. "Once when he jabbed out harpoon-fashion with his fork to pinion a biscuit the weapon nearly impaled the hand of the Easterner which had been stretched quietly out for the same biscuit." The Swede has become so transformed, in fact, that in the card game played at his insistence he supplants the cowboy at exuberant "board-whacking."

Like many a confident voyager before him, the Swede has begun his quest with preconceived notions about the extraordinary world he has now entered. He is not aware that "few people even know the true definition of the term 'West,' " as George Catlin wrote in the 1840s, for "phantom-like it flies before us as we travel."[10] But the Swede, who begins by insisting that Fort Romper is the West (he knows that "there have been a good many men killed" in the front room of the Palace Hotel), also learns something new. He learns from Scully a lesson in camaraderie. The agent of that lesson turns out to be whiskey. Yet the whiskey, when it comes, is surprising, for there is no liquor in Scully's front room, where guests, visitors, and inhabitants sit before the stove and play cards. The only whiskey in the place appears to be the bottle the innkeeper keeps hidden under his bed. It seems as if the blue hotel is being palmed off as a temperance inn, a place that pays obeisance (at least lip service) to the temperance cause. If something like this is going on, then there is much cultural irony that this "temperance" inn is being run by an Irishman, given the Irishman's reputed appetite for strong drink. Moreover, Scully reverts to the stereotype of the secret, solitary drinker. He "dropped suddenly to the floor and thrust his head beneath the bed. The Swede could hear his muffled voice. 'I'd keep it under me piller if it wasn't for that boy Johnnie. Then there's the old

9. Brenda Murphy traces Crane's source to Mark Twain in " 'The Blue Hotel': A Source in *Roughing It*," *Studies in Short Fiction*, 20 (Winter 1983), 39–44.

10. Geo. Catlin, *Letters and Notes on the Manners, Customs, and Condition of the North American Indians*, 2nd ed. (New York: Wiley and Putnam, 1842), I, 62.

woman—Where is it now? I never put it twice in the same place.' " At this moment Scully proves to be an avatar, not of the model hotel keeper described earlier but of the alcoholic landlord so viciously depicted by the temperance workers and sympathizers in the nineteenth century. Phebe Cary's poem "The Landlord of 'The Blue Hen,' " reprinted in temperance readers, offers a typical account of what might be seen as the as yet unfulfilled life of the landlord of the blue hotel. It is not necessary to quote the entire poem, but a few lines, beginning at the third stanza, will serve to give a sense of the whole:

> He sold barrels of liquor, but still the old "Hen"
> Seemed never to flourish and neither did Ben,
> For he drank up his profits, as everyone knew,
> Even those who were drinking their profits up too.
>
> Even poor Ben himself could not drink of the cup
> Of fire-water forever without burning up;
> He grew sick, fell to raving, declared that he knew
> No doctors could help him, and they said so too.
>
> He told those about him, the ghosts of the men
> Who used in their lifetime to haunt The Blue Hen,
> Had come back, each one bringing his children and wife,
> And trying to frighten him out of his life.
>
> Now he thought he was burning; the very next breath
> He shivered and cried he was freezing to death;
> That the peddler lay by him, who long years ago
> Was put out of The Blue Hen and died in the snow.
> . . . .
> " 'Twasn't liquor that killed him" some said, "that was plain.
> He was crazy, and sober folks might be insane!"
> " 'Twas *delirium tremens*," the coroner said;
> But whatever it was, he was certainly dead.[11]

The blue hotel's landlord, faced with the problem of what to do about his guest's asocial behavior, reaches back for a solution. That he knows his man becomes apparent when with the offer of the whiskey we find "the weak-kneed Swede . . . about to eagerly clutch this element of strength." Something stops him, though, for "he suddenly jerked his hand away and cast a look of horror upon Scully." The lure of the whiskey, however, wins out over his fear

11. Phebe Cary, "The Landlord of 'The Blue Hen,' " in *Readings and Recitations, No. 2,* 21–22.

and his horror. And as it turns out, his fear that Scully would poison him is unwarranted. The whiskey does not affect him in that way. On the contrary. Drink so props up this "Dutchman" that he begins to believe he *can* function in the West. His immobilizing fear has metamorphosed into belligerence. Full of Dutch courage—his "pot-valor" enhanced by alcohol—he now embraces his new knowledge of himself as a man fully comfortable in the West, where a man like him can be a man among men.[12] The Swede has now seen this, and in a narration dominated by visual imagery, from the "snow-crusted engine" announcing the imminence of a blizzard to the saloon cash register, he is encouraged to accept and to learn from what he sees (or thinks he sees).

It was Ralph Waldo Emerson, the prophet of self-reliance, who extolled time and again the beautiful necessity of personal growth gained through expanding visual perception. "The eye is the first circle; the horizon which it forms is the second; and throughout nature this primary figure is repeated without end," begins "Circles." "It is the highest emblem in the cipher of the world. . . . There is no outside, no inclosing wall, no circumference to us."[13] Later Emerson radically scaled down his assessment of man's potential, but never did he admit that the very acquisition of knowledge can pose danger for the individual. It took a later prophet to pinpoint the risks to a person "overcome by knowledge or by some new realization." Quoting Saint Paul to the effect that "knowledge puffeth up"—that any new knowledge feeds self-conceit—Jung notes that such "inflation has nothing to do with the *kind* of knowledge, but simply and solely with the fact that any new knowledge can so seize hold of a weak head that he no longer sees and hears anything else. He is hypnotized by it, and instantly believes he has solved the riddle of the universe," an illusion that, without his being dishonest to what he has seen, is

12. Compare the following excerpt from the anonymous temperance piece "Determination Essential to Success": "Moral courage will nerve the weakest arm in the hour of danger, and make the faint-hearted stout in the day of battle. The being that needs to have Dutch courage poured down his gaping throat, is not likely to stand to his post in the hour of peril" (in *Readings and Recitations, No. 1*, ed. L[izzie] Penney [New York: National Temperance Society and Publication House, 1877], 56).

13. Ralph Waldo Emerson, "Circles," in *Essays, First Series, The Complete Works of Ralph Waldo Emerson*, 12 vols., ed. Edward Waldo Emerson (Boston: Houghton Mifflin, 1903–4), II, 301, 304. Crane knew Emerson's work well enough to quote from it. "As Emerson said," he once noted, " 'There should be a long logic beneath the story, but it should be kept carefully out of sight' " (Letter, Crane to John Northern Hilliard, [1897?], quoted in the *New York Times*, Supplement, July 14, 1900, 467; *The Correspondence of Stephen Crane*, ed. Stanley Wertheim and Paul Sorrentino [New York: Columbia University Press, 1988], I, 323). He also wrote: "In the top-most and remotest studio there is an old beam which bears this line from Emerson in half-obliterated chalk-marks: 'Congratulate yourselves if you have done something strange and extravagant and broken the monotony of a decorous age.' It is a memory of the old days" ("The Art Students' League Building," in *Tales, Sketches, and Reports*, Volume VIII of *The University of Virginia Edition of the Works of Stephen Crane*, ed. Fredson Bowers, intr. Edwin H. Cady [Charlottesville: University Press of Virginia, 1973], 315).

"equivalent to almighty self-conceit."[14] It goes without saying that such dogged fidelity to what one knows is no assurance that one has discovered truth and thereby guaranteed one's safety.

The Swede's problem exactly. Having survived his bouts with fear before both supper and his fistfight with the hotel keeper's son, the Swede is ready to take on the universe, and the mismatch suits him fine. He now becomes, again in Emerson's terms, one of nature's "proud ephemerals." "Fast to surface and outside," he scans "the profile of the sphere."[15] "Fresh from the pounding of Johnnie's fists, [his face] felt more pleasure than pain in the wind and the driving snow." As the Swede moves through what might have been "a deserted village," Crane offers a sardonic overview of the Swede as a proud ephemeral holding fast to the surface of the world's sphere:

> We picture the world as thick with conquering and elate humanity, but here, with the bugles of the tempest pealing, it was hard to imagine a peopled earth. One viewed the existence of man then as a marvel, and conceded a glamour of wonder to these lice which were caused to cling to a whirling, fire-smote, ice-locked, disease-stricken, space-lost bulb. The conceit of man was explained by this storm to be the very engine of life. One was a coxcomb not to die in it. However, the Swede found a saloon.

"One was a coxcomb not to die in it. However, the Swede found a saloon." These sentences call for comment. Particularly important is the function, at first puzzling, of the adverb at the beginning of the last sentence—that "however."

Crane's snowstorm has some literary precedents. Emerson's, for example, is "announced by all the trumpets of the sky." "The whited air / hides hills and woods, the river, and the heaven," "veil[ing] the farm-house at the garden's end" and stopping "the sled and traveller"; everyone is driven indoors to sit "around the radiant fireplace, enclosed / In a tumultuous privacy of storm."[16] Emerson's poem then swerves away from the experience of those who depend upon a fireplace-centered house to shelter them from the storm, but John Greenleaf Whittier would appropriate the hinting possibilities for "Snow-

14. C. G. Jung, *Two Essays on Analytical Psychology*, trans. R. F. C. Hull (New York: Meridian, 1956), 318.

15. Emerson, "Circles," in *Essays*, 299.

16. Emerson, "The Snow-Storm," in *Poems, Complete Works*, IX, 41–42. In *Swinton's Fifth Reader and Speaker* (New York and Chicago: Ivison, Blakeman, 1883), the headnote to "The Snow-Storm" describes it as a "vivid descriptive poem" by "the most subtle of American thinkers," one whose "volumes of Essays have had a wide influence on all young and aspiring minds" (137).

Bound," his celebration of the virtues of human friendship and companionship. In "The Blue Hotel" it is as if Crane, having endured the Nebraska storm, has nevertheless availed himself of Emerson's depiction and Whittier's sense of the need for community to render an action totally alien to the two earlier works. For the Swede, exposed to minimal community—supper with a few men and a friendly card game—ends by bungling badly. And he bungles it all because of his fidelity to the truth of what his eyes have seen. Indeed, the Swede's discovery that he has been cheated at cards is followed immediately by what he readily sees as justification of his new sense of personal power and efficacy: his vanquishing of his opponent, the cheat, in a fair, if brutal, fight. Small wonder that the Swede feels more pleasure than pain as he strides through the driving snow. It may be a bad night for others, but, he boasts, "it's good enough for me." Perhaps "one was a coxcomb not to die" in this storm; but because "the conceit of man" is discovered to be "the very engine of life," it is all to the good (but only up to a point) that the Swede acts as if, like Jung's man of new knowledge, he "has solved the riddle of the universe." That self-conceit, which sustains man on this "space-lost bulb," carries him through the storm—his victory over Johnnie occurs outside on "heavily-encrusted grass," and his moment of greatest well-being takes place as he walks through the desertlike town—but the Swede has the misfortune to come across another man-made shelter.

"One was a coxcomb not to die" in the storm, suggesting that seemingly only foolishness and conceit enable one to survive in a storm of this magnitude; "however" (read "unfortunately"), this particular coxcomb "found a saloon." It might have been a second refuge for the Swede. But—now puffed up with his new knowledge—he turns it into the place of his ultimate defeat. If Scully's hotel, bellowing its intemperate blue, is the setting for the Swede's transformation from a fear-stricken tenderfoot into a bullying coxcomb, the saloon, its "indomitable red light" (then the typifying color for a saloon)[17] tinting the snowflakes "blood-color," becomes the setting for his death. The whiskey, which had not killed him at Scully's hotel, has worked to poison him by feeding his new knowledge. Because whiskey had seemed to promote community among strangers at the blue hotel, it should work in the same way—he thinks—at the saloon. Inflated with the realization that the West—climate and people alike—is "good enough" for him and that *he* is good enough for it, the Swede confronts another group of cardplayers, including this time "a professional gambler of the kind known as 'square.'" Rebuffed by those he invites

---

17. For the stereotype of the saloon as the alcoholic's den of temptation, see John B. Gough, "How to Break the Chain," in *Readings and Recitations, No. 2*, ed. L[izzie] Penney (New York: National Temperance Society and Publication House, 1878), 18; E. Wentworth, "The 'Blue Ribbon,'" in *Readings and Recitations, No. 2*, 14–15.

to drink with him, the Swede wildly overreacts. In a narrative in which the author's very style of exaggeration serves to convey the notion of a "West" that lives only in overstatement, it is to be expected that the gambler's quiet refusal to drink will enrage the Swede. When the gambler says coldly, "My friend, I don't know you. . . . take your hand off my shoulder and go 'way and mind your own business," the Swede, grasping the gambler "frenziedly at the throat," drags him from his chair. After all, to the powerful Swede, whose prowess as a brawler has just been established, the gambler—"a little slim man"—would seem to pose little threat.

But the unfolding of events is unpredictable. If Emerson celebrated his place in nature as one of generous and safe exposure—"I expand and live in the warm day like corn and melons"[18]—the reader of "The Blue Hotel" discovers something else: "There was a great tumult, and then was seen a long blade in the hand of the gambler. It shot forward, and a human body, this citadel of virtue, wisdom, power, was pierced as easily as if it had been a melon. The Swede fell with a cry of supreme astonishment."[19] It is the last bit of knowledge that comes his way. He was not after all doomed to die in Scully's intemperate temperance hotel; he would purchase his own fate. "The corpse of the Swede, alone in the saloon," Crane sums up his parable of debt and payment, "had its eyes fixed upon a dreadful legend that dwelt a-top of the cash-machine. 'This registers the amount of your purchase.' " This legend replies to the question posed in a familiar temperance poem: " 'Ten cents a glass!' Does any one think / That that is really the price of a drink?" And no wonder that "The Blue Hotel" works out to this ironic legend, for Crane's story has still other affinities with this poem:

> The price of a drink? Let that one tell
> Who sleeps to-night in a murderer's cell . . .
> "*Ten cents a glass!*" How Satan laughed,
> As over the bar the young man quaffed
> The beaded liquor; for the demon knew
> The terrible work that drink would do.
> And before the morning the victim lay

18. Ralph Waldo Emerson, *Nature*, in *The Collected Works of Ralph Waldo Emerson, Volume I, Nature, Addresses, and Lectures*, ed. Robert E. Spiller and Alfred R. Ferguson (Cambridge, Mass.: Harvard University Press, 1971), 35.

19. Abraham Lincoln is quoted: "The citadels of this great adversary [alcohol] are daily being stormed and dismantled; his temples and his altars, where the rites of his idolatrous worship have long been performed, and where human sacrifice has long been wont to be made, are daily desecrated and deserted" ("Abraham Lincoln on Temperance," in *Readings and Recitations, No. 5*, ed. L[izzie] Penney [New York: National Temperance Society and Publication House, 1884], 29). In "The Bride Comes to Yellow Sky," Crane refers to Jack Potter's house as a "citadel."

With his life-blood swiftly ebbing away;
And that was the price he paid, alas!
For the pleasure of taking a social glass.[20]

In so dramatizing the Swede's last transaction, Crane seems to subscribe sardonically to Emerson's explanation that there is a necessary relationship between person and event, one that anticipates Crane's own *grammatical* explanation for the relation between persons and events. "The secret of the world is the tie between person and event," explains Emerson. "Person makes event, and event person. . . . He thinks his fate alien, because the copula is hidden. But the soul contains the event that shall befall it; for the event is only the actualization of its thoughts. . . . The event is the print of your form. It fits you like your skin."[21] This leads, in the final section of "The Blue Hotel," to the conversation, months after the Swede's death, between the Easterner and the cowboy. The Easterner has just learned that the gambler has been given three years—a "light sentence"—for killing the Swede. The two of them continue to discuss the circumstances that led to the Swede's death until the Easterner turns on the complacent cowboy to announce that the Swede had been right after all—Johnnie had indeed been cheating—and hence not everything had been "square" in the events preceding the fistfight. Therefore, he concluded, the Swede's death was the result of social complicity, an illustration of Emerson's notion that "Society everywhere is in conspiracy against the manhood of every one of its members."[22] The Easterner, hitting hard at the notion of their complicity, charges: " 'We are all in it! This poor gambler isn't even a noun. He is kind of an adverb. Every sin is the result of a collaboration. We, five of us, have collaborated in the murder of this Swede. Usually there are from a dozen to forty women really involved in every murder, but in this case it seems to be only men—you, I, Johnnie, old Scully, and that fool of an unfortunate gambler came merely as a culmination, the apex of a human movement, and gets all the punishment.' " This rhetorical burst comes from the same observer, it will be recalled, who, along with the cowboy and the hotel keeper, had "burst into a cheer" at Johnnie's one successful moment when "his fist sent the over-balanced Swede sprawling" but who, after Scully and his son had conceded defeat, felt "indifferent to the condition of the vanquished man."

Knowing that the Easterner is partly based on Crane himself and that "The Blue Hotel" might have grown out of Crane's imaginative recreation of his experiences as an observer of fistfights in Western saloons, readers have too often and too readily assumed that the Easterner's speech conveys the author's

20. Josephine Pollard, "The Price of a Drink," in *Readings and Recitations, No. 5*, 57–58.
21. Emerson, "Fate," in *The Conduct of Life, Complete Works*, VI, 39–40.
22. Emerson, "Self-Reliance," in *Essays, First Series, Complete Works*, II, 49.

own unequivocal interpretation of the circumstances leading to the death of the Swede.[23] Yet there is strong evidence to support the contention that the Easterner speaks only for himself, for the narrator's final words characterize the Easterner's speech as a "fog of mysterious theory." Even if it is argued that this "mysterious theory" is a "fog" to the cowboy, it is notable that there is nothing in the sentence to suggest that it fogs only the cowboy. As theories go, this one is rather comforting because it implies that someone could have done something to keep the Swede from meeting his fate. The theory calling for communal guilt and social complicity, if accepted, implies the existence of shared responsibility and the potential for social efficacy. Indeed, this bit of theory—a parade of new knowledge—so puffs up the Easterner that he ignores several facts: that the cowboy had not seen anyone cheating, that perhaps he was alone in knowing that the Swede's accusation was warranted, and that, despite his knowledge of the cheating, he also wanted to see the upstart Swede thrashed. Further evidence that "knowledge puffeth up," this piece of rhetoric illustrates the additional observation that the Swede has no monopoly on self-inflation and conceit, for the Easterner also acts as if he has "solved the riddle," not of the "universe" but of the ways of society.

But what about the Easterner's passing remark that in every murder there are involved "usually . . . a dozen to forty women." This puzzling remark—especially the numbers—makes some sense if one puts it into a temperance movement context. The WCTU grew out of the Woman's Temperance Crusade and never did abandon its highly successful tactic of closing down saloons by swooping down on them in groups and demanding pledges of temperance—both from the drinkers and the sellers. It will be recalled, too, that Scully's wife and daughters swoop down on the men after the Swede and Johnnie have fought. "The sad quiet was broken by the sudden flinging open of a door that led toward the kitchen. It was instantly followed by an inrush of women. They precipitated themselves upon Johnnie amid a chorus of lamentation. Before they carried their prey off to the kitchen, there to be bathed and harangued with that mixture of sympathy and abuse which is a feat of their sex, the mother straightened herself and fixed old Scully with an eye of stern reproach. 'Shame be upon you, Patrick Scully!' she cried. 'Your own son, too. Shame be upon you!' " Like the fury-like women of temperance who left their kitchens to invade the domain of men in order to shame them into action, Scully's women rush from the kitchen and into the men's parlor. Rallying to

23. Whether critics have found the final section of the story to be successful, thematically or structurally, most of them have accepted, for good or ill, the Easterner's conclusions as the author's own. The various interpretations of "The Blue Hotel" are summarized in Michael W. Schaefer, *A Reader's Guide to the Short Stories of Stephen Crane* (New York: G. K. Hall, 1996), 10–59. But see also *The Blue Hotel*, ed. Joseph Katz (Columbus: Merrill, 1969), especially the comments by Starrett, Shroeder, Stallman, Satterwhite, Greenfield, Stein, Maclean, Gleckner, and Klotz.

their mother's slogan, the girls "sniffed disdainfully in the direction of those trembling accomplices" of Scully, the secret drinker and the dispenser of the demon alcohol.

Although all of this is so, one question remains unanswered. What is the effect, finally, of Crane's choosing to conclude his tale with the Easterner's analysis of consequences traced to cause and his somewhat haughty assumption of complicity for himself and his erstwhile cohorts? The final section of "The Blue Hotel," I would suggest, offers an instance of Crane's psychological acumen. Man will not, perhaps cannot, readily accept the mystery of things and events. He would, it is apparent, puzzle out matters, even if his solutions are at best little more than appealing rationalizations. The Easterner will ponder on the past, he will figure things out; and, sure of it all at last, full of himself, he will allocate blame because—Crane implies—such allocations are what humankind wants. He will, ex post facto, feign necessity by forging a link, even if spurious, between collective social behavior and personal fate.

3

Consider this bit of sermonizing from a temperance publication.

It has been difficult to regard white mice seriously. One hears of their performing tricks, but that is not a sufficient excuse for their being. Some sing sweetly, but they are rare, and almost anyone would prefer a bird. But with modern inventions comes a profession for white mice so important that it commands government pay—a shilling a week—in the English Navy. Every submarine vessel carries a cage of white mice. At the least leakage of gasoline the little creatures feel uncomfortable, and begin to squeal. This serves as a warning, which is quickly heeded.

Many young men seem to have less gray matter in their brains than these white mice—at least they do not make so good a use of it. The very first drop of gasoline is seen by these little sentinels to be a cause for alarm. And fearless fighters do not belittle the danger but heed the warning, and take instant steps to stop the dangerous leak. How sad the contrast afforded by young men who do not even take alarm at their first intoxication, but cry in foolhardiness, "I am not afraid!" and go straight on to shipwreck. Go to the white mice, O tippler; consider her ways and be wise![24]

24. Anonymous, "Danger Signals," *World Book of Temperance* (Abridged ed.), comp. Dr. and Mrs. Wilbur F. Crafts (Washington, D.C.: International Reform Bureau, 1908), 109.

In April 1898 Crane published two "Mexican" stories. "The Wise Men" appeared in the *Ludgate Monthly* and "The Five White Mice" in the *New York World*.[25] In the same month they were collected in *The Open Boat and Other Stories* (London) and *The Open Boat and Other Tales of Adventure* (New York). A few reviewers of the volumes singled out these two stories. One reviewer wrote that in "The Five White Mice" and "The Wise Men" Crane showed that he had "not yet outgrown a rather immature cynicism."[26] And while another reviewer thought that although "farcical comedy . . . riots amusingly . . . the foot-race between the two barkeeps is not elevating,"[27] a reviewer in Chicago complained: "When the author takes us into the dives of a Mexican city, and introduces us to the ways of two fast and dissolute young men from America, we rebel." Tellingly, this last reviewer concludes: "The pictures may be realistic enough, but we object to contact with vice, except for sanitary and disinfectant purposes."[28]

These are hardly Crane's purposes. Perhaps "The Wise Men" is a mere "amusement," as Berryman calls it,[29] but there is enough drinking and gambling in it to rile the average temperance worker. Much of the story is set in two bars, one of which bears its temperance identity in its name. The "Café Colorado" is an avatar of the temperance worker's "red saloon."[30] Its "long billiard hall," stretching "back to a vague gloom," would itself have been cause enough for complaint to the WCTU worker who wrote: "The pool and billiard rooms, with their obscenity and profanity, are the training schools in which our boys may take the first steps in vice, and becoming infatuated with gaming, render themselves victims to a passion which is soul destroying, and

25. Stephen Crane, "The Wise Men," in *Tales of Adventures*, Volume V of *The University of Virginia Edition of the Works of Stephen Crane*, ed. Fredson Bowers, intr. J. C. Levenson (Charlottesville: University Press of Virginia, 1970), 26–38, and "The Five White Mice," ibid., 39–52.

26. Anonymous, "Fiction" [*The Open Boat and Other Tales of Adventure*], *New York Tribune Illustrated Supplement* (Apr. 24, 1898), 17.

27. "Droch" [Robert Bridges], "Books for Summer Readers" [*The Open Boat and Other Tales of Adventure*], *Life*, 31 (May 26, 1898), 446.

28. Anonymous, [*The Open Boat and Other Tales of Adventure*], *Advance* (Chicago), 35 (June 2, 1898), 742. The reviewer for the *Isle of Wight* saw it differently: "Many of the stories deal with life in Texas and Mexico, and are stamped with that verisimilitude which comes from the eye-witness. Some of them are rather thin, 'The Wise Men,' to wit. This is simply a story of two 'kids,' one from 'Frisco and the other from New York, who are going free in a Mexican town, and they back one saloon-keeper to race another at a hundred yards and their man wins. A thin enough thread to hang a story on, especially when there is nothing very realistic in the telling of it" (Anonymous, [*The Open Boat and Other Stories*], July 20, 1898, clipping, Stephen Crane Collection, Columbia University, New York, New York).

29. John Berryman, *Stephen Crane* (New York: William Sloane, 1950), 112.

30. Gough, "How to Break the Chain," 18.

from whose toils few ever escape."[31] The author of this attack was Crane's mother.

"The Wise Men" is a comedic story in which drunkenness, despite the saloons and the Kids' all-night hours, leads to no tragic consequences, and in which gambling takes no vicious turn. The Kids turn out to have been the "wise" men all along. There is no shipwreck for them here. "The Five White Mice" is a different matter.

The reviewers did not much like the second of Crane's Mexican tales either. One of them, as we have seen, found it objectionable for its "rather immature cynicism."[32] Another reviewer dismissed it as a story of "dice-throwing that results in a visit to the circus (the whole accompanied by much drink)," which, like most of the other stories in the volume, "no good qualities of form redeem from failure."[33]

One reviewer, however, praises "The Five White Mice" as "an active bit of Mexican experience by Americans, and picturesque in much; but its most notable feature is the psychic completeness of the mental and physical attitudes of three young men confronting an equally numbered foe. It is both amusing and impressive."[34] Speaking of Crane's writing to date, one last reviewer recognizes that "Mr. Stephen Crane has made the psychology of peril and terror his own."[35]

"The Five White Mice" has not caught on with Crane's critics, though there are early exceptions, for example, Thomas Beer, Crane's first biographer, and H. E. Bates, the English fiction writer and perceptive student of the short story. Deciding that in this "fanciful" story "one sees Crane himself, recording his own pulse before a shadow" to which "he refused to kneel and worship," Beer writes:

The boy of "Five White Mice" stands with a drunkard on each hand and the cloudy group of Mexicans before him, speculating on his friend's atti-

31. Mrs. M. H. Crane, "Change of Base," *Ocean Grove Record* (Mar. 15, 1884), 3; reprinted in *Stephen Crane's Career: Perspectives and Evaluations*, ed. Thomas A. Gullason (New York: New York University Press, 1972), 36. Crane's father's view on the billiard parlor is also worth quoting: "It is expected that the idler and the spendthrift will be attracted to the place; and in the crowd the seller of alcohol will find customers, and the swindler victims. Billiards figure very low in the scale of amusements. Associated as it generally is with late hours, confined air, smoking and drinking, the game is detrimental to health, to morals, and to mind" (Rev. J. T. Crane, *Popular Amusements* [Cincinnati: Hitchcock and Walden/New York: Carlton and Lanahan, 1870], 118–19).

32. Anonymous, [*The Open Boat and Other Tales of Adventure*], *New York Tribune Illustrated Supplement*, 17.

33. Anonymous, [*The Open Boat and Other Stories*]. *Sunday Special* (Apr. 24, 1898), 6.

34. Caroline T. Pilsbury, "Literature" [*The Open Boat and Other Tales of Adventure*], *Boston Ideas*, 12 (June 18, 1898), 6.

35. Anonymous, "Literature: Notes on New Novels" [*The Open Boat and Other Stories*], *Illustrated London News*, 112 (May 7, 1898), 662.

tude after the slaughter. "The other Kid would mourn his death. He would be preternaturally correct for some weeks, and recite the tale without swearing. But it would not bore him. For the sake of his dead comrade he would be glad to be preternaturally correct and to recite the tale without swearing." Then the tortured thought veers off to a memory of a summer hayfield and to the wonder of a distant crooning stream. And then he steps forward and the great death steps back. The Mexicans retire up the dim street. Nothing has happened. The emotion has projected its intensity against nonsense, against a posture of some loungers. It is the last point in futility, the hurtle of mighty chords on an unhearing ear. . . . That this work was outside the mood of his time and his nation everybody knows.[36]

Berryman's astute comments on Beer's interpretation will be taken up shortly, but first there is H. E. Bates.

No one has approached Bates in enthusiasm for "The Five White Mice." His high opinion of the story might stem, at least partly, from the fact that as late as 1926 it was the only Crane story he had read.[37] "In the very early nineteen-twenties, as a boy of sixteen or seventeen, I picked up a story of Crane's called 'Five White Mice,' " he writes, "and was electrified and troubled by that curious feeling, which you get sometimes on hearing a piece of music, of renewed acquaintance, of having taken the thing out of the storage of my own mind. I have no doubt now that this was purely the result of a certain quality of inevitability in Crane . . . where again and again the order of words and sounds has the air, most notably in Shakespeare and Mozart, of having been preordained."[38] (Four years later Carl Van Doren included "The Five White Mice" among the twenty stories he chose for his Crane collection. He called it "an invented story," one showing "Crane at his most intense in the passage describing the New York Kid's sensations as he faces the Mexican knife."[39])

Berryman's brilliant commentary on "The Five White Mice" plays off against what he considered to be Beer's misreading. "Beer's misunderstanding of the ironic sentence with which Crane concludes the story surpasses his misrepresentation," begins Berryman. The story is not about futility, he insists. "Nothing has happened except that a young man has learned, first, that he is

36. Thomas Beer, *Stephen Crane: A Study in American Letters*, intr. Joseph Conrad (New York: Knopf, 1923), 118–19.

37. Letter, H. E. Bates to Edward Garnett, Feb. 10, 1926, Harry Ransom Humanities Research Center, University of Texas, Austin, Texas; quoted in Dean R. Baldwin, *H. E. Bates: A Literary Life* (Selinsgrove, Pa.: Susquehanna University Press, 1987), 77.

38. H. E. Bates, *The Modern Short Story: A Critical Survey* (London: Thomas Nelson, 1941), 65.

39. Carl Van Doren, Introduction to *Twenty Stories by Stephen Crane*, ed. Carl Van Doren (New York and Cleveland: World, 1945), xiii.

not isolated in his fear—everybody is afraid; and second, that his fear need not prevent his controlling his fate." Significantly, in a story in which virtually everyone else, including his friend Benson, is drunk, the Kid is sober. "At the end, when the Mexicans have vanished, Benson comes to and observes with pain that the New York Kid is 'shober.' Benson 'passed into a state of profound investigation. "Kid shober 'cause didn't go with us. Didn't go with us 'cause went to damn circus. Went to damn circus 'cause lose shakin' dice. Lose shakin' dice 'cause—what make lose shakin' dice, Kid?" The New York Kid eyed the senile youth. "I don't know. The five white mice, maybe." ' " It is the reader "not determined on nihilism" who will "recognize without diffi-culty that Crane intended something by this rigmarole." Berryman explains: "The sequence of unforeseeable, fortuitous events has turned out well: the Kid enjoyed the circus, and has had an important experience, and neither of the Kids is dead. He was right to trust the mice. But is it really owing to the mice that things have turned out well? Perhaps in drawing his revolver—Crane says—the Kid 'had unconsciously used nervous force sufficient to raise a bale of hay.' This is not quite the work of the mice; all they have done is to provide the situation and the soberness. Soberness is an agreeable provision, just here."[40] Berryman calls attention to the Kid's sobriety at the moment when he perceives the threat from the Mexicans and faces them down (his revolver emerges "as if it were greased," arising "like a feather"), but he does not pursue the importance of this temperance clue.

Alcohol is central to the story. The Kid's having lost his bet at dice compels him to attend the circus and precludes his going off with his drinking friends to tie one on. The possibility might be considered that the white mice, not having come through for him at the gaming table, have nevertheless had a stake in his moment of courageous truth with the Mexicans. Elsewhere in Crane's work, at least twice, mice are associated with Chance or Providence. In "The Open Boat" the submerged image of mice in the reference to men who have been "dragged away" as they were "about to nibble the sacred cheese of life" gives body to the narrator's sense of futility, and in the poem "A man adrift on a slim spar" it is for the mice that "The Hand" that "beckons" turns oceans into gray ashes.[41] As we shall see in chapter 11, embedded in the language of the poem are references to drinking and temperance. So it is that the "white mice" of chance the Kid believes in bring forth their implications for danger, drink, courage, and sobriety, serving the Kid while "other animals—rabbits,

40. Berryman, *Stephen Crane*, 109–11.

41. Stephen Crane, "The Open Boat," in *Tales of Adventure*, Volume V of *The University of Virginia Edition of the Works of Stephen Crane*, ed. Fredson Bowers, intr. J. C. Levenson (Charlottesville: Univer-sity Press of Virginia, 1970), 68–92; Stephen Crane, "A man adrift on a slim spar," in *Poems and Literary Remains*, Volume X of *The University of Virginia Edition of the Works of Stephen Crane*, ed. Fredson Bow-ers, intr. James B. Colvert (Charlottesville: University Press of Virginia, 1975), 83.

dogs, hedgehogs, snakes, oppossums"—just will not do. As for the possibility that these tipplers will become "wise" by mending their ways—or "changing their base," to adapt Mrs. Crane's advice—Crane had already implicitly rejected that notion in "The Wise Men."[42]

4

"Twelve O'Clock" appeared in the *Pall Mall Gazette* in December 1899, six months before Stephen Crane's death. It was collected posthumously in *The Monster and Other Stories*, published in 1901. The *Academy*'s unidentified reviewer praises the author and the book overall: "The quick, nervous, prehensile mind that in an instant could select the vital characteristics of any scene or group, is notably here; and here also in superabundance is the man's grim fatalism, his saturnine pleasure in exhibiting (with bitter, laughing mercilessness) the frustrations of human efforts, the absurd trifles which decide human destiny." The story he singles out for specific praise is "Twelve O'Clock," which "tells how a young cowboy's excitement on hearing a cuckoo-clock for the first time led indirectly to murder—all done with perfect credibility." "Nothing but a kind of savage impatience with the accidentalism of the scheme of things," he concludes, "could have caused a man to set down this particular story; but it is finely done—a triumph of narrative art."[43]

Fifty years later, insisting that in "Twelve O'Clock" there is something of considerable psychological significance going on for its author in the last year of his life, Berryman noticed that on November 1, 1899, Crane turned twenty-eight and "his mind was blazing with death." He ties these facts in with the publication, the next month, of "Twelve O'Clock." He describes it as "a Western nightmare of spreeing cowboys" who wait in a hotel "for a cuckoo-clock to strike and the bird to come out that one has seen."[44]

Placer sits there in the hotel he has named after himself, writing in his ledger. Arriving on the scene is Big Watson, a drunk. There is a quarrel. Watson shoots Placer in the throat, gets himself killed, and someone else is also shot dead. "Placer, in some dying whim," writes Crane, "had made his way out from be-

42. Walter Benn Michaels reads "The Five White Mice" as a puzzle about gambling and its risks (*The Gold Standard and the Logic of Naturalism: American Literature at the Turn of the Century* [Berkeley: University of California Press, 1987], 224–26). See also Charles W. Mayer, "Two Kids in the House of Chance: Crane's 'The Five White Mice,' " *Research Studies*, 44 (1976), 52–57; Michael J. Collins, "Realism and Romance in the Western Stories of Stephen Crane," in *Under the Sun: Myth and Realism in Western American Literature*, ed. Barbara Howard Meldrum (Troy, N.Y.: Whitston, 1985), 139–48; and Schaefer, *Reader's Guide*, 143–58.

43. Anonymous, [*The Monster and Other Stories*], *Academy*, 60 (Mar. 16, 1901), 230.

44. Berryman, *Stephen Crane*, 248.

hind the pink counter, and, leaving a horrible trail, had travelled to the centre of the room, where he had pitched headlong over the body of Big Watson."[45] Then the wooden cuckoo bird comes out, as if to survey the bloody scene caused by its novelty in this wild part of the West. This tableau is reminiscent of the tableau in the saloon the Swede found in the midst of the storm.

"Twelve O'Clock" starts out with an epigraph: "Where were you at twelve o'clock, noon, on the 9th of June, 1875?" It is identified as a "question on intelligent cross-examination," suggesting that it is a part of a trial or inquest into the events of that morning leading up to noon, particularly those taking place in and around Placer's Hotel. There is shooting in the office of Placer's Hotel. The owner is shot dead. This killing attracts the local citizenry, who in large numbers rush to the hotel. More shots are fired, and one cowboy, attempting to flee on horseback, "suddenly slump[s] over on his pony's neck, where he held for a moment like an old sack, and then slid to the ground, while his pony, with flapping rein, fled to the prairie."

Such an inquest might begin by addressing the questions of how and why this killing of the owner of Placer's Hotel came about in the first place. One response is to blame everything that ensues on the cuckoo clock displayed in Placer's office. It captures the attention of a twenty-five-year-old cowboy who has never before seen such a thing. As he stands there negotiating a dinner for his cowboy outfit (at one dollar a head), the machinery of the cuckoo clock on the wall begins to whirr and the wooden bird emerges to cry out eleven times. Told what the clock is called, the cowboy runs out into the street to bring news of this marvel to the other cowboys who have just come to town. Not all of them are surprised at his description (the mother of one of them, back in Philadelphia, owns such a clock), but some of them are not only amused at Jake's enthusiasm but skeptical enough to think that "the eccentric Jake had been victimized by some wise child of civilization." Old Man Crumford suggests that Jake has been drinking. "You ben drinkin' lonely an' got up agin some snake-medicine licker," he accuses, "a bird a-tellin' ye th' time!" Infuriated, Jake enters into bets with some of the cowboys over the clock. They march to the hotel in a group, arriving before it is time for the clock to cry out again. There's a stir near the door and a drunken cowboy from the second outfit that has come into town that morning—Big Watson of the Square-X outfit—shoulders his way through the crowd and demands to know what is going on. Told that it is none of his business, he "whip[s]" out "his revolver half out of its holster," bringing about a similar reaction from Jake, who threatens to kill Watson for sure. The men glare "murder at each other, neither seeming to breathe, fixed like statues." A third party intercedes. Placer himself stands behind his bright pink counter, a revolver in each hand. " 'Cheese it!' " he says. " 'I won't have no fightin' here. If you want to fight, git out in the street.' "

45. Stephen Crane, "Twelve O'Clock," in *Tales of Adventure*, 171–78.

Big Watson laughs, and "speeding up his six-shooter like a flash of blue light," he shoots Placer "through the throat." He "shot the man as he stood behind his absurd pink counter with his two aimed revolvers in his incompetent hands." Jake then hits Watson over the head with his heavy weapon, knocking him "sprawling and bloody." Placer's fall behind the counter brings down on him "his ledger and his inkstand, so that one could not have told blood from ink." Something like this ending has occurred elsewhere in Crane's work. The single final image of body, ledger, and inkstand recalls the Swede's body, "its eyes fixed upon a dreadful legend that dwelt a-top of the cash-machine. 'This registers the amount of your purchase.' "[46] Coincidentally, Scully's "blue hotel" was actually called the Palace Hotel, which turns out to be only slightly more civilized than Stevenson's Palace Hotel in "Moonlight on the Snow" or Placer's Hotel in "Twelve O'Clock," even though the latter was the "best hotel within two hundred miles."

The unnamed town in "Twelve O'Clock" appears to be in no immediate danger of invasion by the ever-threatening temperance worker. But the germinating seeds for great change are already there. In Yellow Sky, as will be seen, Scratchy Wilson is identified as the last member of an old gang that used to hang around those parts. It is not the same kind of gang Scratchy belonged to that on June 9, 1875, rides into town in "Twelve O'Clock," but the reactions of the rational citizenry to its periodic rampages are pretty much the same. " 'Excuse *me*,' said Ben Roddle with graphic gestures to a group of citizens in Nantucket's store. 'Excuse *me*. When them fellers in leather pants an' six-shooters ride in, I go home an' set in th' cellar. That's what I do. When you see me pirooting through the streets at th' same time an' occasion as them punchers, you kin put me down fer bein' crazy. Excuse *me*.' " These men have come into the town to drink and cut loose. It will take them less than a half hour to riot, predicts Ben Roddle accurately. They will also murder.

Crane's clock is an obvious sign of the invasion of civilization from the East (all the way from Germany, this time, where the cuckoo clock was invented). The comic possibilities of a narrative in which western cowpunchers first encounter the marvels of a cuckoo clock turn sour with the murderous gunfire. These are not yet the "watchful" (targeted in the temperance literature) who will put on their watches "mottoes"—"The hour is flying; pray" or "On this moment hangs eternity"—to remind them that "there are dangers—moral dangers, especially, in every hour."[47]

"God's Clock Strikes," the title of a short temperance piece favored by Frances E. Willard, acknowledges that "saloon power is a political power." To

---

46. Crane, "The Blue Hotel," 169.

47. Anonymous, "Drugging the Guards," in *World Book of Temperance*, 3rd enlarged and rev. ed., comp. Dr. and Mrs. Wilbur F. Crafts (Washington, D.C.: International Reform Bureau, 1911), 125.

counter that power, the writer calls for "the organization of an anti-saloon party." "Brethren, let us do our duty in this matter," she exhorts. "Twenty-five years ago God spoke to the conscience of this nation for the last time on the subject of human slavery. His time-clock struck twelve, and rang out the sound full and clear. It said, God's time has come at last to destroy human slavery." Now the evil is drink. "Once more the time-clock of God Almighty is ringing out the hour of high noon. God is summoning His troops from all parties, and bids us strike this evil—a thousand times greater than slavery—down to the earth, bind it and cast it out and down into hell, where it belongs."[48] Is it God's time that has struck through the cuckoo? Certainly littering the lobby floor of Placer's Hotel are the wages of the sin that is drink.

The disaster at Placer's Hotel took place on "the 9th of June, 1875." Incidentally, the WCTU's first national convention was held November 18–20, 1874, while its second was held November 17–19, 1875, placing the action of Crane's story on a day that falls almost exactly between these two important early dates in the history of the WCTU. The WCTU could not have been, in 1875, too far behind Placer's "civilized" hotel with its modern appointments.

One final observation. The first sentence of "The Blue Hotel" begins: "The Palace Hotel at Fort Romper was painted a light blue, a shade that is on the legs of a kind of heron."[49] That heron can be related to the cuckoo of "Twelve O'Clock." In both stories the sense that there is something forbidden and foreboding associated with liquor (and smoking—the young man, who originally wanted only to buy some tobacco, possesses a "remarkably clear eye" resulting "from perhaps a period of enforced temperance") is enhanced by what might be deep-seated references to scriptural imprecations. The Old Testament lists both the cuckoo and the heron as abominations that "shall not be eaten" (Leviticus 11:16–19; Deuteronomy 14:15–18), and the temperance writer warns that the "two chief perils of the mouth" are "liquor and tobacco."[50] Liquor and tobacco, it will be recalled, are similarly the twin staples of Bleecker's table in *George's Mother*: "There were upon it a keg of beer, a long row of whiskey bottles, a little heap of corn-cob pipes, some bags of tobacco, a box of cigars, and a mighty collection of glasses, cups, and mugs. Old Bleecker had arranged them so deftly that they resembled a primitive bar."[51] George Kelcey's *Walpurgisnacht* had begun.

48. Rev. George F. Pentecost, "God's Clock Strikes," in *Frances E. Willard Recitation Book, Werner's Readings and Recitations, No. 18* (New York: Edgar S. Werner, 1898), 132–34.

49. Crane, "The Blue Hotel," 142.

50. "Drugging the Guards," 128.

51. Stephen Crane, *George's Mother*, in *Bowery Tales*, Volume I of *The University of Virginia Edition of the Works of Stephen Crane*, ed. Fredson Bowers, intr. James B. Colvert (Charlottesville: University Press of Virginia, 1969), 142.

10

The New Estate

The National Convention of the T.P.A. [Travelers' Protective Association of America] will be held this month in San Antonio, the metropolis of Texas. . . . The "boys" will fall in love with San Antonio, because, like themselves, it is broad-gauged, hospitable, little addicted to the vice of hypocrisy. Many of them who come from the older states will probably expect to find a wild and woolly frontier town, where bad whisky's four-bits a drink and the festive cowboy chases the elusive longhorn through the principal streets, shoots out the kerosene street-lamps, and rides his broncho up to the bar when yearning for a compound of tarantula-juice and creosote; to be met at the train by a deputation of leading citizens who wear their pants in their boots and boycott their barbers, and welcomed by Mayor Elmendorf from the hurricane deck of a cayuse. . . . But those who come expecting to "rough it" will be happily disappointed. They will find a cultured city possessing all the modern improvements, including a municipal debt.

—William Cowper Brann, "The American Drummer: Apostle of Civilization" (1896)

It was not politically harmonious to be reminded that but for his wife's liquor a number of fine young men, with nothing save youth untrained and health the matter with them, would to-day be riding their horses instead of sleeping on the hill.

—Owen Wister, *Lin McLean* (1897)

1

In *Active Service* (1899), the last novel Stephen Crane completed, there is a curious incident in which Rufus Coleman, a news correspondent on his way to covering a war, looks at the corpse of a dead Turk. Suddenly "a snake ran out from a tuft of grass at his feet and wriggled wildly over the sod," but it did not get away. "One of the soldiers put his heel upon the head of the reptile and it flung itself into the agonized knot of death." Then "the whole crowd pow-wowed, turning from the dead man to the dead snake." Coleman turns the incident into a threatening allegory involving the safety of the woman who is on his mind. Then he abandons the notion. "The incident of the snake and the dead man had no more meaning than the greater number of the things which happen to us in our daily lives," he decides. "Nevertheless it bore upon him"— even as it did on Crane.[1] This cluster of images—snake, woman, and death— makes several appearances in Crane's work, notably "The Snake" and "The Bride Comes to Yellow Sky."

2

In "The Snake," a quasi-fable published in several newspapers in June 1896, a man, out walking with his dog, comes upon a rattlesnake, whose "dry shrill whistling rattle . . . smote motion instantly from the limbs of the man and the dog."[2] "Like the fingers of a sudden death, this sound seemed to touch the man at the nape of the neck, at the top of the spine, and change him, as swift as thought, to a statue of listening horror, surprise, and rage." "His fingers un-guided," the man seeks out and finds a stick. "With a blanched face, he sprang backward and his breath came in strained gasps, his chest heaving as if he were in the performance of an extraordinary muscular trial. His arm with the stick made a spasmodic defensive gesture. . . . The snake, tumbling in the anguish of final despair, fought, bit, flung itself upon this stick which was taking its life. . . . In the formation of devices hideous and horrible," marvels the narrator, "nature reached her supreme point in the making of the snake, so that priests who really paint hell well, fill it with snakes instead of fire. These curving forms, these scintillant colorings create at once, upon sight, more relentless ani-mosities than do shake barbaric tribes." Hence the power, one infers, of the snake in paintings, heuristic religious writings, and, in the Crane family house-

1. Stephen Crane, *Active Service*, in *The Third Violet and Active Service*, Volume III of *The University of Virginia Edition of the Works of Stephen Crane*, ed. Fredson Bowers, intr. J. C. Levenson (Charlottesville: University Press of Virginia, 1976), 111–328.

2. Stephen Crane, "The Snake," in *Tales, Sketches, and Reports*, Volume VIII of *The University of Virginia Edition of the Works of Stephen Crane*, ed. Fredson Bowers, intr. Edwin H. Cady (Charlottesville: University Press of Virginia, 1973), 65–68. For a complementary consideration of "The Snake" as an encoded rendering of Crane's anxieties over the performative act of writing, see Michael Fried, *Realism, Writing, Disfiguration: On Thomas Eakins and Stephen Crane* (Chicago and London: University of Chicago Press, 1987), 152–55.

hold of Elizabeth and Port Jervis, in those tales in temperance readers intended to terrify drinkers and would-be drinkers alike into signing cold-water pledges, with their snake-filled visions of the drunkard in the throes of the delirium tremens. " 'Well Rover,' said the man, turning to the dog with a grin of victory, 'we'll carry Mr. Snake home to show the girls.' " It is almost as if the man has conquered the snake of intemperance so that he can present his trophy to women.[3] Certainly, killing this snake is something that is done for Rufus Coleman, that George Kelcey could never do, and that Scratchy Wilson of "The Bride Comes to Yellow Sky" will have to learn to do if he is to survive in the New West.

3

"The Bride Comes to Yellow Sky," published in February 1898, was written in England shortly after Stephen Crane and Cora Howarth (Taylor) Stewart had settled in, as husband and wife, at Ravensbrook, Surrey, during the summer of 1897. Crane boasted to his literary agent that the "Bride" was "a daisy," warning him not to "let them talk funny about" it.[4] The magazines bought the story rather quickly. In February 1898 it was out on both sides of the Atlantic.[5] By April it was collected in the United States in *The Open Boat and Other Tales of Adventure*.[6] Five months later Cora complained that the story had been "plagiarized." It had been reprinted, unauthorized, in *Illustrated Bits*.[7] One of Crane's major themes in this story was in the air. It had been treated in *Lin McLean*, Owen Wister's Western novel published on December 7, 1897. In *Lin McLean* rambunctious cowboys—"playful, howling horsemen" who "made it

3. *The Snake*, a pamphlet promoting prohibition, in which the Volstead Act in 1920 is seen allegorically as cutting off the head of the snake, with the further need now to finish off the snake's "writhing and twisting," was published by O. J. McClure of Chicago (*ca.* 1932) at twenty-five cents a copy, with discount prices for multiple copies.

4. Letter, Stephen Crane to Paul Revere Reynolds, October 1897, *The Correspondence of Stephen Crane*, ed. Stanley Wertheim and Paul Sorrentino (New York: Columbia University Press, 1988), I, 305.

5. Stephen Crane, "The Bride Comes to Yellow Sky," *McClure's Magazine*, 10 (Feb. 1898), 377–84; *Chapman's Magazine*, 9 (Feb. 1898), 115–26.

6. In England the book was entitled *The Open Boat and Other Stories*. There "The Bride Comes to Yellow Sky," along with other Western and Mexican stories, was grouped under the rubric "Minor Conflicts." But that Crane might have thought of the events in Yellow Sky as something more than minor "news" is suggested by David Halliburton, who writes: "Crane's title is like an abbreviated version of newspaper headline that, in the format Crane knew well, might have read: BRIDE COMES TO YELLOW SKY / SHOOT-OUT FIZZLES / ROWDY ROUTED BY GUNLESS LAWMAN" (*The Color of the Sky: A Study of Stephen Crane* [Cambridge, Eng., Cambridge University Press, 1989], 228).

7. Letter, Cora Crane to Paul Revere Reynolds, Sept. 29, 1898, Crane, *Correspondence*, ed. Wertheim and Sorrentino, II, 376, 376 n.

their custom to go rioting with pistols round the ticket-office, educating the agent,"[8] and whose potshots perforate the town of Separ's water tank—are brought up short when they come up against a young woman who has been brought to town to become the railroad's telegraph operator. "The innocent door stood open wide to any cool breeze or invasion, and Honey Wiggen tramped in foremost, hat lowering over eyes and pistol prominent," writes Owen Wister. "He stopped rooted, staring, and his mouth came open slowly; his hand went feeling up for his hat, and came down with it by degrees as by degrees his grin spread. Then in a milky voice, he said: 'Why, excuse me, ma'am! Good-morning.' "[9] Thus was the periodic ritual of shooting up the water tank brought abruptly to an end. It had worked out just as the narrator had predicted. "Put that girl in charge of Separ, and," he promised, "the boys'll quit shooting your water-tank."[10]

Most of the reviews of *The Open Boat and Other Tales of Adventure* focused on the title story. A scant three or four of them mentioned the Western stories. The *Independent*, a New York weekly, described the Western stories as "highly colored and extremely melodramatic reflections of besotted border life in the Southwest." The "pages smell of whisky," wrote the reviewer, "and are lurid with the flashing of pistols."[11] In Crane's West—like Mark Twain's of an earlier generation—there was still free-flowing whiskey—civilization's avant-garde and pioneer. But whiskey is not always the entirely destructive force—the "monster"—that the temperance workers insisted it was. The Weary Gentle-man saloon in Yellow Sky hardly fits the stereotype imagined by the temperance workers of Crane's day. Already somewhat tamed by creeping civility, Yellow Sky's saloon has become the kind of place that fits right in with what Crane calls the town's "new estate." It has precious few of the lurid requisites of "the red saloon," the bane of the temperance worker.[12]

If there is an "enemy" in the "Bride" it is the conventional, popular-maga-zine view of an American West romanticized. The *Independent*'s reviewer had described Crane's Western stories as "literature pretty evenly mixed of the 'dime dreadful' and the Bret Harte elements," while missing the point.[13] Crane had anticipated by several months the reviewer's charge by identifying his pri-mary literary target in his next Western story, "The Blue Hotel" (completed in February 1898), in which he impugns the Swede's perception of reality by suggesting that he is a reader of "dime-novels."

8. Owen Wister, *Lin McLean* (New York and London: Harper, 1908), 171.

9. Ibid., 223.

10. Ibid., 217.

11. Anonymous, [*The Open Boat and Other Tales of Adventure*], *Independent*, 50 (June 2, 1898), 727.

12. John B. Gough, "How to Break the Chain," in *Readings and Recitations, No. 2*, ed. L[izzie] Penney (New York: National Temperance Society and Publication House, 1878), 18.

13. Anonymous, [*The Open Boat and Other Tales of Adventure*], *Independent*, 727.

But "The Bride Comes to Yellow Sky" works through its points of direct satire to a much broader vision of the American West. With intentions different from Bret Harte's (or Owen Wister's), Crane works out his vision of the American West through the stylized form of lawman versus outlaw in a contest ending in a bittersweet gun-down in the open street. Crane's approach, enabling him to manipulate his audience's preconceptions concerning basic Western materials, leads to the undermining of conventional forms rather than their fulfillment—after the turmoil and the promise of violence the showdown peters out into a talk-down.

Jack Potter, town marshal, brings home to Yellow Sky the bride he has gone to San Antonio to marry. The town is deserted when they arrive and he hopes to slip her into town unawares. But they run into Scratchy Wilson, who has been looking for the marshal to challenge him to a shoot-out. The drunken Scratchy stops in his tracks at the sight of the bride, totally defeated by what he takes to be the marshal's failure to observe the rules of the ritualistic gunfight that the two of them engage in from time to time. The marshal does not even have his gun with him. Scratchy, this "simple child of the earlier plains," picks up "his starboard revolver, and, placing both weapons in their holsters," walks away, his feet making "funnel-shaped tracks in the heavy sand."[14]

By 1897, when Crane wrote the "Bride," much of the frontier quality of the West had disappeared in the face of encroachment from the East. This historical fact is reflected in the Olympian vision of the opening paragraph: "the plains of Texas," seen from the moving train, "pouring eastward." The single outlaw's ceremonial dress is composed in part of a shirt "purchased for purposes of decoration and made, principally, by some Jewish women on the East Side of New York" and a pair of boots whose "red tops with gilded imprints" make them "of the kind beloved in winter by little sledding boys on the hillsides of New England." Besides their inflationary intent, such phrases reveal Crane's perception that technology and eastern mercantilism have overcome the less ordered economy of the West. Even in Crane's day this secondary theme would not have been striking, but it serves a larger purpose.

Crane's tale deals with metamorphoses—personal and communal. It is not casual that the adjective appearing most frequently in it is *new*. What is old is the old West epitomized in periodic lawlessness fired by whiskey. Motif-like, the word *new* is invariably associated with the marshal, his marriage, and the signs of an emerging new order. If the narrative begins with a sense of movement and rush threatening full destruction—in dreamlike flood, besides "the plains of Texas," flats, spaces, frame houses, and tender trees sweep "over the

14. Stephen Crane, "The Bride Comes to Yellow Sky," in *Tales of Adventure*, Volume V of *The University of Virginia Edition of the Works of Stephen Crane*, ed. Fredson Bowers, intr. J. C. Levenson (Charlottesville: University Press of Virginia, 1970), 109–20.

horizon, a precipice"—it closes with the vestigial "child" of an earlier time moving slowly away. Opening with a vision of the double strand of civilization and nature sweeping before "the great Pullman," the "Bride" ends with the demise of the individual who at the end stands alone for an older alliance of man with nature. He is the sole reminder, in fact, of an attenuated, if still unbroken, connection.

Fundamental oppositions structure the story. Under the rubric society-nature, the conflict appears as domestication-wildness, order-chaos, and law-disorder. On the surface the opposing details appear as silence, speech, and reason versus noise, music, and emotion. In turn, these details are aligned, dramatically, with house and street, railroad and river, and, finally, in the epitome of external conflict, marshal and drunkard.

Crane divides his story into four sections. In Part I, Marshal Potter and his bride ride the train from San Antonio. They appear to be out of place. In the parlor car, the "environment" of their greatest discomfort, they are "bullied" gently by the porter. The parlor car, the icon for the "new estate" in Part I, is transformed into the Weary Gentleman saloon of Parts II and III. As a sign of the established order of Yellow Sky, the saloon opposes the street. Within the saloon, identified imagistically with the parlor car, the "town" is incarcerated at Wilson's pleasure. Still the climactic confrontation must take place, on one level, between the marshal and the badman, and, on the other, between the temperate man and the drunkard. Therefore, while Wilson himself does not appear in Part I, the porter assumes his functions when he answers Potter's own laughter as he flees the coach by "chuckling fatuously" behind him. In this contest it is the marshal who is vanquished. In Parts II and III, Marshal Potter does not appear, while Wilson himself gains victory over the inmates of the saloon as well as over the barkeeper's dog, with whom Wilson later associates the marshal. In Part IV Potter finally encounters Wilson, and the man who has been bullied by the porter of the "new estate," now committed to that estate, wins out over the badman who had bullied the entire town. The action of the tale, along with its designated parts, turns on a series of conflicts between bullies armed with guns or manners, depending upon the occasion, and victims at total disadvantage.

The particular code by which each individual wishes the conflict to be fought determines whether he is victim or victor. In the parlor-car world Potter is victim because, having chosen to live by the manners and mores of that world, he is at the moment less qualified to do so than the porter or the passenger who, amused at the bridal couple, "winked at himself in one of the numerous mirrors." In the scene played out in front of the saloon Wilson effectively cows those within only because the townsmen when informed that Wilson is drunk do not even consider the possibility of merely leaving by the back door as the peripheral Mexicans do. Appropriately, the drummer, closer to the world of parlor cars and marriages than the townsmen, decides to stay within easy access of the back door should he want to emulate the Mexicans' retreat from a conflict that the others accept so readily. In this world the weapon is the gun, not manners and mores, because the townsmen accept it as such. But in the final scene new mores come smack up against the world of the gun. When Potter refuses to revert to the old terms of conflict, Wilson is defeated. The manners of the "new estate," because the bride stands right there, defeat the accepted form of periodic conflict. The new alliance of the marshal and the parlor-car world has won out.

This action has further reverberations. Potter and Wilson have been described as one another's "ancient antagonist." Admittedly feeling about his marriage as if he has sinned in darkness, Potter, as marshal of Yellow Sky, is nevertheless identified with daylight. Wilson, on the other hand, a "midnight cat" on a tear, turns the town, except for the street, into darkness. At this moment, with Wilson raging drunk, the solemnity of darkness pervades the saloon.

The drunken badman's outbreak, subverting the traditional role of authority and order, suggests that this action in Yellow Sky can be likened to a Saturnalia. Dionysian drink turns Wilson into a Lord of Misrule standing for dark and demonic forces customarily kept in tight rein, assuming omnipotence. His reign occurs, as Frazer's *Golden Bough* tells us such reigns do occur, in an intercalary period between the old and the new. This vessel of drunkenness and revelry, opposing the forces of reason and order, parodying the figure of normal authority, and doomed to a short reign, is deposed, as expected, by the traditional figure of power and law. His reign, an interlude of indulgence, unleashes the forces effectively controlled by constituted rule. But even though this seizure of dark power for disorder offers a not unexpected release, it poses a threat. Quickly becoming unbearable, it must be succeeded by the reestablishment of the restraints of law, custom, and morality.

The nature of this rite of subversion and superseding suggests an Apollonian-Dionysian opposition. Apollonian force, based on the *principium individuationis*, insists upon morals, forms, limits, borders, and categories and imposes the image of finite humanity upon the disorder of experience. Its counterpart, the Dionysian spirit, recognizes the unity of nature and experience. Knowing neither limits nor measures, the Dionysian spirit persists in excess, exuberant expression, and amorality. Opposed to Apollonian limits and morality, Yellow Sky's outlaw becomes the vessel of Dionysian spirit. During periods of condoned misrule, the marshal waits for the town to have had enough of the ruling fool. He then re-creates order. This is his role, performed cyclically and rhythmically.

Apollonian-Dionysian ordering moves subtly through the story in still other ways. The Apollonian temper is associated with reason and speech, the Dionysian with drunkenness, noise, and music. With the god Dionysus, Nietzsche writes in *The Birth of Tragedy*, "an entirely new set of symbols springs into being. . . . All the symbols pertaining to physical features: mouth, face, the spoken word, the dance movement which coordinates the limbs and bends them to rhythm."[15] Hence the importance of Crane's description of Wilson: "The little fingers of each hand played sometimes in a musician's way. Plain from the low collar of the shirt, the cords of his neck straightened and sank, straightened and sank, as passion moved him." Rather than Arion's affective music, which *tamed* waves and sea, Wilson's sounds—"chanting Apache scalp-music"— express unruly primeval forces. Furthermore, when the marshal does face Wilson, his new power of speech deserting him for the moment, there is the silence of death: "Potter's mouth seemed to be merely a grave for his tongue." But earlier, Wilson's vociferous demand, coming at the full, is described as follows—"he yelled, and these cries rang through a semblance of a deserted village, shrilly flying over the roofs in a volume that seemed to have no relation to the ordinary vocal strength of a man. It was as if the surrounding stillness formed the arch of a tomb over him." To use Nietzsche's formulation, it is "as though nature were bemoaning the fact of her fragmentation, her decomposition into separate individuals."[16]

Wilson's shrill cries and "wild yowls" set him off against Potter, the man of speech and reason. In "maroon-colored" shirt, "red-topped" boots, and with face "flaming in a rage begot of whiskey," Wilson's appearance suggests a rampant demonism. Armed with ominously "blue-black" revolvers, this familiar prowler becomes for an hour the last Dionysian reveler in the washed-out wilderness of Yellow Sky. Yet Potter's new suit is black, and his hands— "constantly performing in a most conscious fashion"—"brick-colored." These hands, a reminder of the inflaming possibilities within himself that in his prior battles enabled him to overcome his opponent, reappear in a simile revealing his new allegiance. Unlike Wilson, who turns "loose with both hands," Potter sits "with a hand on each knee, like a man waiting in a barber's shop." To end an earlier outburst the marshal had "shot Wilson up once—in the leg," but now Potter himself waits, Samson-like, to be shorn of his hair and of a kind of power. Later, when the porter brushed his "new clothes," "Potter fumbled out a coin and gave it to the porter as he had seen others do. It was a heavy and muscle-bound business, as that of a man shoeing his first horse." This gesture reveals the nature of the change going on within Potter, for parlor cars, porters, and tips are part of the psychological and social domestication essential to the "new estate."

15. Friedrich Nietzsche, *The Birth of Tragedy*, in *The Birth of Tragedy and The Genealogy of Morals*, trans. Francis Golffing (Garden City: Doubleday, 1956), 27–28.

16. Ibid., 27.

The second simile, "as that of a man shoeing his first horse," rhetorically and thematically echoing "like a man waiting in a barber's shop," intimates that Potter's domestication serves a greater utility; that for Potter, just as for such a horse, traditionally indicative of body, energy, sexuality, rampant forces have been controlled. The conjunction of these similes suggests something like the sexual sublimation of bodily force necessary, it is sometimes argued, for the development of human culture.

Herein lies the importance of the coming of the bride to Yellow Sky. The first person this invading stranger meets is Wilson; she stands "a slave to hideous rites, gazing at the apparitional snake." It is as if she, not the drunkard, is experiencing delirium tremens. At this moment the snake refers to Wilson, of course, and the revolver he thrusts "venomously forward." But the snake in this tale tempts not the new bride; Crane does not use his Edenic myth quite that directly. Rather, the snake, tempting the man, recalls his darker, unconscious self. At the moment of encounter Potter, "exhibit[ing] an instinct to at once loosen his arm from the woman's grip," "dropped the bag to the sand." It is of great importance, imagistically and thematically, that when Wilson finally returns the revolver to its holster, the marshal lifts "his valise." At the end, the gun, indicating erotic force and natural chaos, is useless to Wilson and to Potter, unnecessary. Potter has survived the first challenge to his "new estate," but only with the bride present is the confrontation between Potter and Wilson seen as the manifestation of "hideous rites." It takes the bride as symbol of control, form, and conscience to give this episode its new meaning as the satanic threat to the other world from which Wilson is exempted. A double counter disperses Wilson's shadowy threat: the unmasking of Jack Potter as bridegroom and the uncoiling force of marriage.

For the town the new order, signaled finally in the marriage, has its harbinger in the "new-comer" whose tales dominate the townsmen drinking in the saloon. His power comes through speech (unlike the "Texans who did not care to talk" and the "Mexican sheep-herders who did not talk as a general practice"), just as later the marshal, bolstered by the bride, *talks* Wilson down. The drummer, like "a bard who has come upon a new field," is also identified imagistically with the world of the parlor car, which is a strikingly topical image of an Apollonian world (*parlour*, from the French, making the parlor car a place for talk and conversation—the sign indicative of the new order and, consequently, the marshal's "new estate").

Just as the bard's performance has held the men by engaging their interest in the new and different, so too does Wilson later contain them, in a parody of order, by resurrecting the familiar and customary. With noise and gunfire (rather than speech), he expresses his authority most dramatically in his control over the dog which acts as surrogate for the men within. In fact, when Wilson approaches the saloon, the barkeeper, still not an effective part of the new "world," motions to the drummer to remain silent. Since talk counts for nothing at this moment, the barkeeper takes "a Winchester from beneath the bar," which might count. Consequently, the dog episode, besides functioning as the traditional demonstration of the gunman's shooting skills prior to a final confrontation, anticipates, in Wilson's turning the barkeeper's dog into something "like an animal in a pen," the drunkard's desire to control Yellow Sky, and realizes imagistically the success of the marshal, whose "nice job" it is to contain Wilson. Wilson's parody of the order invested in the marshal becomes, in larger scope, a parody of man's desire to overcome his natural environment.

Still other images indicate domestication and control. The Weary Gentleman saloon, turned by "heavy wooden shutters" into a "solemn, chapel-like gloom," becomes a sanctuary from the disorder in the street—"out there" where "there's a fight just waiting." Potter's own house presents "the same still, calm front" to Wilson "as had the other adobes." Wilson, "howl[ing] a challenge," faces blankly a building that "regarded him as might a great stone god." Of course, the parlor car remains, beginning and end, the crucial sign of the new order; but it has its counterpart in the town saloon attacked directly by Wilson. There, in the midst of fear, the drummer finds consolation in a quasi-vision. Crane describes the drummer's reaction in language suggestive of the parlor car's interior: "Balm was laid upon his soul at sight of various zinc and copper fittings that bore a resemblance to armor-plate." The marriage itself, the new order manifested in its own ritual, in dealing death to the passion of the old order "weigh[s] upon" Jack Potter "like a leaden slab." Adobes, saloon, bronze, brass, brilliantly polished wood, and leaden slab, all suggest the metallic and heavy constructions of order, stability, and *deathlike* protection. Yet stone house, saloon, and parlor car, shelters from the drunken violence exhibited by Wilson, stand also for man's portion of permanence through his civilization. As such each of these requires a protector against an uncongenial invader. Consequently, in the context of the parlor car, even the marshal, despite his new status as bridegroom, must be defended against, for at that moment he still threatens the manners and mores of the parlor-car estate.

Buildings, manifesting human order, relate directly to the marshal's recent marriage, and specifically to the bride. Identifications occur through carefully worked-out clusters of imagery. Crane's initial description of the bride hints at rigidity, hardness, and formality. A mixture of femininity and hard control, "she wore a dress of blue cashmere, with small reservations of velvet here and there and with steel buttons abounding. She continually twisted her head to regard her puff sleeves, very stiff, straight, and high." Resemblance in imagery, skillfully transmuted, identifies bride with parlor car: "[Potter] pointed out to her the dazzling fittings of the coach, and in truth her eyes opened wider as she contemplated the sea-green figured velvet, the shining brass, silver, and glass, the wood that gleamed as darkly brilliant as the surface of a pool of oil. At one end a bronze figure sturdily held a support for a separated chamber, and at convenient places on the ceiling were frescos in olive and silver." If this connection between parlor car and bride of "new estate" is not immediately apparent, Crane makes it explicit when the husband-marshal wavers before Wilson's temptation. For some moments Potter rises to familiar bait: "He was stiffening and steadying, but yet somewhere at the back of his mind a vision of the Pullman floated, the sea-green figured velvet, the shining brass, silver, and glass, the wood that gleamed as darkly brilliant as the surface of a pool of oil—all the glory of the marriage, the environment of the new estate." A montage of metal and velvet, dark brilliance, and "the glory of their marriage" carries Potter through the town's crisis and his personal ordeal.

But this individual and communal victory is not without alloy. Steel buttons counter the velvet of the bride's dress; the marriage brings happiness and shame, self-assertion and "new cowardice," pleasure and pain—Potter "laughed, and groaned as he laughed." This antinomy, this doubleness, insisted upon throughout, inheres brilliantly in what Berryman calls Crane's *tenderness* theme—quoting, from the story, "A sense of mutual guilt invaded their minds and developed a finer tenderness"—where tenderness is gentle *and* sore, innocent *and* wounded.[17] Yellow Sky's rich triumph destroys an honored ritual.

Confrontation of reveler and marshal—remember that *marshal* has within its compass the meaning also of "one who regulates rank and order at a feast or other assembly, one who directs the order of a procession"—offers nothing new to Yellow Sky. The first report of Wilson's eruption moves the townspeople immediately to position.

> The information had made such an obvious cleft in every skull in the room that the drummer was obliged to see its importance. All had become instantly morose. "Say," said he, mystified, "what is this?" His three companions made the introductory gesture of eloquent speech; but the young man at the door forestalled them.
>
> "It means, my friend," he answered, as he came into the saloon, "that for the next two hours this town won't be a health resort."
>
> The bar-keeper went to the door and locked and barred it. Reaching out of the window, he pulled in heavy wooden shutters and barred them. Immediately a solemn, chapel-like gloom was upon the place. The drummer was looking from one to another.

Except for the drummer, and for the Mexicans, who are outsiders, the patrons of the Weary Gentleman saloon accept the inevitability of Scratchy's ("devil's") theatrical performance, cowering in anticipation of its familiar notes: "Pre-

---

17. John Berryman, *Stephen Crane* (New York: William Sloane, 1950), 196.

sently they heard from a distance the sound of a shot, followed by three wild yowls. It instantly removed a bond from the men in the darkened saloon." Appropriately, Crane sets his ritual in terms of the theater: "Across the sandy street were some vivid green grass-plots, so wonderful in appearance . . . they exactly resembled the grass mats used to represent lawns on the stage." This ritual-like, theatrical quality, expressed also in Crane's references to the barkeeper in terms of his function, "the man of bottles," and Wilson in terms of his, "he of the revolver," is developed by the bartender's admission: "This here Scratchy Wilson is a wonder with a gun—a perfect wonder—and when he goes on the war-trail, we hunt our holes—naturally." Indicating further that the ritual is strongly atavistic, his statement provides another telling metaphor, for the world of nature is Wilson's province; according to the barkeeper, "he's about the last one of the old gang that used to hang out along the river here."

The same metaphor emerges in the story's final scene. Incredulous that his antagonist has no gun, Wilson calls the marshal a "whelp," a term that recalls Wilson's natural world by relating the marshal to the "fear-stricken" dog before the saloon.

At sight of the dog, the man paused and raised his revolver humorously. At sight of the man, the dog sprang up and walked diagonally away, with a sullen head and growling. The man yelled, and the dog broke into a gallop. As it was about to enter an alley, there was a loud noise, a whistling, and something spat the ground directly before it. The dog screamed, and, wheeling in terror, galloped headlong in a new direction. Again there was a noise, a whistling, and sand was kicked viciously before it. Fear-stricken, the dog turned and flurried like an animal in a pen. The man stood laughing, his weapons at his hips.

This incident has a sacrificial cast. As the locus of rebellion, Wilson implicitly fixes the town's malady in its principles of order; hence his animus toward houses and public buildings. But in his choice of the dog as scapegoat comes his most protracted challenge to order. Harassed as the embodiment of the town's ills (ills only in the eyes of the drunkard, who stands, of course, for quite a different order of things), the dog provides a temporary outlet for Wilson's violence. But more important, the dog, turned finally into a "penned-up" animal, becomes exactly what Wilson himself has been to the town: the last of the old gang—partly domesticated but with natural wildness still his most potent element. In short, Wilson not only attributes his own qualities and vices to his scapegoat but ends by turning the animal into his own metaphorical substance. The animal reacts finally to being "penned-up," much as, in a different mode, Wilson has reacted. Yet Wilson's derisive laughter, directed in part at his normal *role* within the town's diurnal course, is also self-directed, for it aims ironically at his own impending defeat. Wilson's inebriated laughter reminds us further of the behavior of the porter, who, in an action symbolically like Wilson's, had skillfully "bullied" Potter. Oppressed, the bride and the marshal—"with a hang-dog glance"—finally leave the train. But just "behind them the porter stood, chuckling fatuously." If "historically there was supposed to be something infinitely humorous in their situation," so too is there humor in Wilson's badgering the dog and in the prospect of the town's manhood cowed by the "nicest fellow in town"—when not liquored up, that is.

Accurate insofar as it reflects the marshal in the dining car, the sign of a relatively supra-order of being, Wilson's equation of Potter and dog proves inaccurate as a prediction of final outcome. Wilson hopefully tries to make his connection stick, but, finally, he is the one who moves away beaten, like an animal. Kenneth Burke talks of the "scapegoat as a 'suppurating' device (that brings the evil 'to a head')."[18] Wilson's action has such an effect; but evil has not been so clearly discriminated as one would normally expect in a scapegoat ritual. The temporary ambivalence of good and evil suggests a reason for Crane's use of the double scapegoat. While Wilson appropriately chooses the more archaic form—animal scapegoat—the marshal, tacitly attributing his own vices and temptations to the delegated vessel, designates Wilson as human scapegoat for the entire town and for himself.

The tensions are individual and cultural. To some degree the nature of Wilson's public aggression has been considered. But we have still to discern the import of Crane's emphasis on the marshal's reticence and guilt. Writing about Apollo and Dionysus in *Life Against Death*, Norman O. Brown concludes: "The path of cumulative sublimation is also the path of cumulative aggression and guilt, aggression being the revolt of the baffled instincts against the desexualized and inadequate self."[19] Such a formulation helps to account for the nexus of Wilson's aggression against the town, Potter's—and the bride's—sense of complicity and feelings of "mutual guilt," and the symbols of personal and institutional desexualization that designate the sublimation necessary to the emergence, growth, and fostering of culture.

If we recognize that in psychological terms Wilson is the public manifestation of the marshal's unconscious self, and that in such a sense Wilson is the "outlaw" marshal, we see that the marshal's sense of betrayal and shame is directed not only toward the town that he has served officially as a particular kind of person but also toward the outlaw who has periodically initiated the ritual of maintaining order. Without Wilson there can be no ritualistic reestablish-

18. Kenneth Burke, *The Philosophy of Literary Form: Studies in Symbolic Action*, rev. ed. (New York: Vintage, 1957), 40.

19. Norman O. Brown, *Life Against Death: The Psychoanalytical Meaning of History* (New York: Random House, 1960), 174.

ment of communal order. Hence the marshal's marriage, along with his abandoning of the gun for the "little silver watch" purchased in San Antonio (a purchase that, in temperance terms, makes him a "watchful" man[20]) betrays the "ancient" ways of Yellow Sky. But because Wilson appears to be a smaller, darker, "blue-black" version of the marshal, Jack Potter's shame, guilt, and sense of treachery are also directed toward this primitive version of himself. In marrying he has denied the town's badman his sporadic occupation; he has, in effect, destroyed a former self.

Grant this and it becomes important to note that the marshal, in systematically controlling this part of himself, has in the past also resorted to violence. With murderous possibilities equal for both men, the drunkard's outbursts have created "an obvious cleft in every skull" ultimately satisfied by ritual. Now, although intercepted in his journey to his "safe citadel" from which "he could issue some sort of a vocal bulletin," Potter does overcome his adversary's rage, but he does so through talk and "so much enforced reasoning." Thus, in a larger cultural sense, Wilson's Dionysian excess brought under control by Apollonian force keeps Yellow Sky distinct from the old river home of the intemperate outlaw.

The marshal, like the community, stands between forces of attraction. His temptation in the face of the "hideous rites," hardly casual, involves a decision on his part which will have ramifications for "his corner." But the exact nature of these attractions shows forth in still another way in two passages offering the basic conflict, at times in fundamentally similar terms and at others in their opposites. The first comes early in the narrative: "He, the town marshal of Yellow Sky, a man known, liked, and feared in his corner, a prominent person, had gone to San Antonio to meet a girl he believed he loved, and there, after the usual prayers, had actually induced her to marry him, without consulting Yellow Sky for any part of the transaction. He was now bringing his bride before an innocent and unsuspecting community." Potter's passion has taken the form of love. Having gone to San Antonio to get the girl he loved to marry him, he finds, "after the usual prayers," that his orderly suit is successful.

The marshal's courtship has its complement. In absentia he is himself wooed by the disorderly Wilson.

The name of Jack Potter, his ancient antagonist, entered his mind, and he concluded that it would be a glad thing if he should go to Potter's house and by bombardment induce him to come out and fight. He moved in the direction of his desire, chanting Apache scalp-music.

When he arrived at it, Potter's house presented the same still, calm

20. Anonymous, "Drugging the Guards," in *World Book of Temperance*, 3rd enlarged and rev. ed. comp. Dr. and Mrs. Wilbur F. Crafts (Washington, D.C.: International Reform Bureau, 1911), 125.

front as had the other adobes. Taking up a strategic position, the man howled a challenge. But this house regarded him as might a great stone god. It gave no sign. After a decent wait, the man howled further challenges, mingling with them wonderful epithets.

This passage also expresses a suit of passion, but rather than love *desire* wells forth. Wilson's challenge is really a suit to an empty house. (Recall the imagistic identification of house—parlor car-bride.) If the "usual prayers" are the prelude to Potter's proposal, the aftermath of Wilson's unsuccessful suit is marked by the howling of "challenges" and "wonderful epithets." Hence *induce* appears in both passages (and nowhere else). The conjunction of these passages defines the opposing claims made upon the marshal while discovering the similarity of their basis, for Wilson's suit of violence and desire in the streets of Yellow Sky stands in demonic parody to the marshal's proposal in the parlors of San Antonio.

The personal drama in this case parallels the larger human conflict of civilization and primitive nature. The intercalary state of Yellow Sky, still in transition between the human chaos which is unruled nature and a human-controlled, ordered, perhaps mechanized, civilization, is rendered imagistically: "To the left, miles down a long purple slope, was a little ribbon of mist where moved the keening Rio Grande. The train was approaching it at an angle, and the apex was Yellow Sky." The topographical apex that is Yellow Sky not only depends upon the physical–spiritual forces of railroad and river but appears suspended between them. Crane charts the contest of these forces; forces present in the framework of the town in the specifically acknowledged opposition of the marshal and the remaining member of "the old gang." Consequently, with Wilson explicitly identified with the river and Potter with the railroad, Yellow Sky ultimately moves away from the order of brute nature.

Hinted at throughout, this shift is discernible in the cumulative effect of three references to the river. As the "newly married pair" approaches Yellow Sky, the river is identified as the "keening Rio Grande." Later, when the narrative turns to the "new-comer" in the saloon, there is a reference to the effect that "the fresh-cut bank of the Rio Grande circled near the town." The third reference associates Wilson with the river: "He's about the last one of the old gang that used to hang out along the river here." Like Potter, "a man waiting in a barber's shop," the river has been, in part, domesticated. And the dirgelike sound of the "new" river with its "fresh-cut bank" anticipates the demise of Wilson, the "simple child of the earlier plains." If the town, along with the marshal, leans toward the "new estate," it is also clear that the California Express has made grave inroads on the old world of the river. But nature cannot be wholly domesticated, cannot be brought entirely under control, any more than can Potter's darker self be wholly exorcised. Even what at first seems like a cursory detail about the railroad—Potter's observation, "They have to take water here," made "from a constricted throat and in mournful cadence, as one announcing death"—suggests that under the shifts of power and dominance lies a bedrock of permanent forces in elementary opposition.

Still the old conditions of interaction have disappeared. The "drowning woman at the other man's side" has survived. "His starboard revolver" tamely returned to holster, the drunkard moves away, leaving a wake of "funnel-shaped tracks in the heavy sand." With the surging forces of sea and river echoing cynically, and sadly, in *starboard* and *funnel-shaped*, Yellow Sky at this moment realizes pacification. The marshal "knew full well that his marriage was an important thing to his town." In fact, "it could only be exceeded by the burning of the new hotel."

What Crane finds no need to name is temperance, even though—make no mistake about it—the advent of the bride is the beginning of a new and more temperate dispensation for Yellow Sky. The message is clear in the very environment when it is read aright, according to the temperance worker. "A new significance is given to the old term 'water power' when we read how water is used to remove mountains in California," one worker put it. "As man learns better how to use the forces of Omnipotence, so 'the reform wave,' the union of the cold water forces, enlisting god's omnipotence, is sweeping away the seemingly insurmountable obstacles to world-wide prohibition."[21] Given the strong and powerful role women were playing in the temperance movement, new meaning is taken on by the marshal's cold (and oddly predictive) assurance to the bride: "They have to take water here." As for Crane's attitude, suffice it to say that it was made "as one announcing death." In "The Bride Comes to Yellow Sky," Crane looked deeply into how human needs, drives, and functions were affected by social transformation and demographic change. It was a searching, probing look that was inconceivable to those armies waging righteous war against the monsters of intemperance.

4

Published in *Frank Leslie's Popular Monthly* in April 1900, "Moonlight on the Snow" shares themes with "The Bride Comes to Yellow Sky." It also recycles two of that story's principals—Jack Potter and Scratchy Wilson—who intervene significantly in events toward the end of the story.

Following Robert W. Stallman's hint that "Moonlight" parodies Bret Harte's work, especially his California tales, Eric Solomon shows how this

---

21. Ella Wheeler Wilcox, "Water Power," in *World Book of Temperance*, 3rd ed., 176.

story supports his theory that parody forms the basis of Crane's realism.[22] With that much a given, it is useful to go beyond that parody of the West which Solomon has charted, in order to define the theme that both underlies and potentiates the parody.

Alcohol is a given in "Moonlight." The Crystal Palace houses the bar, the center of power and conviviality and recreation in War Post, Texas. Discussions are held there and decisions reached about the collective aspirations for the town and its citizenry. The "popular barkeeper" is listened to and accepted as a leader in meting out justice. But their occasional moral spokesman is Billie Simpson ("somewhere in his past he had been a Baptist preacher"), a "bleareyed old ruffian" with "a fatal facility of speech when half drunk."[23] "War Post used him on those state occasions when it became bitten with a desire to 'do the thing up in style.' " The owner of the gambling house ("the biggest institution in War Post"), a man who "had been educated somewhere," makes cryptic speeches regarding the townspeople's perception of their town's needs. Over War Post, a town whose sole fixed asset is a reputation for violence and lawlessness, now hovers "the serene-browed angel of peace." That seductive angel holds out glowing rewards for War Post if its people will create the conditions proper to financial exploitation. Faced with the mushroom growth of surrounding towns—those that have already embraced the new finance—War Post's first citizens resolve that it is their civic duty to find a way to attract a generous portion of that wealth. "Well, when all this here coin is floatin' 'round, it 'pears to me we orter git our hooks on some of it," announces the citizen "who whirled roulette." "Them little tin horns over at Crowdger's Corner are up to their necks in it, an' we ain't yit seen a centavo. Not a centavetto. That ain't right," he whines. "It's all well enough to sit 'round takin' money away from innercent cowpunchers s'long's ther's nothin' better; but when these here speculators come 'long flashin' rolls as big as waterbuckets, it's up to us to whirl in an' git some of it." But the gambler, Tom Larpent, reminds them, "The value of human life has to be established before there can be theatres, water-works, street cars, women and babies."

Deciding that a system of law and precedent will provide the semblance of that visible order necessary to the successful courtship of any outside investment, they formulate a plan to be implemented immediately. "A great meeting was held," writes Crane, "at which it was decreed that no man should kill another man under penalty of being at once hanged by the populace. All the influential citizens were present, and asserted their determination to deal out a

22. Robert Wooster Stallman, *Stephen Crane: An Omnibus* (New York: Knopf, 1952), xxvii; Eric Solomon, *Stephen Crane: From Parody to Realism* (Cambridge, Mass.: Harvard University Press, 1966), 276–81.

23. Stephen Crane, "Moonlight on the Snow," in *Tales of Adventure*, 179–81.

swift punishment which would take no note of an acquaintance or friendship with the guilty man." The next morning, as if on schedule, Larpent, the gambler who is a "chief factor in the life of the town," shoots and kills a fellow cardplayer who has the temerity to accuse him of cheating.

This killing puts War Post's public resolution to its first test. Everything goes awry. First, the townsmen who are to hang the murderer in accordance with the law against killing fail to arrest Larpent as quickly as he himself reasonably expects. The immediate result is that the murderer disgustedly leaves the Crystal Palace's gambling hall for his room, where, he announces, he can await his captors in comfort, pouring himself a drink of the rye whiskey ("of a brand which he specially and secretly imported from the East") and taking up "an old copy of Scott's *Fair Maid of Perth*." When the lynching mob does arrive, its members are individually reluctant to arrest the murderer. Their behavior bespeaks a lack of the will to accept the consequences of their dedication to the new values of land speculation and economic prosperity. Collectively embarrassed and guilt-ridden, the mob falls an easy victim to Larpent's rapid current of sarcasm. Drawing on their individual friendship for him and playing shrewdly on their clanlike loyalties, he baits them, individually and collectively, until he has whipped them into resuming their hangman's business. Before they manage to carry out the hanging, however, they are interrupted by the arrival of a stage full of easterners who are passing through on their way elsewhere. Abetted by the women in his company (we are reminded of Larpent's speech about a future with theater, women, and babies), a clergyman (answering a call to Crowdger's Corner) objects righteously enough to the proposed hanging to immobilize the War Post citizenry a second time. This impasse continues until the prisoner himself suggests, partly because he is bored, that they postpone his execution until these eastern meddlers have left War Post. His suggestion is immediately adopted by his would-be executioners, who release Larpent until the conditions for his hanging are more propitious.

Before the townsmen can collect him a second time for the communal hanging that is now his due, however, the outside world again interferes in War Post's affairs. This time the interference comes in the form of a county sheriff, who arrives with an arrest warrant charging Larpent with grand larceny. Since the sheriff's action is viewed as an invasion of War Post and as such will set an undesirable precedent, the overriding question now becomes whether War Post can afford to allow the vested representatives of a higher law to impinge upon their sovereignty by whisking away their friend and fellow citizen, or whether it must collectively stiffen to prevent the sheriff and his deputy from taking Tom Larpent, thereby preserving War Post's integrity as an autonomous seat of violence and disorder.

One of its leaders speaks out for the "new" War Post when he argues that Larpent's arrest by "outsiders" will accomplish exactly what War Post's hanging of him would: it will help to persuade the outside world that War Post has become a lawful, orderly community. But this idea in turn finds immediate opposition among those who raise the fearful possibility that someone else—not War Post—will get to hang Larpent. As members of the two factions argue, the sheriff and his deputy quietly back out of the Crystal Palace, taking along the county's latest prisoner. Finally, in clan loyalty, one of War Post's leaders makes the point that no outside authority will ever succeed in hanging Larpent for the War Post murder because there will be no witnesses to convict him. Of course, no one from War Post, he insists, will ever testify against War Post's own Tom Larpent. So concludes Crane's Western fable: greater law and outside authority encroach even as the clan thinks it has successfully reasserted its traditional values.

The "threat" of civilization has come to War Post in two related ways: the money to be made by following the lure of land speculation and the weakening of civic autonomy through the extension of organized law enforcement on a scale larger than the town has ever before known. That the two threats seem to arrive coincidentally is one of Crane's most effective strokes. For the story implies clearly that law and civilization have come whether War Post knows it or wants it. In a way it is War Post's fortune that its saloon-engendered cupidity has made it easier for its citizenry to rationalize away the significance of their capitulation in the Tom Larpent affair. One of Crane's points is that in reality the town can do no more than endorse the social process that has overtaken it. Just as a lynching mob of private citizens now gives way to the county sheriff and his sober deputy, so too must War Post go the way of Yellow Sky.

The structure of the story bears this idea out. Hard upon the town's hurriedly devised resolution come three tests, almost as if Crane has transformed the entire town into an anthropomorphized hero on a quest. Can War Post, it might be asked, survive those tests and threats to its sovereignty?

War Post fails all three tests, of course; yet each failure has the effect of pushing the town further along the way it thinks it wants to go—toward law and greater civilization: first, dragging its collective heels in the proposed execution of Larpent, the town wishes to revert to the values of friendship and personal privilege before the law; second, assailed by the righteous complaints of outraged Easterners, War Post's best citizens are rendered immobile through confusion and embarrassment; third, the county sheriff's "invasion" of War Post territory brings opposition that succeeds only in dividing the town into factions—those who would revert to clan values and loyalties and those who would see in the "invasion" an aid in the fulfillment of War Post's ambition to become the respectable town capable of attracting investment that it thinks it should be.

There are ironic turns here. Desiring a new image, the town of War Post is nevertheless forced to assert exactly what would hurt that image. A resolution in favor of objective law puts its citizens in the position that forces them to fall back on the clan values of local loyalty. Only by falling back on those loyalties, however, is the town able to rationalize the collective behavior that enables it to move toward the objectives of a law purporting to be equal and nonpersonal. It is a wry comment on that law and the society it enables that while the sheriff arrests Larpent for a crime against *property*, he takes no apparent interest in the crime against *life* that Larpent has just committed.

Evident as well is the social specialization that is a principle in the evolution of societies. While the vigilante citizens of War Post would at one fell swoop, as it were, arrest, judge, and execute their murderer, the sheriff's visit is so described that we realize that there are limits to his authority. Although his authority now exceeds that of anyone in War Post, that authority is restricted to arresting the thief and bringing him back to stand trial. The division of power and the specialization and professionalization of functions are clearly indicated by the fact that the sheriff's action is legal only because it has been empowered by a court-issued warrant. The specific nature of the emblematic events in War Post—communal greed; resolution for greater law; tests of both by the conjunction of a murder, Eastern moral righteousness, and county law—indicates that even at the end of the events depicted, War Post has not yet developed to the point at which Yellow Sky had already arrived when Jack Potter made his secretive visit to San Antonio. It is reasonable to expect, however, that hard on the sheriff's heels there will appear another "bride" to stake out this "new estate."

Appropriating both Jack Potter, the ex-marshal of Yellow Sky and now the county sheriff, and Scratchy Wilson, the ex-drunkard now sufficiently rehabilitated to have become his deputy, "Moonlight" offers a variation on one of the earlier story's major themes—the necessary, if sorrowful, passing of one type of society into a society of a more complex sort. The ambivalence of the drama engendered by the social and political evolution of a small Western town is another way to describe the theme that joins "The Bride Comes to Yellow Sky" to "Moonlight on the Snow."

There is an interesting matter left. What is the reader to make of Larpent's highhanded, theatrical behavior? Like the sot Scratchy, who periodically shot his way through Yellow Sky, Larpent is himself the serpent who would tempt War Post into falling again into its old ways. The murder he commits comes so quickly after the town has launched its plan for respectability that one tends to see the act as one of defiance and scorn. In effect, he has offered himself up as a scapegoat for the town's past sins, an offer intended to put his fellow townsmen to the test. Larpent's literary descent may be of help here. It leads back to the *Adventures of Huckleberry Finn* (1885). Like Mark Twain's Colonel Sherburn, who guns down Boggs, the town drunkard, War Post's murderer reads his townsmen perfectly, probing their weaknesses as individuals and as elements of a mob. To this, Larpent adds the touch of playing directly upon personal as well as mob sentimentalities. The thing Larpent fails to consider, apparently—a possibility missing from Mark Twain's novel—is that there might be outside intervention in the affairs of the hitherto entirely self-ruling War Post.

Thus with Tom Larpent's arrest at the hands of a *county* sheriff working out of Yellow Sky, the old War Post silently becomes, if unwittingly and unexpectedly, the new War Post. But no one should be entirely surprised at the author's conclusion: that in its growing consciousness of financial potential, War Post has already betrayed signs of having moved from a kind of barbarity to a crude expression of its desire to be a "law-abiding" place.[24]

No question. The arrival of the 3:42 carrying Jack Potter's dowdy (but deadly) bride from San Antonio to new territory started shock waves that moved through a good deal of Crane's whiskey-soaked Western fiction.

24. Larpent's reading of Sir Walter Scott's *Fair Maid of Perth* gives the attentive reader an early clue. Scott's theme is Crane's: the inevitable, yet not for that reason entirely desirable, evolution from a tribal state of communal existence into a more complex system that subsumes justice to law, not loyalty. The novel traces the painful stages of the transitional period in which the mores of the clan give way to the more "objective" ways of a lawful society. Scott's novel turns on the conflict between the old barbarism of continuous warfare and the new and far more conciliatory society that has evolved from it. Spinning out to lengthy conclusion, *The Fair Maid of Perth* asserts the secondary theme that social and political evolution is by no means all gain; that such evolution, if it brings gain, will exact loss as well. As Crane saw things, War Post, Texas, was drifting toward the rudimentary dictates of a more conventional order. What it was losing, however, was its bravura and independence, along with something that one could call its tribal innocence.

11

Blue Skies

Instead of sending forth a fleet strong enough to sweep the cruel pirates from the sea, we are working with a little life-boat, glad when we are able to pick up a wounded man thrown overboard from a burning ship, or to give decent burial to a corpse of some poor victim.

—Rev. J. T. Crane, *Arts of Intoxication* (1870)

She is launched on the wave—the good ship Prohibition,
   The wave of Humanity boundless and free;
Around her stomach gunwale in fierce ebullition,
   The mad waters foam as she heads out to sea . . .

—Lide Meriwether (1887)

Then could attentive ears hear the cold breakers muttering their rebellious fugue to the glory of the Creator.

Louis Zara, *Dark Rider* (1961)

Thomas Beer opens chapter 5 of his study of Crane with this gnomic sentence: "He loved babies, horses, oceans or anything that offered an enigmatic surface to his thought."[1] He might have stressed further that Crane, especially taken with the sea, was uncommonly adept at seascapes. Conrad thought so. "The Open Boat" made him "horribly" envious. "Confound you—you fill the blamed landscape—you—by all the devils—fill the sea-scape," he wrote. "The boat thing is immensely . . . fundamentally interesting to me. Your tem-

---

1. Thomas Beer, *Stephen Crane: A Study in American Letters*, intr. Joseph Conrad (New York: Knopf, 1923), 139.

perament makes old things new and new things amazing."[2] Several times Crane tried his hand at seascapes. "The Open Boat" is his major achievement. But two other attempts are worth consideration, the poem "A man adrift on a slim spar" and the sketch "Dan Emmonds."

1

"Dan Emmonds" begins with the arrival of the Irishman Dan in New York City, where his father has opened a saloon. Unable to support his son, the father decides to send him to sea. Dan's shipboard experiences are covered in three paragraphs, and by the seventh paragraph Dan's ship, already approaching Australia, runs into a storm. When the ship is wrecked Dan finds himself alone in the water clutching desperately to a hen coop. Drifting aimlessly, he comes upon the carcass of a pig. He manages to get to it and then bobs along with firm hold on both hen coop and carcass until he encounters a fishing smack filled with "strange people." Sensing trouble, he addresses them in a long speech which is apologetic and, he hopes, conciliatory. But the occupants of the smack, who are probably cannibals, seem not to understand him. They take him aboard. The tale ends abruptly with Dan's adieu to the pig's carcass in sentences that echo "The Open Boat": " 'Good fortune be with you, Bartholomew,' said I addressing the distance. 'You are better off than I am indeed, if I am going to be killed after taking this long troublesome voyage.' "[3]

It is useful to begin by comparing "Dan Emmonds" with "The Open Boat." The latter is a work of tragic import; the former is nothing if not comic. The intensity that builds tonally and stylistically in "The Open Boat" is countered by the bantering, flippant tone in which Dan records his high jinks. In "The Open Boat" names are not used. The sunken ship is not identified. Its survivors are known only as the captain, the cook, and the correspondent. Only the oiler is identified by name, and he is called simply Billie. In "Dan Emmonds" everyone is named, from the title character to Bartholomew, the dead pig bobbing along on the main, to the *Susan L. Terwilleger*, the ship that goes down in the storm. Anonymity is one way of making characters and situations more typical and universal. In "The Open Boat" characters are devoid of biography. Nothing is said, not even about the life aboard the ship they have just abandoned. In "Dan Emmonds," however, a good half of the

2. *The Collected Letters of Joseph Conrad, Volume I, 1861–1897*, ed. Frederick R. Karl and Laurence Davies (Cambridge, Eng.: Cambridge University Press, 1983), 415.

3. Stephen Crane, "Dan Emmonds," in *Poems and Literary Remains*, Volume X of *The University of Virginia Edition of the Works of Stephen Crane*, ed. Fredson Bowers, intr. James B. Colvert (Charlottesville: University Press of Virginia, 1975), 112–17.

tale is concerned with Dan's relationship with his father in New York and with his weeks of drunkenness aboard ship. The entire narrative of "The Open Boat," on the other hand, takes place after the sinking of the ship.

Mindful of Crane's own view of "Dan Emmonds" as a piece "strong in satire," one critic defines it as "a wild spoof of many aspects of sea fiction."[4] Besides being directed at the more romantic forms of sea fiction, however, Crane's satire aims at themes and motifs widely promulgated through popular evangelical hymns and the writings of the temperance movement. In the 1890s Crane could safely assume that those objects of his satire were familiar enough to his readers to evoke from them an appropriate response.

In "Dan Emmonds" much is made of its Irish hero's drunkenness. It is his dissipation that compels his saloon-keeper father to send Dan to sea. But the thief is now in the hen coop, for aboard ship Dan falls in with the ship's captain and other drinking sailors. Now he does nothing but drink. "The captain's rum and tobacco were good," he recalls, "and he was a first-class companion with a bottle between him and me." "We became great philosophers," he continues, "and conversed deeply upon many things that were not usually understood, cocking up our legs and puffing and letting the ship go to ruin."

That shipwreck and alcohol are often linked is a commonplace of sea lore and fiction. In *Captains Courageous*, for example, one of Kipling's fishermen says of a sinking ship that it "'must ha' been spewin' her oakum fer a week, an' they never thought to pump her. That's one more boat gone along o' leavin' port all hands drunk."[5] That shipwreck will follow drunkenness is the theme of many versified accounts of disaster on the high seas. Crews often behaved badly. Failing to react as God-fearing Christians, they, like Crane's Dan Emmonds, resort to drink. "Instead of calling 'upon the Lord in their trouble,' that He might 'bring them out of their distresses,' they drink and are drunken." Out of this despair, however, comes hope at last, in the form of a lifeboat launched from shore. "Quickly she takes the drowning wretches from the drifting spars [a fate happier than that of the castaway of Crane's poem "A man adrift on a slim spar"], giving back to them life and hope." But those "not yet sobered, will not be saved," for those manning the lifeboat would save the sober but not the drunk. The principle is clear: for these Christians sobriety stands next to godliness. But the drunkards sin to a fault, for they fail to apprehend their situation. Unlike Dan, who mistakenly takes the approaching, smiling natives for rescuers—discovering only later that he has fallen among cannibals—the

4. Eric Solomon, *Stephen Crane: From Parody to Realism* (Cambridge, Mass.: Harvard University Press, 1966), 149.

5. Rudyard Kipling, *"Captains Courageous": A Story of the Grand Banks* (New York: Century, 1897), 128.

emblematically drunken sailors, refusing to leave their raft, "take the 'life-preservers' for pirates, that have come to take and sell them for slaves."[6]

Similar stories of drunkenness and shipwreck were included in temperance readers. One such tale, "The Pirate Alcohol," presents an allegory of drunken sailors on an "intemperance" ship who not only cannot save their ship during a violent storm but murder their would-be rescuers on "the temperance boat." Now "the drunken ship" fills with water. There is "not a man at the pumps, not an arm at the helm."

> Having destroyed their friends, the crew fall upon each other. Close under their bow rave the breakers of a rocky shore, but they hear them not. . . . In this terrible extremity Independence is heard to refuse help and boasts of his strength. Friendship and Parental Love rail at thoughts of affection. Language trumpets his easy yarn, and grows garrulous as the timbers crack one after another. Rage and Revenge are now the true names of Firmness and Courage. Silly Mirth yet giggles a dance, and I saw him astride the last timber as the ship went down, tossing foam at the lightning. Then came a sigh of the storm, a groaning of waves, a booming of blackness, and a red, crooked thunder-bolt shot wrathfully blue into the suck of the sea where the ship went down.

Then comes the explication and the moral. "I asked the names of those rocks, and was told: God's stern and immutable Laws. And I asked the name of that ship, and they said: Immortal Soul. And I asked why its crew brought it there, and they said: Their Captain Conscience and Helmsman Reason were dead. And I asked how they had died, and they said: By one single shot from Pirate Alcohol; by one charmed ball of Moderate Drinking. On this topic, over which we sleep, we shall some day cease to dream."[7] Such ship and ocean metaphors were singularly apt to Crane's perception of the human situation. If the temperance worker located the source of virtually all human misery in pirate alcohol and demon whiskey, Crane saw misery as endemic to the human condition. He transformed temperance metaphors and transvalued the movement's millennial rhetoric so as to convey his vision of man's plight in an indifferent universe. In poem VI of *Black Riders* he satirizes those who put their credence in a benevolent, caring Creator:

6. Rev. William Holmes and John W. Barber, "The Life-Boat," in *Religious Allegories: Being a Series of Emblematic Engravings*, Improved ed. (Boston: L. P. Crown, 1854), 48.

7. Rev. Joseph Cook, "The Pirate Alcohol," in *Readings and Recitations, No. 3*, ed. L[izzie] Penney (New York: National Temperance Society and Publication House, 1879), 53–54.

GOD FASHIONED THE SHIP OF THE WORLD CARE-
FULLY.
WITH THE INFINITE SKILL OF AN ALL-MASTER
MADE HE THE HULL AND THE SAILS,
HELD HE THE RUDDER
READY FOR ADJUSTMENT.
ERECT STOOD HE, SCANNING HIS WORK
PROUDLY.
THEN——AT FATEFUL TIME——A WRONG CALLED,
AND GOD TURNED, HEEDING.
LO, THE SHIP, AT THIS OPPORTUNITY, SLIPPED
SLYLY,
MAKING CUNNING NOISELESS TRAVEL DOWN THE
WAYS.
SO THAT, FOREVER RUDDERLESS, IT WENT UPON
THE SEAS
GOING RIDICULOUS VOYAGES,
MAKING QUAINT PROGRESS,
TURNING AS WITH SERIOUS PURPOSE
BEFORE STUPID WINDS.
AND THERE WERE MANY IN THE SKY
WHO LAUGHED AT THIS THING.[8]

2

The poem "A man adrift on a slim spar" went unpublished in its author's life-
time. It is not known when it was written exactly, but it appears, as "A man
afloat on a slim spar," on a list of magazine acceptances sometime before June
1898, when the poem "The Blue Battalions," which is also on the list, was
published in the *Philistine*.[9] This paradigmatic poem was not published until
1929, when it appeared in the *Bookman*:

A man adrift on a slim spar
A horizon smaller than the rim of a bottle
Tented waves rearing lashy dark points
The near whine of froth in circles.
God is cold.

8. Stephen Crane, *The Black Riders and Other Lines* (Boston: Copeland and Day, 1895), 6–7.
9. Daniel Hoffman, *The Poetry of Stephen Crane* (New York and London: Columbia University
Press, 1957), 94 n.

The incessant raise and swing of the sea
And growl after growl of crest
The sinkings, green, seething, endless
The upheaval half-completed.

God is cold.

The seas are in the hollow of The Hand;
Oceans may be turned to a spray
Raining down through the stars
Because of a gesture of pity toward a babe.
Oceans may become grey ashes,
Die with a long moan and a roar
Amid the tumult of the fishes
And the cries of the ships,
Because The Hand beckons the mice.

A horizon smaller than a doomed assassin's cap,
Inky, surging tumults
A reeling, drunken sky and no sky
A pale hand sliding from a polished spar.

God is cold.

The puff of a coat imprisoning air.
A face kissing the water-death
A weary slow sway of a lost hand
And the sea, the moving sea, the sea.

God is cold.[10]

It is possible that Crane took his hint for this poem from "A Tragedy of the Sea," an excerpt from Victor Hugo's *Les Misérables* published in school readers during Crane's formative years. "A man overboard! What matters it? The ship does not stop. The wind is blowing. That dark ship must keep on her destined course. She passes away." The man disappears beneath the waves, reappears, plunges, and rises again to the surface. He calls out. Hugo then elaborates on the man's actions and growing panic as he despairs for his life. He delves in detail into the psyche of the floundering man, who "implores the blue vault, the waves, the rocks," all of which are deaf to his cries. "He thinks of the shadowy adventures of his lifeless body in the limitless gloom. The biting cold para-

---

10. Stephen Crane, "A man adrift on a slim spar," in *Poems and Literary Remains*, Volume X of *The University of Virginia Edition of the Works of Stephen Crane,* ed. Fredson Bowers, intr. James B. Colvert (Charlottesville: University Press of Virginia, 1971), 83.

lyzes him. His hands clutch spasmodically, and grasp at nothing. Winds, clouds, whirlwinds, blasts, stars,—all useless." "What shall he do?" the castaway asks. Or is it the author who questions? "He yields to despair: worn out, he seeks death; he no longer resists; he gives himself up; he abandons the contest, and he is rolled away into the dismal depths of the abyss for ever."[11]

Crane's poem seems to follow from this final sentence, finding in this "tragedy of the sea" an opportunity to look once again into the theme of man and Providence. Yet to the literary text he might have remembered from his textbook reader Crane added something from Charles Lamb ("the slave of alcohol"[12]) that he found quoted in his father's work.

The waters have gone over me. But out of the black depths, could I be heard, I would cry out to all those who have but set a foot in the perilous flood. Could the youth to whom the flavor of his first wine is delicious as the opening scenes of life, or the entering upon some newly discovered Paradise, look into my desolation, and be made to understand what a dreary thing it is when a man shall feel himself going down a precipice with open eyes and a passive will—to see his destruction and have no power to stop it, and yet to feel it all the way emanating from himself.

Lamb then offers up himself as an example of drunkenness and pathos: "Could he see my fevered eye, feverish with last night's drinking, and feverish by looking for this night's repetition of the folly; could he feel the body of the death out of which I cry hourly with feebler and feebler outcry to be delivered—it were enough to make him dash the sparkling beverage to the earth in all the pride of its mantling temptation."[13] Besides the language and symbols he borrowed from Lamb and Hugo, there was also something from the temperance worker's lexicon or arsenal.

Take the "doomed assassin's cap," for instance. Daniel Hoffman observes that line 20—"A horizon smaller than a doomed assassin's cap"—shifts the point of view of the poem back to the man on the spar so that the reader can "see his dying moment through his eyes." Later, explaining Crane's comparison of the castaway's shrinking horizon to a "doomed assassin's cap," Hoffman suggests the possibility that Crane is referring to "a fez or stocking cap."[14] Since both of these are ordinarily worn *on* the head and not *over* the head and face and, consequently, are not visible to the wearer, the image Hoffman's explana-

---

11. Victor Hugo, "A Tragedy of the Sea," in *Swinton's Fifth Reader and Speaker* (New York and Chicago: Ivison, Blakeman, 1883), 163, 165.

12. Rev. J. T. Crane, *Arts of Intoxication: The Aim, and the Results* (New York: Carlton & Lanahan/San Francisco: E. Thomas/Cincinnati: Hitchcock & Walden, 1870), 206.

13. Quoted in ibid., 195–96.

14. Hoffman, *Poetry*, 96, 99.

tion conjures up would seem to be at odds with his earlier suggestion that line 20 returns us to the castaway's point of view. Rather than a fez or a stocking cap, however, Crane may be referring to the cap described in "Tales of the Revolution": "On the day of his [the condemned man's] execution, the fatal cap was drawn over his eyes, and he was caused to kneel in front of the whole army."[15] Such a cap, pulled *over* the head, would be fully consistent with Crane's shift at line 20 to the castaway's claustrophobic point of view.

It is even more likely, however, that Crane knew about the strategies of the temperance worker who depicted the inevitable demise of the alcoholic with "the last drop on the gallows." There is a temperance cartoon, taken from the *Watchman*, which is captioned "Beware of the First Drop," and continues, " 'Come in and take a drop.' The first drop led to other drops. He dropped his position, he dropped his respectability, he dropped his fortune, he dropped his friends, he dropped finally all his prospects in this life, and his hopes for eternity; and then came the last drop on the gallows. BEWARE OF THE FIRST DROP."[16] The drunkard has over his head the "doomed assassin's cap." The connection between "assassin" and intoxication was explained by Crane's father in *Arts of Intoxication*: "The Turkish name of the preparation of hemp being *hasheesh*, and those addicted to the use of it being called hashasheen, it is supposed that the English word *assassin* originated in the time of these wars [the Crusades], and in the murderous deeds which the baleful drug instigated."[17]

Although Crane's poem centers on what the poet takes to be God's indifference to man's plight, the vision of the "man adrift" is characterized by images appropriate to the temperance worker's vocabulary descriptive of the drunkard. The man sees his horizon to be diminished to less than "the rim of a bottle." In a pun the circling froth nearly "whine[s]." The sinkings of the sea are (bottle?) "green." The sky itself is "reeling, drunken." What Crane's poem does not reveal are the circumstances of how this man came to be adrift in the first place. In the sketch "Dan Emmonds" it is the wholesale drunkenness of the captain and his crew that causes shipwreck. The handbook *Weapons for Temperance Warfare* offers a quotation from the "Captain of a Great Steamship Line": "Many a time has a glass of whiskey wrecked a ship." Indeed, on the so-called "temperance ships," insurance costs were reduced. The poet John Greenleaf Whittier invoked such ships: "Freighted with love our temperance ship / Around the world shall sail; / Take heart and hope, dear mariners; /

15. "Old Soldier," "Tales of the Revolution," in *Collections, Historical and Miscellaneous*, ed. J. Farmer and J. B. Moore (Concord, July 1824), III, 210–12.

16. Anonymous, "The First Drop. The Last Drop," in *World Book of Temperance* (Abridged ed.), comp. Dr. and Mrs. Wilbur F. Crafts (Washington, D.C.: International Reform Bureau, 1908), 49.

17. Crane, *Arts of Intoxication*, 91. Hoffman offers a similar explanation but does not trace Crane's knowledge of the etymology of the word *assassin* to his father's work (*Poetry*, 98–99).

God's errands never fail."[18] With proper education in the dangers of alcoholic liquors, it was argued, "even the sea would lose its terrors, and the families of seafaring men would look serenely over the stormy waters, confidently expecting the return of their loved ones."[19]

But it is God's indifference (coldness) to man that Crane makes the theme of his poem. God's errands are to turn oceans into raining spray in pity for a babe or to scorch them into ashes to save some mice. It is not Rimbaud's drunken boat that Crane adduces but a drunken sky. It is not an alcohol-death man kisses but a "water-death." (So much for the salvific claims of the "cold-water" army.) It is man's condition and situation that he is shipwrecked in an environment characterized by alcoholic drink, one whose reeling, drunken sky narrows down to the rim of a (green) bottle. As usual with Crane, he employs their language—words and images—against the righteous messengers of temperance on their self-appointed errands. God the executioner brings about man's "last drop." As Hoffman puts it, "The 'slim spar' that fails him is the debris of the wreck from which he has been cast adrift: the 'ship of the world' which God had abandoned in the *Black Riders* (VI)."[20] Crane's target is Isaiah's Lord (40:12), "who hath measured the waters in the hollow of his hand, and meted out heaven with the span."

And yet Crane was also capable of playing with the notion that man was sinful enough to share in the blame for his fate, as in poem LXII of *Black Riders*.

> THERE WAS A MAN WHO LIVED A LIFE OF FIRE.
> EVEN UPON THE FABRIC OF TIME,
> WHERE PURPLE BECOMES ORANGE
> AND ORANGE PURPLE,
> THIS LIFE GLOWED,
> A DIRE RED STAIN, INDELIBLE;
> YET WHEN HE WAS DEAD,
> HE SAW THAT HE HAD NOT LIVED.[21]

One temperance reader prints a piece that opens with an anecdote about a burning ship going over the falls at Niagara. This incident opens out into an allegory of human sinfulness. No reader could have doubted that the cataract of water stands for the cataract of alcohol inundating the sinner beset. "In 1812 there was a vessel, just above Niagara Falls, set on fire and unloosened from its

18. Quoted in Belle M. Brain, *Weapons for Temperance Warfare* (Boston and Chicago: United Society of Christian Endeavor, 1897), 43.

19. Julia Colman, "One Way to Make Money," in *Readings and Recitations, No. 2*, ed. L[izzie] Penney (New York: National Temperance Society and Publication House, 1878), 87.

20. Hoffman, *Poetry*, 99.

21. Crane, *Black Riders*, 69.

moorings, and in the night it came down through the rapids and over the falls. It was said to be a scene of overwhelming grandeur. But there are thousands of people in our midst who are on fire with evil habits, going down through the rapids in the awful night of temptation to the eternal plunge."[22] But the fire resulting from evil habit is embraced in poem XLVI of *Black Riders*. Sinfulness appears to be his natural condition and thus the source of the "red muck" out of which the poet writes:

> MANY RED DEVILS RAN FROM MY HEART
> AND OUT UPON THE PAGE.
> THEY WERE SO TINY
> THE PEN COULD MASH THEM.
> AND MANY STRUGGLED IN THE INK.
> IT WAS STRANGE
> TO WRITE IN THIS RED MUCK
> OF THINGS FROM MY HEART.[23]

3

Coming at last to the conclusion that man's freedom lies somewhere between Fate and, as he termed it, a "Beautiful Necessity," Emerson turned to the figure of shipwrecks and castaways to convey his sense of the individual human being's precarious hold upon life within the province of nature. "I seemed in the height of a tempest to see men overboard struggling in the waves, and driven about here and there," he wrote. "They glanced intelligently at each other, but 'twas little they could do for one another; 'twas much if each could keep afloat alone. Well, they had a right to their eye-beams, and all the rest was Fate."[24]

For Emerson the metaphor of shipwreck remained a personal metaphor, though when he first put together his lecture "Fate" he had just experienced something of its awesome literalness in the shipwreck off Fire Island that took Margaret Fuller's life. For Stephen Crane, however, shipwreck was to become a literal reality when the *Commodore*, an American ship carrying arms to the Cuban insurrectionists, sank off the Florida coast on New Year's Day 1897. Cast in the dual roles of reporter and author, the survivor made two major attempts at transmitting his personal sense of the experience: "Stephen Crane's Own Story," which appeared within the week in the *New York Press* and an-

22. Rev. T. De Witt Talmage, "True Help," in *Readings and Recitations, No. 3*, ed. L[izzie] Penney (New York: National Temperance Society and Publication House, 1879), 18.

23. Crane, *Black Riders*, 49.

24. Ralph Waldo Emerson, "Fate," in *Selections from Ralph Waldo Emerson: An Organic Anthology*, ed. Stephen E. Whicher (Boston: Houghton Mifflin, 1957), 352, 338.

other half-dozen or so newspapers, and "The Open Boat," published in June 1897 in *Scribner's Magazine*.

Probably because it is based on Crane's own experience, readers of "The Open Boat" generally minimize the richness of its figural quality. That the story has resonance beyond the experience depicted is readily acknowledged for the most part, but that that meaning bodies forth in a *type* for the human being in extremis goes unattended. When readers move back from the close focus on details of rowing and bailing away from the bone-weariness of those who battle an endless series of waves so that they can take a more panoramic view of the entrapped boat, they begin to see that that detailed representation of life is actually the sketching in of the typological image of a human being sheltered from natural forces by the "egg-shell" of a lifeboat.

Crane makes convincingly real to us just how precarious and tentative man's hold upon life actually is. What wastes away in the course of events is the unexamining man's sense of his own self-assurance, comfort, and safety. Quoting Schopenhauer, Nietzsche confirms the ordinary human situation: "Even as on an immense, raging sea, assailed by huge wave crests, a man sits in a little rowboat trusting his frail craft, so, amidst the furious torments of this world, the individual sits tranquilly, supported by the *principium individuationis* and relying on it."[25]

The concept of *principium individuationis* helps us to understand how human beings so order their portion of experience that they can believe they control it. The logical categories that the human being ordinarily lives by—a linear sense of time, meaningful sequences of cause and effect, the measurement of possibilities and probabilities—these, and others, enable him to keep on an even keel for most of his waking hours. Seldom does he acknowledge the fragility of these distinctions and categories. Useful as they usually are, these props are the first things to fail him in his crises. "Shipwrecks," decides Crane's narrator, "are *apropos* of nothing." "The ship goes down" and it is like "when, willy-nilly, the firm fails, the army loses."[26] In a shipwreck little survives of what a person formerly believed he could accomplish under those circumstances. Reason thwarted and expectations repeatedly frustrated, he soon discovers that his efforts go, not merely unrewarded, but, it sometimes seems, actually punished. What such survivors have learned to expect of experience can largely be discounted. Human activity, reduced to rowing and bailing, turns out to be Sisyphean:

25. Arthur Schopenhauer, *The World as Will and Idea*; quoted by Friedrich Nietzsche, *The Birth of Tragedy*, in *The Birth of Tragedy and The Genealogy of Morals*, trans. Francis Golffing (Garden City: Doubleday, 1956), 22.

26. Stephen Crane, "The Open Boat," in *Tales of Adventure*, Volume V of *The University of Virginia Edition of the Works of Stephen Crane*, ed. Fredson Bowers, intr. J. C. Levenson (Charlottesville: University Press of Virginia, 1970), 68–92.

A singular disadvantage of the sea lies in the fact that after successfully surmounting one wave you discover that there is another behind it just as important and just as nervously anxious to do something effective in the way of swamping boats. In a ten-foot dinghy one can get an idea of the resources of the sea in the line of waves that is not probable to the average experience, which is never at sea in a dinghy. As each slaty wall of water approached, it shut all else from the view of the men in the boat, and it was not difficult to imagine that this particular wave was the final outburst of the ocean, the last effort of the grim water. There was a terrible grace in the move of the waves, and they came in silence, save for the snarling of the crests.[27]

Each wave appears to be "the final outburst of the ocean," but the brutal fact that they learn and relearn is that the store of such apocalyptic waves is endless.

At every point knowledge hinders perception. The cook and the correspondent argue about ways of differentiating between a lifesaving station and a house of refuge, but the reality, though they do not then know it, is that in the vicinity neither exists, just as there is no lighthouse within miles when the men convince themselves that they have seen one. The men, experiencing the effect that the breaking day has on the waves that come toward them, know not the "color of the sky" but only the "colors of the sea," while the "process of the breaking day was unknown to them." Indeed, their knowing the *process* would have been a way of reaffirming the idea that, in some measure at least, the *principium individuationis* is related to human efficacy, but even that consolation is withheld from them. Their moment of elation is quickly punctured.

Having "seen" a house of refuge, "the four waifs rode impudently in their little boat, and with an assurance of an impending rescue shining in their eyes,

27. Here Crane draws ironically on verses from the hymn "God's wonders on the deep," included under the rubric "Mariners" in *Hymns for the Use of the Methodist Episcopal Church*, rev. ed. (New York: Carlton & Lanahan, 1871), 623.

> Up to heaven their bark is whirl'd,
> On the mountain of the wave;
> Down as suddenly 'tis hurl'd
> To the abysses of the grave.
>
> Then unto the Lord they cry;
> He inclines a gracious ear,
> Sends deliv'rance from on high,
> Rescues them from all their fear.
>
> O that men would praise the Lord,
> For his goodness to their race;
> For the wonders of his word,
> And the riches of his grace.

puffed at the big cigars and judged well and ill of all men. Everybody took a drink of water." But their sense of well-being arises from a collective misreading of reality, and when they realize that this is so, Crane writes: "They then briefly exchanged some addresses and admonitions," just in case, the captain cautions, they "don't all get ashore." "As for the reflections of the men, there was a great deal of rage in them"—

> "If I am going to be drowned—if I am going to be drowned—if I am going to be drowned, why, in the name of the seven mad gods who rule the sea, was I allowed to come thus far and contemplate sand and trees? Was I brought here merely to have my nose dragged away as I was about to nibble the sacred cheese of life? It is preposterous. If this old ninny-woman, Fate, cannot do better than this, she should be deprived of the management of men's fortunes. She is an old hen who knows not her intention. If she has decided to drown me, why did she not do it in the beginning and save me all this trouble? The whole affair is absurd. . . . But no, she cannot mean to drown me. She dare not drown me. She cannot drown me. Not after all this work." Afterward the man might have had an impulse to shake his fist at the clouds. "Just you drown me, now, and then hear what I call you!"

Ordinarily man views Fate, destructive though it might be, as a sober thing. Fate that tantalizes and taunts, however, is rather nasty. It wears on the collective sense of that propriety with which it should guide the cosmos in its conduct of human affairs.

Knowing only the caprices of Fate, the captain decides ruefully that the men must brave the surf individually before they become too weak "to do anything" for themselves. One assumption underlying his order is, of course, that human physical strength has some relation to survival of the individual, that logically the chances for survival are greatest for those who are strong and skillful. The strongest and most skillful of the four occupants of the boat, "a wily surfman," is the oiler. Just as he is the source of the few useful suggestions for survival in the ten-foot dinghy, so too is he the one who is physically best prepared to battle the unpredictable surf. Shortly after having tumbled out of the boat into the sea, the correspondent notices without surprise that "the oiler was ahead in the race. He was swimming strongly and rapidly." But it is exactly when each of the four swimmers has struck out for himself that the last shred of the correspondent's understanding of his experience disappears. He is sucked up in the "grip" of a "strange new enemy—a current," and recognizing that he is helpless in the matter of his own survival, he gives himself up to his fate. Yet death is not to be his portion—not this time, anyway. "Later a wave perhaps whirled him out of this small deadly current, for he found suddenly that he could again make progress toward the shore." The waves, which had brought "the babes of the sea" so much sustained fear, now inexplicably become agents of salvation. But the boat, which was the means of their surviving the sinking of the ship, now is a thing of danger. "An overturned boat in the surf is not a plaything to a swimming man," the narrator warns us. When the correspondent unwillingly moves perilously close to the bouncing dinghy, however, it is a wave that flings him "with ease and supreme speed completely over the boat and far beyond it." Weak and weary beyond measure, the correspondent has his life given back to him twice.

Yet the waves that spare the correspondent take their ransom in the person of the strong swimmer who was well "ahead in the race." That the oiler dies while the others survive is as inexplicable as the passage in Ecclesiastes which his death recalls.[28] To the survivors the only reality is that four of them have nibbled at the "sacred cheese of life," but the "old hen" who is Fate has turned on one of them. Crane's tale startles us into recognizing the high degree of optimism built into those Darwinian ideals of natural selection and the survival of the fittest.

Stripping his account down to the twenty-hour aftermath of shipwreck,

---

28. Phyllis Frus argues that "The Open Boat" must be read continuously with the news story Crane filed immediately after the sinking of the *Commodore* and that he refers to his *donnée* for the short story only in the sentence, "The history of life in an open boat for thirty hours would no doubt be very instructive for the young, but none is to be told here now." Otherwise, she insists, the oiler's death and the ending of Crane's story remain "merely mysterious":

> Unless the reader considers the events told of in "Stephen Crane's Own Story," she cannot understand the reference in the sixth paragraph of "The Open Boat" to the "scene in the grays of dawn of seven turned faces" that has impressed itself on the captain's face. This is the only reference in "The Open Boat" to the seven men aboard the *Commodore* or on one of the two makeshift rafts when it sank, whom the four have abandoned. Readers who treat the two narratives as continuous and on the same historical level can explain why the men feel they can be interpreters: they may understand the oiler's death to be the appropriate sacrifice of their best in order to propitiate a vengeful Nature or God, and thus begin to alleviate their guilt at having survived. Thus what the men will "interpret" to others is the appropriateness of the ending, the meaning that is provided by the oiler's death" ("Writing After the Fact: Crane, Journalism, and Fiction," in *The Politics and Poetics of Journalistic Narrative: The Timely and The Timeless* [Cambridge, Eng.: Cambridge University Press, 1994], 37–38).

It might reasonably be supposed that Crane could have expected the attentive reader to notice immediately that he was referring to those who remained on the ship as it sank without counting on the likelihood that readers of the story in *Scribner's Magazine* in June 1897 would recall what he had reported in the newspaper as far back as January. Moreover, judging from the vantage of the whole of Crane's work, it seems unlikely that Crane would have seen the death of the oiler as the sacrifice exacted from four men suffering collectively from guilt. Such "sacrifices" to "propitiate a vengeful God or Nature"—if they might be called sacrifices—would inspire only irony in Crane. If nothing else, for example, an attentive reading of *Black Riders*, especially those many lines directed against the gods of vengeance should be enough to put Frus's "reflexive" reading in serious doubt.

Crane tells us almost nothing of the past lives of the men in the boat. Apart from the "subtle brotherhood of men that was here established on the seas" and the fact that for the correspondent, who "knew even at the time [this comradeship] was the best experience of his life," we simply do not know how this experience relates to the past. For Crane himself, however, we can speculate on the matter with some assurance. In this experience Crane found new cause for his rigorous and somewhat systematic repudiation of an unquestioning faith in a protective Christ. To see this in a story whose only apparent references to religion come in a repeated complaint addressed to the "seven mad gods who rule the sea" and in threats leveled at a "temple" that does not exist, may be, at least at first, somewhat surprising. But Crane's practice in "The Open Boat" exemplifies Ernest Hemingway's discovery that in writing fiction "you could omit anything if you knew that you omitted and the omitted part would strengthen the story and make people feel something more than they understood."[29] What Crane omitted from this story, I would suggest, was his explicit answer to a Christian's interpretation of the meaning of what, he would agree, was a most emblematic experience: that in adversity Christ is the believer's certain protector. Crane's details in "The Open Boat" were drawn from actual experience, of course, but they are details resonant with meaning, especially when they are viewed against the background of nineteenth-century evangelical Christianity.

In working out the emblematic nature of "The Open Boat," it is instructive to take into account the fact that in the nineteenth century there was a way, a late manifestation of a centuries-old tradition, of seeing the allegorical import of "The Life-Boat."[30] Compiled by the Reverend William Holmes in collaboration with John W. Barber, *Religious Allegories: Being a Series of Emblematic Engravings* (1854) presented the reader with emblems and allegories "Designed to Illustrate Divine Truth, in Accordance with the Cardinal Principles of Christianity."[31] The full import of the emblem of the lifeboat is given succinctly: "O what is this but a picture of the goodness of our God in Christ, in establishing his Church on the earth. The tempestuous sea is this world, the wreck is man; the life-boat is the Church, and the multitudes on shore may represent the heavenly host who look with interest into the affairs of man's redemption."[32] Testing it at every turn, Crane's story literalizes this emblematic figure, even in particulars. Although there is nothing explicitly Christian about him, the naked man who rushes into the surf (representing "the multitudes on shore," who "may represent the heavenly host") is described: "He was naked, naked as a

---

29. Ernest Hemingway, *A Moveable Feast* (New York: Scribners, 1964), 75.
30. Holmes and Barber, "The Life-Boat," 46–51.
31. Holmes and Barber, *Religious Allegories,* title page.
32. Holmes and Barber, "The Life-Boat," 48.

tree in winter, but a halo was about his head, and he shone like a saint." The overall result is a demythologizing of those "Cardinal Principles of Christianity."

There is no documentary evidence that Crane knew Holmes and Barber's *Religious Allegories*. But he could have found the same figure, the "Life-Boat," in the evangelical hymns popular in his day or in the temperance readers, where the Life Boat would emanate from the Ship of Temperance. The Sunday school hymnals used during Crane's childhood constitute a rich source for several poems and stories. Hymnals were generously salted with celebrations of Christianity's protective power, a buoyant message that Crane rejected time and again. *George's Mother*, for example, can be read, as we have seen, as a reply to the sentiments of Isaac Watts's hymn "Holy Fortitude," the primary message of which is that life's trials enable the Christian to grow strong in faith.[33] A second example of a reply to a widely known hymn is Crane's castaway poem, "A man adrift on a slim spar." This poem has already been considered twice, but this time it may be looked at for its affinity with "The Open Boat." Its central stanza reads:

> The seas are in the hollow of The Hand;
> Oceans may be turned to a spray
> Raining down through the stars
> Because of a gesture of pity toward a babe.
> Oceans may become grey ashes.
> Die with a long moan and a roar
> Amid the tumult of the fishes
> And the cries of the ships.
> Because The Hand beckons the mice.[34]

The conceit in the line "the seas are in the hollow of The Hand," though ultimately deriving from Isaiah (40:12), would have been just as familiar to Crane from lines in the Wesleyan hymn included especially for "Mariners" in the Methodist hymnals. "Embarking" starts out: "Lord, whom winds and seas obey, / Guide us through the watery way; / In the hollow of thy hand / Hide, and bring us safe to land."[35] But just as the poem recalls William Cowper's "The Cast-Away," so too is it that the poem offers a reply to hymns of deep affirmation like Cowper's own "Light Shining Out of Darkness":

33. "Holy Fortitude; or, The Christian Soldier," in *The Psalms, Hymns, and Spiritual Songs, of the Rev. Isaac Watts, D.D.*, ed. Samuel Worcester (Boston: Crocker and Brewster, 1838), 563.

34. Stephen Crane, "A man adrift on a slim spar," in *Poems and Literary Remains*, 83.

35. *Hymns*, 621. The phrase "In the hollow of His hand" occurs also in the hymn "Safe with Jesus in the ship" (622). See also "He holdeth the waters in His hand" (624).

God moves in a mysterious way
  His wonders to perform;
He plants his footsteps in the sea,
  And rides upon the storm . . .
Blind unbelief is sure to err,
  And scan his work in vain:
God is his own interpreter,
  And he will make it plain.[36]

That "God is his own interpreter" recalls, of course, the final sentence of "The Open Boat," which tells us that the survivors, having survived, "felt that they could then be interpreters." And both Cowper's poem and Crane's story, different as they are in sentiment, can be seen as responses to Elihu's words to Job (33:23–24): "If there be a messenger with him, an interpreter, one among a thousand, to show unto man his uprightness: Then he is gracious unto him, and saith, Deliver him from going down to the pit; I have found a ransom."

Nineteenth-century Protestant hymns regularly employed the familiar metaphor of Christianity as the lifeboat of salvation, and a surprisingly large number of those hymns were favorites of those who compiled evangelical hymnals. Favorites among the favored were hymns such as P. P. Bliss's two treatments of the metaphor, "Sailing into Port"[37] ("Sailor, though the darkness gathers, / Though the cold waves surge and moan, / Trust thy bark to God's great mercy, / Falter not, sail on, sail on") and "The Life-Boat," known best as "Pull for the Shore." For the moment let us defer consideration of the latter hymn.

Bliss himself, a great success on the evangelical circuit, compiled several exceedingly popular Sunday-school collections. If it were necessary to choose one of them as the one that the young Crane, child of late nineteenth-century Methodism, would most likely have encountered during his formative years, the prime candidate would have to be Bliss's *Sunshine for Sunday-Schools*, first published in 1873 and frequently reprinted. Beside Watts's "Holy Fortitude" and Bliss's own "Pull for the Shore," it contains E. E. Rexford's lyrics for "Your Father's at the Helm," the uplifting lines of which read:

In the night when storm and tempest
Howls about your little bark,
And no ray of light to guide you,
Glimmers faintly thro' the dark,

---

36. William Cowper, "Light Shining out of Darkness," in *Cowper: Verse and Letters*, ed. Brian Spiller (Cambridge, Mass.: Harvard University Press, 1968), 154.

37. P. P. Bliss, "Sailing into Port," in *Memoirs of Philip P. Bliss*, ed. D. W. Whittle, intr. D. L. Moody (New York, Chicago, and New Orleans: N.p., 1877), 119.

Then remember, tho' the billows
Threaten all to overwhelm,
That the beacon star is shining,
And your Father's at the helm.

. . . .

Never yet was vessel stranded
On the rocks and shifting sands,
If its course was wholly trusted
To the heavenly Pilot's hands;
He will guide you thro' the tempest
To his own delightful realm,
So be calm amid the danger,
For your Father's at the helm.[38]

Although it is no more than probable that Crane knew this hymn, there can be no doubt that he knew Bliss's "The Life-Boat," the hymn (referred to in Crane's story "A Little Pilgrim" as "Pull for the Shore," its alternate title) that Whilomville's children are made to sing in Sunday school.[39] Here is something of Bliss's text:

Light in the darkness, sailor, day is at hand!
See o'er the foaming billows fair Haven's land.
Drear was the voyage, sailor, now almost o'er;
Safe within the life-boat, sailor, pull for the shore.

Pull for the shore, sailor, pull for the shore!
Heed not the rolling waves, but bend to the oar;
Safe in the lifeboat, sailor, cling to self no more!
Leave the poor old stranded wreck and pull for the shore.

Trust in the life-boat, sailor, all else will fail
Stronger the surges dash and fiercer the gale,
Heed not the stormy winds, tho' loudly they roar;
Watch the "bright and morning star," and pull for the shore.[40]

Crane might have known that the ultimate source for Bliss's shipwreck-salvation metaphor was Paul's account of his three survivals of shipwreck, but Paul's

38. E. E. Rexford, "Your Father's at the Helm," in *Sunshine for Sunday-Schools*, collected by P. P. Bliss (Cincinnati: John Church/Chicago: George F. Root, 1873), 52–53.

39. Stephen Crane, "A Little Pilgrim," in *Tales of Whilomville*, Volume VII of *The University of Virginia Edition of the Works of Stephen Crane*, ed. Fredson Bowers, intr. J. C. Levenson (Charlottesville: University Press of Virginia, 1969), 235–39.

40. P. P. Bliss, "Pull for the Shore," in *Sunshine for Sunday-Schools*, 68–69.

evidence was to him as unconvincing as the assertions of Bliss's hymn. "I know what Saint Paul says," Crane is reputed to have said in another context, "but I disagree with Saint Paul."[41]

In "The Open Boat" Crane successfully fulfilled the dictum that he had found in Emerson and had (mis)quoted with approval: "There should be a long logic beneath the story, but it should be kept carefully out of sight."[42] He matched his personal experiences of shipwreck against the essentialist, allegorical teachings of nineteenth-century Protestantism as he knew them, and he found their optimism decidedly wrongheaded. While the hymns talk of Christianity as the lifeboat which in itself provides safety and salvation, Crane's story tells of a dinghy that at the last becomes as dangerous to human life as the sea itself. And while the temperance readers warned only of the dangers of embarking on the Intemperance Ship, Crane found that as far as nature was concerned there was no difference between that one and the Temperance Ship. The men in the dinghy drink only water. There's not a drop of alcohol in the whole story, though intemperance does rear its head when the men light up celebratory cigars to celebrate the rescue that they mistakenly think is imminent.

But the story of the vitalizing sources of "The Open Boat" does not end with the hymns and the Sunday-school parables and exemplary tales. There remains the probable influence of other texts, including the school readers. In this context, three texts—one poetic, one expository, and one visual—can be adduced.

In an early review of *The Open Boat and Other Stories*, the London *Academy* called Crane "an analytical chemist of the subconscious."[43] To give "a faint notion of the curious and convincing scrutiny to which, through some forty pages, the minds of the crew are subject" in the book's title story, the anonymous reviewer quotes two passages: the first is the "if I am going to be drowned—if I am going to be drowned" question that the correspondent poses to himself at various moments; the second is the correspondent's meditation on the "soldier of the Legion who lay dying in Algiers." It is the second instance that interests us here.

Having long since enlisted in his so-called beautiful war for realism, the

---

41. Quoted in John Berryman, *Stephen Crane* (New York: William Sloane, 1950), 21.

42. Letter, Stephen Crane to John Northern Hilliard, 1897?, *The Correspondence of Stephen Crane*, ed. Stanley Wertheim and Paul Sorrentino (New York: Columbia University Press, 1988), I, 323.

43. Anonymous, "Reviews" [*The Open Boat and Other Stories*], *Academy*, 53 (May 14, 1898), Supplement, 522. The *Academy*'s anonymous reviewer anticipates Bill Brown's overall assumption, if not the details of his project, in *The Material Unconscious: American Amusement, Stephen Crane, and the Economies of Play*. Brown's interest in Crane's story lies in the notion that "the play between agony and play, labor and leisure, pain and pleasure—this is what activates the other story that 'The Open Boat' has to tell" (Cambridge, Mass.: Harvard University Press, 1996, 119).

young author nevertheless had reached back, as he had for the *Red Badge*, to a schoolboy's memory of Caroline Norton's poem "Bingen." "A verse mysteriously entered the correspondent's head," writes Crane; "he had even forgotten that he had forgotten this verse, but it suddenly was in his mind":

> A soldier of the Legion lay dying in Algiers,
> There was lack of woman's nursing, there was dearth of woman's tears;
> But a comrade stood beside him, and he took that comrade's hand,
> And he said: "I never more shall see my own, my native land."

These, the opening lines of Caroline Norton's poem, with some twenty words silently omitted at the very middle of the verse, Crane drew upon to render the emotional state of his castaway narrator. It was the pathos of the soldier, dying far from his homeland, in the throes of defining his hopeless situation and his unavoidable fate, that came suitably to the writer's hand. Crane tells us that the correspondent "had been made acquainted" with the soldier dying in Algiers "in his childhood," even as Crane had probably discovered Caroline Norton's poem, its title expanded to "Bingen on the Rhine," in his grade-school readers.[44]

It is equally clear, however, that Crane's knowledge of Caroline Norton's poem went beyond the unadorned reprintings in grade-school texts, for his description of the dying soldier and the setting for his death elaborate on Norton's text. Crane expands: "The correspondent plainly saw the soldier. He lay on the sand with his feet out straight and still. While his pale left hand was upon his chest in an attempt to thwart the going of his life, the blood came between his fingers. In the far Algerian distance, a city of low square forms was set against a sky that was faint with the last sunset hues." There is nothing in the lines Crane quotes to validate the correspondent's view of the dying soldier, though the clause "the blood came between his fingers" expresses concretely what the poem, in a clause omitted by the correspondent, states more abstractly as "while his life-blood ebb'd away." It could be argued, of course, that in having the correspondent elaborate on the original lines of "Bingen," Crane was merely exercising a writer's legitimate license. It is more likely, however, that Crane was also familiar with a particular reprinting of Caroline Norton's poem, an edition in 1883 featuring illustrations by several artists—William T. Smedley, Frederic B. Schell, Alfred Fredericks, Granville Perkins, J. D. Woodward, and Edmund H. Garrett. Published in Philadelphia by Porter & Coates, this edition appeared more than three decades after the first publication of the

44. On my bookshelves I have copies of three such readers—*National Fifth Reader* (1870), *Lippincott's Fifth Reader* (1881), and *Swinton's Fifth Reader* (1883)—and in what must be a measure of the poem's popularity and usefulness, each of them prints "Bingen on the Rhine."

poem and six years after the poet's death.[45] Crane's paragraph of "elaboration," it seems likely, draws directly on illustrations by Smedley keyed to the lines "a Soldier of the Legion lay dying in Algiers" and "His voice grew fainter and hoarser." Since the soldier does not hold his hand over his heart, as Crane has it, it is unlikely that Crane had Smedley's illustration before him as he wrote—though it is possible, one should note, that the "light" patch just below the soldier's throat might well have been remembered by Crane as the soldier's "pale left hand." But the soldier's feet, both in story and illustration (if not in the poem), are "out straight and still." And the soldier's death in both story and illustration (though not in the poem) plays itself out against "the far Algerian distance, a city of low square forms. . . . set against a sky that was faint with the last sunset hues." It should surprise no one that we have here still another instance of Crane's translation of visual experience into the stuff of fiction.

The major lines of Crane's imagination were set by his familial concerns with matters of religion and warfare, particularly as that imagination shaped his early work. Indeed, when Crane saw the events within and without the "open boat" as ironically bringing to question the tenets of Christian consolation, he did so in the broadest context, playing off the configuration of events against the trope of the Pilot-God and his Ship-World. Parables of man (a pilgrim) sailing in a lifeboat (belief in Christianity) on the rough seas (life in the world), dating from the Middle Ages, were abundant in Crane's time in religious tracts and emblem books. Such parables also appeared in textbooks used in the public schools. These latter, however, were demythologized. There were no Christian referents in stories of shipwreck in the grade-school readers issued by Lippincott or Swinton. Typical of these is the following excerpt, the concluding paragraphs of an account entitled "A Ship in a Storm," taken from a standard grade-school reader:

On the dangerous points along our sea-coast are light-houses, which can be seen far out at sea, and serve as guides to ships. Sometimes the fog is so dense that these lights can not be seen, but most light-houses have great fog-bells or fog-horns; some of the latter are made to sound by steam, and can be heard for a long distance. These bells and horns are kept sounding as long as the fog lasts.

There are also many life-saving stations along the coast where trained men are ready with life-boats. When a ship is driven ashore they at once go to the rescue of those on board, and thus many valuable lives are saved.[46]

45. Caroline E. S. Norton, *Bingen on the Rhine* (Philadelphia: Porter & Coates, 1883).

46. Anonymous, "A Ship in a Storm," in *McGuffey's Fourth Eclectic Reader*, rev. ed. (Cincinnati and New York: Van Antwerp, Bragg, 1879), 57–58.

This account stresses not loss of life but the saving of it. The efficacy of strategically placed lighthouses and lifesaving stations is indicated, the implication being that man is capable of mitigating and diminishing the dangers posed for him by a destructive sea. Many valuable lives are otherwise saved because of man's foresight in creating and skillfully deploying lifesaving stations. This is the lesson of this grade-school account, and it is a lesson remembered (and subsequently tested) by the correspondent and his companions—babes of the sea—in the open boat.

"There's a house of refuge just north of the Mosquito Inlet Light, and as soon as they see us, they'll come off in their boat and pick us up."

"As soon as who see us?" said the correspondent.

"The crew," said the cook.

"Houses of refuge don't have crews," said the correspondent. "As I understand them, they are only places where clothes and grub are stored for the benefit of shipwrecked people. They don't carry crews."

"Oh, yes, they do," said the cook.

"No, they don't," said the correspondent.

"Well, we're not there yet, anyhow," said the oiler, in the stern.

"Well," said the cook, "perhaps it's not a house of refuge that I'm thinking of as being near Mosquito Inlet Light. Perhaps it's a life-saving station."

"We're not there yet," said the oiler, in the stern.

Nor would they ever get to it if they were thinking of a lifesaving station, for there was not a one on the coast of Florida. (And if they returned their thoughts to houses of refuge, there was none within twenty to thirty miles in either direction, north or south.) Since there were no lifesaving stations on the entire Florida coast, what prompted the cook and the correspondent to think that they might be close to one? And on what basis would the cook later say, "We must be about opposite New Smyrna. . . . Captain, by the way, I believe they abandoned that life-saving station there about a year ago." To which assertion the captain answers only, "Did they?"

It is possible, of course, that the author of "The Open Boat" did not know, just as the cook did not and just as, possibly, the oiler and the captain did not, that there were no lifesaving stations off the coast of Florida. It is further possible that the notion that there would be such stations, even to the extent of the cook's "remembering" the existence of one at New Smyrna, did not derive from personal experience but was the legacy of an elementary school textbook. It is no wonder that they argue over the very existence and the probable location of those stations whose crews will save them, elation and despair following one another as they become sure and less than sure about the accuracy of their senses and the soundness of their information. Ultimately, of course, they will have to jettison their hopes for rescue by those who man such stations because there are no such stations anywhere near them. They will brave the unpredictable waves and the surf as each man is forced to strike out for himself.

A concluding point. The grade-school account had begun with the observation that the sea can have two opposing appearances: it can be blue and calm, the setting for joyous peace; and it can be turbulently destructive to human life. Something like this notion had impressed Crane. In a poem collected in *War Is Kind* (1899), he wrote,

> To the maiden
> The sea was blue meadow
> Alive with little froth-people
> Singing.
>
> To the sailor, wrecked,
> The sea was dead grey walls
> Superlative in vacancy
> Upon which nevertheless at fateful time,
> Was written
> The grim hatred of nature.[47]

In "The Open Boat" Crane wrote wryly of landlubbers, certain of the nature of sport in a boat, who waved gaily at men in a dinghy, recognizing falsely their playful holiday at sea.

"Shipwrecks are *apropos* of nothing," Crane had written. That was not really true. What was *apropos* of Crane's experience was his astonished recognition, like Nietzsche's, that while an immense sea has the potential to assail humanity at every instant, the illusory nature of ordinary existence—the detail of everyday life—seduces us away, with disarming and depressing ease, from confronting that piece of bone-chilling knowledge.

Crane's father, ever the teacher, put it differently. To him the enemy was always intemperance. In language that anticipates his son's more poetic language in "The Open Boat," he concludes his book *Arts of Intoxication*:

We are like the dwellers in a lofty mansion built on some dangerous coast where frequent wrecks occur. Darkness and storm may be without, but we are safe, and full of peace and comfort within. A ship crowded with passengers is going to pieces among the rocks and we know it. We see the red flash of alarm-guns, and hear the booming signal that death is at

47. Stephen Crane, ["To the maiden"], in *Poems and Literary Remains*, 47.

work and help is needed. But we are safe. We look around at the circle of loved ones; we glance at the cheerful fire, the table, the books, the pictured walls. Yes, we are safe. Faintly amid the roar of the winds and the sea we hear imploring voices, but we are safe. We sing our evening song of praise, we say our evening prayer. We retire to our beds and fall asleep to the sound of storm and surf, and imploring voices still more faintly heard, while all through the night, one after another, men, women, and little innocent children are dropping, dropping from the icy wreck, and the busy waves are piling the dead along the shore under our very windows.[48]

After January 1, 1897, Crane could testify that even to the "interpreter" who survived shipwreck, a shipwreck was apropos of nothing.

48. Crane, *Arts of Intoxication*, 263–64.

12

Last Words

Stephen Crane's parents were, each in his own way, teachers of morality. While his father combined pastoral work with religious and theological instruction, his mother more single-mindedly devoted herself to social reform. Each of them promoted the temperance cause. It was in that pragmatically righteous environment that their children, especially Stephen, were raised and educated.

When Stephen was not yet seven, his father spoke at a children's day festival held at the Methodist church. The Reverend Jonathan Townley Crane, whose remarks were reported in the *Port Jervis Evening Gazette* for June 11, 1878, acknowledged "the great difficulties through which the young mind passes before it is properly moulded and prepared to meet the world in its many phases of sin and folly."[1] Part of that molding and preparation in Stephen's case turned out to be the instruction, training, and indoctrination on the personal and social evils unleashed by intemperance. It was effective, though not, perhaps, in the specific ways intended by his militant parents. If his parents' proscriptions against alcohol and tobacco did not ultimately keep Stephen from drinking and smoking, a sense that intemperance had a deleterious effect on individual character and on society itself remained with him to the end. This notion appears frequently, if intermittently, in his journalism, poetry, and fiction. Even more deeply ingrained in his imagination was the grand, apocalyptic style—words, images, metaphors, symbols—employed by temperance workers to describe the pitfalls and dire consequences of intemperance and the Satanic spasmodics of the drunkard afflicted with delirium tremens. The numerous collections of temperance readings and recitation pieces issued by the National Temperance Society and Publication House provided Crane with an archive of situations and language that he would draw on directly and obliquely throughout his career, often enabling him to write effectively about matters and situations that he had not experienced directly. But if "one of the gifts of literature is that the imaginings of one writer become the personal memories of others,"[2] it can be

---

1. Quoted in Linda H. Davis, *Badge of Courage: The Life of Stephen Crane* (Boston and New York: Houghton Mifflin, 1998), 13.
2. Jorge Luis Borges, "North American Literature," in *Twenty-Four Conversations with Borges: Including a Selection of Poems*, interviews conducted by Roberto Alifano (Housatonic, Mass.: Lascaux, 1984), 58.

said as well that those memories are also experiences that can be worked into other works of literature.

In *Stephen Crane's Blue Badge of Courage* I have identified some of the memories and experiences that went into specific pieces of Crane's writing. Our fuller knowledge of those things deepens our understanding of the meaning and purpose of Crane's work as well as our proper appreciation for the achievement of this noble rider of the imagination.

Bibliography

Adams, Henry. *The Letters of Henry Adams, Volume II: 1868–1885.* Ed. J. C. Levenson, Ernest Samuels, Charles Vandersee, and Viola Hopkins Winner. Cambridge, Mass., and London: Harvard University Press, 1982.

Anonymous. "Among the Books: Recent Publications" [*The Blue Badge of Courage*]. *Watchman*, 84 (Nov. 20, 1902), 15.

Anonymous. "Another Crane Sensation" ["The Monster"]. *Newburyport* (Mass.) *News* (July 28, 1898), 6.

Anonymous. "Book Notes" [*The Red Badge of Courage*]. *Peterson Magazine*, n.s. 6 (June 1896), 654.

Anonymous. *A Brief History of the Woman's Christian Temperance Union.* 2nd ed. Evanston: Union Signal, 1907.

Anonymous. "The Charge of the Blue Brigade." In *Readings and Recitations, No. 2.* Ed. L[izzie] Penney. New York: National Temperance Society and Publication House, 1878. 27–28.

Anonymous. "The Cold-Water Army." In *The National Temperance Orator.* Ed. L[izzie] Penney. New York: National Temperance Society and Publication House, 1879. 136–38.

Anonymous. "The Cup-Bearer." In *The Juvenile Temperance Reciter.* New York: National Temperance Society and Publication House, 1880. 53–55.

Anonymous. "Danger Signals." In *World Book of Temperance* (Abridged ed.). Compiled by Dr. and Mrs. Wilbur F. Crafts. Washington, D.C.: International Reform Bureau, 1908. 109–11.

Anonymous. "Determination Essential to Success." In *Readings and Recitations, No. 1.* Ed. L[izzie] Penney. New York: National Temperance Society and Publication House, 1877. 55–56.

Anonymous. "Drugging the Guards." In *World Book of Temperance.* 3rd enlarged and rev. ed. Compiled by Dr. and Mrs. Wilbur J. Crafts. Washington, D.C.: International Reform Bureau, 1911. 125–28.

Anonymous. "Ex-'94." Undated, unsourced clipping. University Archives, Syracuse University Library, Syracuse, New York.

Anonymous. "Fiction" [*The Open Boat and Other Tales of Adventure*]. *New York Tribune Illustrated Supplement* (Apr. 24, 1898), 17.

Anonymous. "The First Drop. The Last Drop." In *World Book of Temperance* (Abridged ed.). Compiled by Dr. and Mrs. Wilbur F. Crafts. Washington, D.C.: International Reform Bureau, 1908. 49.

Anonymous. [*George's Mother*]. *Illustrated London News*, 109 (Oct. 3, 1896), 439.

Anonymous. "God's wonders on the deep." In *Hymns for the Use of the Methodist Episcopal Church.* Rev. ed. New York: Carlton & Lanahan, 1871. 623.

Anonymous. Headnote to "The Snow-Storm." In *Swinton's Fifth Reader and Speaker.* New York and Chicago: Ivison, Blakeman, 1883. 137.

Anonymous. "I Have Drank My Last Glass." In *Temperance Battle Songs!* Compiled by S. W. Straub. Chicago: S. W. Straub, 1883. 50–51.

Anonymous. "The Laureateship." *Critic* (New York), 21 (Nov. 5, 1892), 255–56.

Anonymous. "Literary Notes." *New York Tribune* (July 19, 1891), 14.

Anonymous. "The Literary Week" [*The Monster and Other Stories*]. *Academy,* 60 (Mar. 2, 1901), 177.

Anonymous. "Literature: Notes on New Novels" [*The Open Boat and Other Stories*]. *Illustrated London News,* 112 (May 7, 1898), 662.

Anonymous. "The Logic of Smoking." In *Readings and Recitations, No. 5.* Ed. L[izzie] Penney. New York: National Temperance Society and Book Publications, 1884. 73–74.

Anonymous. "Mr. Stephen Crane." *Publishers' Circular,* 72 (June 9, 1900), 629.

Anonymous. "Modern Fraternities Closed to Liquor Dealers." In *World Book of Temperance* (Abridged ed.). Compiled by Dr. and Mrs. Wilbur F. Crafts. Washington, D.C.: International Reform Bureau, 1908. 38.

Anonymous. [*The Monster and Other Stories*]. *Academy,* 60 (Mar. 16, 1901), 230.

Anonymous. "Oh, Let Me In." In *Temperance Battle Songs.* Compiled by S. W. Straub. Chicago: S. W. Straub, 1883. 56–58.

Anonymous. [*The Open Boat and Other Tales of Adventure*]. *Advance* (Chicago), 35 (June 2, 1898), 742.

Anonymous. [*The Open Boat and Other Tales of Adventure*]. *Independent,* 50 (June 2, 1898), 727.

Anonymous. [*The Open Boat and Other Tales of Adventure*]. *New York Tribune Illustrated Supplement* (Apr. 24, 1898), 17.

Anonymous. [*The Open Boat and Other Stories*]. *Sunday Special* (Apr. 24, 1898), 6.

Anonymous. [*The Open Boat and Other Stories*]. *Isle of Wight* (July 20, 1898). Clipping, Stephen Crane Collection, Columbia University, New York, New York.

Anonymous. "Pier of the suicides / Three Hundred Have Sought to Use It as the Stepping-Off Place to Oblivion / at the Foot of Misery Street / or rather Cherry, Which Is Synonymous—A Man with Broken Legs Who Had a Passion for Life-saving and Who Has Prevented Many from Suicide at This Pier." *New York Recorder* (Nov. 11, 1894), 14.

Anonymous. "Recent Fiction" [*The Red Badge of Courage*]. *Sunday-School Times,* 38 (June 6, 1896), 367–68.

Anonymous. "Reviews" [*The Open Boat and Other Stories*]. *Academy,* 53 (May 14, 1898), Supplement, 522.

Anonymous. "The Saloon." In *Readings and Recitations, No. 1.* Ed. L[izzie] Penney. New York: National Temperance Society and Publication House, 1877. 49–50.

Anonymous. "A Ship in a Storm." In *McGuffey's Fourth Eclectic Reader.* Rev. ed. Cincinnati and New York: Van Antwerp, Bragg, 1879. 55–58.

Anonymous. *The Snake.* Chicago: O. J. McClure, *ca.* 1932.

Anonymous. [Swinburne and the Laureateship]. *Critic* (New York), 21 (Oct. 15, 1892), 213.

Anonymous. "Who Will Be Poet Laureate?" *Atlantic Monthly,* 70 (Dec. 1892), 855–56.

Anonymous. "The World of Story: The Champion of Rum Alley [*Maggie: A Girl of the Streets,* Chapter I]." In *The World Around Us: Fishing Classics Illustrated Publication, No. 34* (June 1961). New York: Gilbertton World-Wide Publications, 1961. 49–53.

Bibliography

Arthur, T. S. *Grappling with the Monster; or, The Curse and the Cure of Strong Drink*. New York: John W. Lovell, *ca.* 1877.

Bacheller, Irving. MS letter to Peggy Manley (Dec. 13? 1944). Baker Library, Dartmouth College, Hanover, New Hampshire.

Bacon, Alice. "Only a Dog." In *Swinton's Fifth Reader and Speaker*. New York and Chicago: Ivison, Blakeman, 1883. 79–87.

Baldwin, Dean R. *H. E. Bates: A Literary Life*. Selinsgrove, Pa.: Susquehanna University Press, 1987.

Bates, H. E. *The Modern Short Story: A Critical Survey*. London: Thomas Nelson, 1941.

Beer, Thomas. *Stephen Crane: A Study in American Letters*. Intr. Joseph Conrad. New York: Knopf, 1923.

Bell, Michael Davitt. *The Problem of American Realism: Studies in the Cultural History of a Literary Idea*. Chicago and London: University of Chicago Press, 1993.

Benfey, Christopher. "Badges of Courage and Cowardice: A Source for Crane's Title." *Stephen Crane Studies*, 6 (Fall 1997), 2–5.

———. *The Double Life of Stephen Crane*. New York: Knopf, 1992.

Berryman, John. *Stephen Crane*. New York: William Sloane, 1950.

Bishop, Elizabeth. *Conversations with Elizabeth Bishop*. Ed. George Monteiro. Jackson: University Press of Mississippi, 1996.

Blair, John. "The Posture of a Bohemian in the Poetry of Stephen Crane." *American Literature*, 61 (May 1989), 215–29.

Bliss, P. P. "Pull for the Shore." In *Sunshine for Sunday-Schools*. Collected by P. P. Bliss. Cincinnati: John Church/Chicago: George F. Root, 1873. 68–69.

———. "Sailing into Port." In *Memoirs of Philip P. Bliss*. Ed. D. W. Whittle. Intr. D. L. Moody. New York, Chicago, and New Orleans: N.p., 1877. 119–20.

Boole, Rev. W. H. "Run Up the Flag—Nail It to the Staff!" In *Readings and Recitations, No. 2*. Ed. Miss L[izzie] Penney. New York: National Temperance Society and Publication House, 1878. 65–66.

Bordin, Ruth. *Woman and Temperance: The Quest for Power and Liberty, 1873–1900*. Philadelphia: Temple University Press, 1981.

Borges, Jorge Luis. "North American Literature." In *Twenty-Four Conversations with Borges: Including a Selection of Poems*. Interviews conducted by Roberto Alifano. Housatonic, Mass.: Lascaux, 1984. 55–59.

Brain, Belle M. *Weapons for Temperance Warfare*. Boston and Chicago: United Society of Christian Endeavor, 1897.

Brann, William Cowper. "The American Drummer: The Apostle of Civilization." In *Brann the Iconoclast: A Collection of the Writings of W. C. Brann*. New York: Brann, 1896. I, 146–55.

———. "Church and Stage." In *Brann the Iconoclast: A Collection of the Writings of W. C. Brann*. New York: Brann, 1896. II, 243–49.

Brooks, Sydney. "In the School of Battle: The Making of a Soldier." *Saturday Review* (London), 81 (Jan. 11, 1896), 44–45.

Brown, Bill. *The Material Unconscious: American Amusement, Stephen Crane, and the Economies of Play*. Cambridge, Mass.: Harvard University Press, 1996.

Brown, Norman O. *Life Against Death: The Psychoanalytical Meaning of History*. New York: Random House, 1960.

Bungay, George W. "The Battle of the Rain." In *Readings and Recitations, No. 3*. Ed. L[izzie]
Penney. New York: National Temperance Society and Publication House, 1879. 40–41.

Burke, Kenneth. *The Philosophy of Literary Form: Studies in Symbolic Action*. Rev. ed. New
York: Vintage, 1957.

Cary, Phebe. "The Landlord of 'The Blue Hen.' " In *Readings and Recitations, No. 2*. Ed.
L[izzie] Penney. New York: National Temperance Society and Publication House, 1878.
20–22.

Catlin, Geo. *Letters and Notes on the Manners, Customs, and Condition of the North American
Indians*. 2nd ed. New York: Wiley and Putnam, 1842.

Chellis, Mary Dwinell. "Polly's Temperance Speech." In *Readings and Recitations, No. 2*. Ed.
L[izzie] Penney. New York: National Temperance Society and Publication House, 1878.
12–14.

Chew, Samuel C. *Swinburne*. Boston: Little, Brown, 1929.

Cigada, Sergio. "Una questione di fonti: George Sand, Leconte de Lisle, Arthur Rimbaud."
Letterature moderne, 9 (July–Aug. 1959), 486–97.

Clendenning, John. "Thomas Beer's *Stephen Crane*: The Eye of His Imagination." *Prose
Studies*, 14 (May 1991), 68–80.

Coleman, Emmet G. "The Prodigal Girl." In *The Temperance Songbook: A Peerless Collection
of Temperance Songs and Hymns for the Women's Christian Temperance Union, Loyal Temperance Legion, Prohibitionists, Temperance Praise Meetings, Medal Contests, etc.* Ed. Emmet G.
Coleman. New York: American Heritage Press, 1971. 8–9.

Collins, Michael J. "Realism and Romance in the Western Stories of Stephen Crane." In
Under the Sun: Myth and Realism in Western American Literature. Ed. Barbara Howard Meldrum. Troy, N.Y.: Whitston, 1985. 139–48.

Colman, Julia. "One Way to Make Money." In *Readings and Recitations, No. 2*. Ed. L[izzie]
Penney. New York: National Temperance Society and Publication House, 1878. 87–88.

Colvert, James B. "*The Red Badge of Courage* and a Review of Zola's *La Débâcle*." *Modern
Language Notes*, 71 (Feb. 1956), 98–100.

———. *Stephen Crane*. San Diego: Harcourt Brace Jovanovich, 1984.

Conant, Rev. H. W. "Is There No Hope?" In *Readings and Recitations, No. 2*. Ed. L[izzie]
Penney. New York: National Temperance Society and Publication House, 1878. 39–40.

Connery, Thomas Bernard. "Fusing Fictional Technique and Journalistic Fact: Literary
Journalism in the 1890s Newspaper." Ph.D. diss., Brown University, 1984.

Conrad, Joseph. *The Collected Letters of Joseph Conrad, Volume I, 1861–1897*. Ed. Frederick
R. Karl and Laurence Davies. Cambridge, Eng.: Cambridge University Press, 1983.

———. Introduction. *Stephen Crane: A Study in American Letters* by Thomas Beer. New
York: Knopf, 1923. 1–33.

Cook, Rev. Joseph. "The Pirate Alcohol." In *Readings and Recitations, No. 3*. Ed. L[izzie]
Penney. New York: National Temperance Society and Publication House, 1879. 51–54.

Cowper, William. "Light Shining out of Darkness." In *Cowper: Verse and Letters*. Ed. Brian
Spiller. Cambridge, Mass.: Harvard University Press, 1968. 154.

Crane, Mrs. Helen. "Rev. Jonathan T. Crane, D.D." *Pennington Seminary Review*, 1 (June
1889), 1–5; reprinted in Thomas A. Gullason, ed. *Stephen Crane's Career: Perspectives and
Evaluations*. New York: New York University Press, 1972. 29–35.

———. "Change of Base." *Ocean Grove Record* (Mar. 15, 1884), 3; reprinted in Gullason,
Stephen Crane's Career, 36.

————. Letter to *New Jersey Tribune* (Feb. 16, 1887), 2; holograph copy in Schoberlin Research Files, Stephen Crane Collection, George Arents Research Library for Special Collections, Syracuse University Library, Syracuse, New York.

Crane, Rev. J. T. *Arts of Intoxication: The Aim, and the Results.* New York: Carlton & Lanahan/San Francisco: E. Thomas/Cincinnati: Hitchcock & Walden, 1870.

————. *Popular Amusements.* Cincinnati: Hitchcock and Walden/New York: Carlton and Lanahan, 1870.

Crane, Stephen. *Active Service.* In *The Third Violet and Active Service.* Volume III of *The University of Virginia Edition of the Works of Stephen Crane.* Ed. Fredson Bowers. Intr. J. C. Levenson. Charlottesville: University Press of Virginia, 1976. 111–328.

————. "The Art Students' League Building." In *Tales, Sketches, and Reports,* Volume VIII of *The University of Virginia Edition of the Works of Stephen Crane.* Ed. Fredson Bowers. Intr. Edwin H. Cady. Charlottesville: University Press of Virginia, 1973. 313–15.

————. "At Clancy's Wake." In *Tales, Sketches, and Reports,* Volume VIII of *The University of Virginia Edition of the Works of Stephen Crane.* Ed. Fredson Bowers. Intr. Edwin H. Cady. Charlottesville: University Press of Virginia, 1973. 38–42.

————. *The Black Riders and Other Lines.* Boston: Copeland and Day, 1895.

————. ["The Blood of the Martyr"]. In *Tales, Sketches, and Reports,* Volume VIII of *The University of Virginia Edition of the Works of Stephen Crane.* Ed. Fredson Bowers. Intr. Edwin H. Cady. Charlottesville: University Press of Virginia, 1973. 735–39.

————. "The Blue Badge of Cowardice." In *Reports of War: War Dispatches: Great Battles of the World,* Volume IX of *The University of Virginia Edition of the Works of Stephen Crane.* Ed. Fredson Bowers. Intr. James B. Colvert. Charlottesville: University Press of Virginia, 1971. 44–48.

————. ["The Blue Battalions"]. In *Poems and Literary Remains,* Volume X of *The University of Virginia Edition of the Works of Stephen Crane.* Ed. Fredson Bowers. Intr. James B. Colvert. Charlottesville: University Press of Virginia, 1975. 82.

————. "The Blue Battalions." In *Spanish-American War Songs: A Complete Collection of Newspaper Verse During the Recent War with Spain.* Compiled by Sidney A. Witherbee. Detroit: Sidney A. Witherbee, 1898. 182–83.

————. "The Blue Hotel." In *Tales of Adventure,* Volume V of *The University of Virginia Edition of the Works of Stephen Crane.* Ed. Fredson Bowers. Intr. J. C. Levenson. Charlottesville: University Press of Virginia, 1970. 142–70.

————. "Bottles and bottles and bottles." In *Poems and Literary Remains.* Volume X of *The University of Virginia Edition of the Works of Stephen Crane.* Ed. Fredson Bowers. Intr. James B. Colvert. Charlottesville: University Press of Virginia, 1975. 89.

————. "The Bride Comes to Yellow Sky." *McClure's Magazine,* 10 (Feb. 1898), 377–84; *Chapman's Magazine,* 9 (Feb. 1898), 115–26.

————. "The Bride Comes to Yellow Sky." In *Tales of Adventure,* Volume V of *The University of Virginia Edition of the Works of Stephen Crane.* Ed. Fredson Bowers. Intr. J. C. Levenson. Charlottesville: University Press of Virginia, 1970. 109–20.

————. ["The chatter of a death-demon from a tree-top"]. *Philistine,* 1 (Aug. 1895), 93.

————. *The Correspondence of Stephen Crane.* Ed. Stanley Wertheim and Paul Sorrentino. New York: Columbia University Press, 1988.

————. "Dan Emmonds." In *Poems and Literary Remains,* Volume X of *The University of*

Bibliography

Virginia Edition of the Works of Stephen Crane. Ed. Fredson Bowers. Intr. James B. Colvert. Charlottesville: University Press of Virginia, 1975. 112–17.

———. "An Experiment in Luxury." In *Tales, Sketches, and Reports*, Volume VIII of *The University of Virginia Edition of the Works of Stephen Crane*. Ed. Fredson Bowers. Intr. Edwin H. Cady. Charlottesville: University Press of Virginia, 1973. 293–301.

———. "An Experiment in Misery." In *Tales, Sketches, and Reports*, Volume VIII of *The University of Virginia Edition of the Works of Stephen Crane*. Ed. Fredson Bowers. Intr. Edwin H. Cady. Charlottesville: University Press of Virginia, 1973. 283–93.

———. "The Fire-Tribe and the Pale-Face: Play." In *Poems and Literary Remains*. Volume X of *The University of Virginia Edition of the Works of Stephen Crane*. Ed. Fredson Bowers. Intr. James B. Colvert. Charlottesville: University Press of Virginia, 1975. 160–64.

———. "The Five White Mice." In *Tales of Adventure*, Volume V of *The University of Virginia Edition of the Works of Stephen Crane*. Ed. Fredson Bowers. Intr. J. C. Levenson. Charlottesville: University Press of Virginia, 1970. 39–52.

———. *George's Mother*. In *Bowery Tales*, Volume I of *The University of Virginia Edition of the Works of Stephen Crane*. Ed. Fredson Bowers. Intr. James B. Colvert. Charlottesville: University Press of Virginia, 1969. 113–78.

———. "Greed Rampant." In *Tales, Sketches, and Reports*, Volume VIII of *The University of Virginia Edition of the Works of Stephen Crane*. Ed. Fredson Bowers. Intr. Edwin H. Cady. Charlottesville: University Press of Virginia, 1973. 7–10.

———. "The Height of the Season at Asbury Park." In *Tales, Sketches, and Reports*, Volume VIII of *The University of Virginia Edition of the Works of Stephen Crane*. Ed. Fredson Bowers. Intr. Edwin H. Cady. Charlottesville: University Press of Virginia, 1973. 562.

———. "I'd Rather Have—" (facsimile). *Syracuse University Library Associates Courier*, 21 (Spring 1986), 4.

———. " 'Intrigue.' " In *Poems and Literary Remains*. Volume X of *The University of Virginia Edition of the Works of Stephen Crane*. Ed. Fredson Bowers. Intr. James B. Colvert. Charlottesville: University Press of Virginia, 1975. 62–69.

———. "The Knife." In *Tales of Whilomville*, Volume VII of *The University of Virginia Edition of the Works of Stephen Crane*. Ed. Fredson Bowers. Intr. J. C. Levenson. Charlottesville: University Press of Virginia, 1969. 184–94.

———. "Lines." *Philistine*, 6 (Apr. 1898), back cover.

———. "A Little Pilgrim." In *Tales of Whilomville*, Volume VII of *The University of Virginia Edition of the Works of Stephen Crane*. Ed. Fredson Bowers. Intr. J. C. Levenson. Charlottesville: University Press of Virginia, 1969. 235–39.

———. *Maggie: A Girl of the Streets (A Story of New York)* (1893) (Norton Critical Edition). Ed. Thomas A. Gullason. New York: Norton, 1979. 1–58.

———. "Making an Orator." In *Tales of Whilomville*, Volume VII of *The University of Virginia Edition of the Works of Stephen Crane*. Ed. Fredson Bowers. Intr. J. C. Levenson. Charlottesville: University Press of Virginia, 1969. 158–63.

———. "A man adrift on a slim spar." In *Poems and Literary Remains*, Volume X of *The University of Virginia Edition of the Works of Stephen Crane*. Ed. Fredson Bowers. Intr. James B. Colvert. Charlottesville: University Press of Virginia, 1975. 83.

———. "Manacled." In *Tales, Sketches, and Reports*, Volume VIII of *The University of Virginia Edition of the Works of Stephen Crane*. Ed. Fredson Bowers. Intr. Edwin H. Cady. Charlottesville: University Press of Virginia, 1973. 159–62.

———. "The Men in the Storm." In *Tales, Sketches, and Reports*, Volume VIII of *The University of Virginia Edition of the Works of Stephen Crane*. Ed. Fredson Bowers. Intr. Edwin H. Cady. Charlottesville: University Press of Virginia, 1973. 315–22.

———. "The Monster." In *Tales of Whilomville*, Volume VII of *The University of Virginia Edition of the Works of Stephen Crane*, ed. Fredson Bowers. Intr. J. C. Levenson. Charlottesville: University Press of Virginia, 1969. 7–65.

———. "Moonlight on the Snow." In *Tales of Adventure*, Volume V of *The University of Virginia Edition of the Works of Stephen Crane*. Ed. Fredson Bowers. Intr. J. C. Levenson. Charlottesville: University Press of Virginia, 1970. 179–91.

———. "An Ominous Baby." *Arena*, 9 (May 1894), 819–21.

———. "On the desert." *Philistine*, 6 (May 1898), 166–67.

———. "The Open Boat." In *Tales of Adventure*, Volume V of *The University of Virginia Edition of the Works of Stephen Crane*. Ed. Fredson Bowers. Intr. J. C. Levenson. Charlottesville: University Press of Virginia, 1970. 68–92.

———. "Parades and Entertainments." In *Tales, Sketches, and Reports*, Volume VIII of *The University of Virginia Edition of the Works of Stephen Crane*. Ed. Fredson Bowers. Intr. Edwin H. Cady. Charlottesville: University Press of Virginia, 1973. 521–22.

———. ["Play Set in a French Tavern"]. In *Poems and Literary Remains*. Volume X of *The University of Virginia Edition of the Works of Stephen Crane*. Ed. Fredson Bowers. Intr. James B. Colvert. Charlottesville: University Press of Virginia, 1975. 129–38.

———. "A Prologue." In *Tales, Sketches, and Reports*, Volume VIII of *The University of Virginia Edition of the Works of Stephen Crane*. Ed. Fredson Bowers. Intr. Edwin H. Cady. Charlottesville: University Press of Virginia, 1973. 109.

———. *The Red Badge of Courage*, Volume II of *The University of Virginia Edition of the Works of Stephen Crane*. Ed. Fredson Bowers. Intr. J. C. Levenson. Charlottesville: University Press of Virginia, 1975. 1–135.

———. "The Snake." In *Tales, Sketches, and Reports*, Volume VIII of *The University of Virginia Edition of the Works of Stephen Crane*. Ed. Fredson Bowers. Intr. Edwin H. Cady. Charlottesville: University Press of Virginia, 1973. 65–68.

———. "Some Hints for Play-Makers." In *Tales, Sketches, and Reports*, Volume VIII of *The University of Virginia Edition of the Works of Stephen Crane*. Ed. Fredson Bowers. Intr. Edwin H. Cady. Charlottesville: University Press of Virginia, 1973. 42–47.

———. ["Spanish-American War Play"]. In *Poems and Literary Remains*, Volume X of *The University of Virginia Edition of the Works of Stephen Crane*. Ed. Fredson Bowers. Intr. James B. Colvert. Charlottesville: University Press of Virginia, 1975. 139–58.

———. *Stephen Crane: Letters*. Ed. R. W. Stallman and Lillian Gilkes. New York: New York University Press, 1960.

———. "Stephen Crane's Own Story." In *Reports of War*, Volume IX of *The University of Virginia Edition of the Works of Stephen Crane*. Ed. Fredson Bowers. Intr. James B. Colvert. Charlottesville: University Press of Virginia, 1971. 85–94.

———. ["To the maiden"]. In *Poems and Literary Remains*, Volume X of *The University of Virginia Edition of the Works of Stephen Crane*. Ed. Fredson Bowers. Intr. James B. Colvert. Charlottesville: University Press of Virginia, 1975. 47.

———. "Twelve O'Clock." In *Tales of Adventure*, Volume V of *The University of Virginia Edition of the Works of Stephen Crane*. Ed. Fredson Bowers. Intr. J. C. Levenson. Charlottesville: University Press of Virginia, 1970. 171–78.

Bibliography

————. *The University of Virginia Edition of the Works of Stephen Crane*. 10 vols. Ed. Fredson Bowers and others. Charlottesville: University Press of Virginia, 1969–76.

————. ["War Is Kind"]. In *Poems and Literary Remains*. Volume X of *The University of Virginia Edition of the Works of Stephen Crane*. Ed. Fredson Bowers. Intr. James B. Colvert. Charlottesville: University Press of Virginia, 1975. 45.

————. "When a people reach the top of a hill." *Philistine*, 7 (June 1898), 9–10.

————. "The Wise Men." In *Tales of Adventure*, Volume V of *The University of Virginia Edition of the Works of Stephen Crane*. Ed. Fredson Bowers. Intr. J. C. Levenson. Charlottesville: University Press of Virginia, 1970. 26–38.

Crowley, John W. *The White Logic: Alcoholism and Gender in American Modernist Fiction*. Amherst: University of Massachusetts Press, 1994.

Cunliffe, Marcus. "Stephen Crane and the American Background of *Maggie*." *American Quarterly*, 7 (Spring 1955), 35–44.

Cuyler, Rev. T. L. "Boys—and the Bottle." In *Readings and Recitations, No. 2*. Ed. L[izzie] Penney. New York: National Temperance Society and Publication House, 1878. 18–20.

Davis, Linda H. *Badge of Courage: The Life of Stephen Crane*. Boston and New York: Houghton Mifflin, 1998.

Delano, Rev. H. A. "The World on Fire!" In *The Temperance Platform, Orations on Abstinence and Prohibition Specially Adapted for Prize Contests, Public Meetings, Social Gatherings, Etc.* Ed. L[izzie] Penney. New York: National Temperance Society and Publication House, 1892. 88–90.

Dickason, David H. "Stephen Crane and the *Philistine*." *American Literature*, 15 (Nov. 1943), 279–87.

Dooley, Patrick K. *The Pluralistic Philosophy of Stephen Crane*. Urbana and Chicago: University of Illinois Press, 1993.

Dowson, Ernest Christopher. *The Poetical Works of Ernest Christopher Dowson*. Ed. Desmond Flower. London: Cassell and John Lane the Bodley Head, 1934.

"Droch" [Robert Bridges]. "Books for Summer Readers" [*The Open Boat and Other Tales of Adventure*]. *Life*, 31 (May 26, 1898), 446.

————. "Stephen Crane's 'The Monster.' " *Life*, 32 (Sept. 1, 1898), 166.

Duchet, Claude. "Autour du 'Dormeur du Val' de Rimbaud." *Revue d'Histoire Littéraire de la France*, 62 (July–Sept. 1962), 371–80.

Edwards, Herbert J., and Julie A. Herne. *James A. Herne: The Rise of Realism in the American Drama*. Orono: University of Maine Press, 1964.

Emerson, Ralph Waldo. "Circles." In *Essays, First Series*. Vol. 2. *The Complete Works of Ralph Waldo Emerson*. 12 vols. Ed. Edward Waldo Emerson. Boston: Houghton Mifflin, 1903–4. 299–302.

————. "Fate." In *The Conduct of Life*. Vol. 6. *The Complete Works of Ralph Waldo Emerson*. 12 vols. Ed. Edward Waldo Emerson. Boston: Houghton Mifflin, 1903–4. 1–49.

————. "Fate." In *Selections from Ralph Waldo Emerson: An Organic Anthology*. Ed. Stephen E. Whicher. Boston: Houghton Mifflin, 1957. 330–52.

————. *Nature*. In *The Collected Works of Ralph Waldo Emerson, Volume I, Nature, Addresses, and Lectures*. Ed. Robert E. Spiller and Alfred R. Ferguson. Cambridge, Mass.: Harvard University Press, 1971. 1–45.

————. "Self-Reliance." In *Essays, First Series*. Vol. 2. *The Complete Works of Ralph Waldo*

Emerson. 12 vols. Ed. Edward Waldo Emerson. Boston: Houghton Mifflin, 1903–4. 43–90.

———. "The Snow-Storm." In *Poems*. Vol. 9. *The Complete Works of Ralph Waldo Emerson*. 12 vols. Ed. Edward Waldo Emerson. Boston: Houghton Mifflin, 1903–4. 41–42.

Fallows, Bishop Samuel. "We Have Not Begun to Fight Yet." In *Readings and Recitations, No. 3*. Ed. L[izzie] Penney. New York: National Temperance Society and Publication House, 1879. 12–13.

Farrar, Canon F. W. "Public Opinion." In *Readings and Recitations, No. 2*. Ed. L[izzie] Penney. New York: National Temperance Society and Publication House, 1878. 25–27.

———. "The Serpent and the Tiger." In *Readings and Recitations, No. 2*. Ed. L[izzie] Penney. New York: National Temperance Society and Publication House, 1878. 10–12.

Fitch, Rev. W. R. " 'My People Shall Be Free!' " In *Readings and Recitations, No. 2*. Ed. L[izzie] Penney. New York: National Temperance Society and Publication House, 1878. 32–34.

Flower, B. O. "The Corrupting Influence of the Liquor Power in Politics, and Outlines of Two Practical Methods for Dealing with the Saloon Evil," in "How to Deal with the Liquor Traffic: A Symposium." *Arena*, 9 (May 1894), 837–44.

Fried, Michael. *Realism, Writing, Disfiguration: On Thomas Eakins and Stephen Crane*. Chicago and London: University of Chicago Press, 1987.

Frus, Phyllis. "Writing After the Fact: Crane, Journalism, and Fiction." In *The Politics and Poetics of Journalist Narrative: The Timely and the Timeless*. Cambridge, Eng.: Cambridge University Press, 1994. 13–52, 238–43.

Fuller, John Overton. *Swinburne: A Critical Biography*. London: Chatto & Windus, 1968.

G. "For What Are We Battling?" In *Readings and Recitations, No. 2*. Ed. L[izzie] Penney. New York: National Temperance Society and Publication House, 1878. 95–96.

Garnett, Edward. "Two Americans." London *Speaker*, 30 (Aug. 6, 1904), 436–37.

Gates, Ellen M. H. " 'Bring Out Your Dead.' " In *Readings and Recitations, No. 1*. Ed. L[izzie] Penney. New York: National Temperance Society and Publication House, 1877. 89–91.

Geismar, Maxwell. *Rebels and Ancestors: The American Novel, 1890–1915*. Boston: Houghton Mifflin, 1953.

Gibson, Donald. "Crane's Own Red Badge: The Origins of That Species." Unpublished paper presented at "One Hundred Years After the Publication of *The Red Badge of Courage*," Nov. 30–Dec. 1, 1995, United States Air Force Academy, Colorado Springs, Colorado.

Gillette, William. *The Illusion of the First Time in Acting*. Intr. George Arliss. New York: Dramatic Museum of Columbia University, 1915.

Golemba, Henry. " 'Distant Dinners' in Crane's *Maggie*: Representing 'The Other Half.' " *Essays in Literature*, 21 (Fall 1994), 235–50.

Gordon, Anna A., ed. *The White Ribbon Birthday Book*. Chicago: Woman's Temperance Publishing Association, 1887.

Gough, John B. "How to Break the Chain." In *Readings and Recitations, No. 2*. Ed. L[izzie] Penney. New York: National Temperance Society and Publication House, 1878. 16–18.

———. "Who Did It?" In *Readings and Recitations, No. 3*. Ed. Miss L[izzie] Penney. New York: National Temperance Society and Publication House, 1879. 73–75.

Bibliography

Gullason, Thomas Arthur. "Tennyson's Influence on Stephen Crane." *Notes and Queries*, n.s. 5 (Apr. 1958), 164–65.

————, ed. "A Family Portfolio: 2. Extracts from the Reverend Crane's Newly Discovered Two-Volume Journal." In *Stephen Crane's Career: Perspectives and Evaluations*. Ed. Thomas A. Gullason. New York: New York University Press, 1972. 11–22.

Hadley, Henry H. *The Blue Badge of Courage*. Akron, New York, and Chicago: Saalfield Publishing, 1902.

Haight, Gordon S. Introduction. *Miss Ravenel's Conversion from Secession to Loyalty* by John William De Forest. New York and London: Harper, 1939. ix–xvi.

Halliburton, David. *The Color of the Sky: A Study of Stephen Crane*. Cambridge, Eng.: Cambridge University Press, 1989.

Harrigan, Edward. "Maggie Murphy's Home." In *Harrigan and Braham's Songs from "Reilly and the 400 Hundred."* New York: Benedict Popular Publishing, [1891?]. 6–7.

Hemingway, Ernest. "Introduction." *Men at War: The Best War Stories of All Time*. Ed. Ernest Hemingway. New York: Crown, 1942. xi–xxxi.

————. *A Moveable Feast*. New York: Scribners, 1964.

Herbert, Annie. "Mulligan's Gospel." In *Readings and Recitations, No. 2*. Ed. L[izzie] Penney. New York: National Temperance Society and Publication House, 1878. 40–42.

Higginson, T. W. "A Bit of War Photography." *Philistine*, 3 (July 1896), 33–38.

————. *Cheerful Yesterdays*. Boston and New York: Houghton Mifflin, 1898.

Hilliard, John Northern. "Stephen Crane: Letters to a Friend." *New York Times*, Supplement (July 14, 1900), 466–67.

Hitchcock, Hiram. "The Hotels of America." In *1795–1895: One Hundred Years of American Commerce*. Ed. Chauncey M. Depew. New York: Haynes, 1895. 1, 149–56.

Hoffman, Daniel. *The Poetry of Stephen Crane*. New York and London: Columbia University Press, 1957.

————. "Talking About Poetry with W. D. Ehrhart." In *Words to Create a World: Interviews, Essays, and Reviews of Contemporary Poetry*. Ann Arbor: University of Michigan Press, 1993. 189–214.

"Holland" [E. J. Edwards]. Editorial. *Philadelphia Press* (Dec. 19, 1894), 8.

Holmes, Oliver Wendell. "Harvard College in the War." In *Speeches by Oliver Wendell Holmes*. Boston: Little, Brown, 1913. 13–15.

————. "Memorial Day, An Address Delivered May 30, 1884." In *Speeches by Oliver Wendell Holmes*. Boston: Little, Brown, 1913. 1–12.

————. "The Soldier's Faith, An Address Delivered on Memorial Day, May 30, 1895, at a Meeting Called by the Graduating Class of Harvard University." In *Speeches by Oliver Wendell Holmes*. Boston: Little, Brown, 1913. 56–66.

Holmes, Rev. William, and John W. Barber. "The Life-Boat." In *Religious Allegories: Being a Series of Emblematic Engravings*. Improved ed. Boston: L. P. Crown, 1854. 46–51.

————. "Passion and Patience." In *Religious Allegories: Being a Series of Emblematic Engravings*. Improved ed. Boston: L. P. Crown, 1854. 70–75.

————. *Religious Allegories: Being a Series of Emblematic Engravings*. Improved ed. Boston: L. P. Crown, 1854.

Holton, Milne. *Cylinder of Vision: The Fiction and Journalistic Writing of Stephen Crane*. Baton Rouge: Louisiana State University Press, 1972.

Howard, June. *Form and History in American Literary Naturalism*. Chapel Hill and London: University of North Carolina Press, 1985.

Howe, Mark De Wolfe, ed. *Holmes-Pollock Letters: The Correspondence of Mr Justice Holmes and Sir Frederick Pollock, 1874–1932*. Intr. John Gorham Palfrey. Cambridge, Mass.: Harvard University Press, 1941.

———. *Touched with Fire: Civil War Letters and Diary of Oliver Wendell Holmes, Jr., 1861–1864*. Cambridge, Mass.: Harvard University Press, 1946.

Howells, W. D. "Frank Norris." *North American Review*, 175 (Dec. 1902), 769–78.

———. "New York Low Life in Fiction." *New York World* (July 26, 1896), 18.

[Hubbard, Elbert]. ["Arrangements have been made"]. *Philistine*, 6 (Feb. 1898), 77.

———. [*The Black Riders*]. *Philistine*, 1 (June 1895), 27.

———. [Stephen Crane Obituary]. *Philistine*, 11 (Sept. 1900), 123–28.

Hugo, Victor. "A Tragedy of the Sea." In *Swinton's Fifth Reader and Speaker*. New York and Chicago: Ivison, Blakeman, 1883. 163–65.

Hyder, Clyde Kenneth. *Swinburne's Literary Career and Fame*. Durham, N.C.: Duke University Press, 1933.

Hymnal of the Methodist Episcopal Church. New York: Phillips & Hunt/Cincinnati: Walden & Stowe, 1883.

Hymns for the Use of the Methodist Episcopal Church. Rev. ed. New York: Carlton & Lanahan, 1871.

Jackson, Holbrook. *The Eighteen Nineties: A Review of Art and Ideas at the Close of the Nineteenth Century*. Intr. Karl Beckson. New York: Capricorn Books, 1966.

Johns, J[oseph]. *St. George and the Dragon: England and the Drink Traffic*. London: S. W. Partridge, [1907?].

Jones, H. P. "Temperance House." *Fountain* (June 26, 1846), 4.

Julian, John, ed. *A Dictionary of Hymnology*. New York: Dover, 1957.

Jung, C. G. *Two Essays on Analytical Psychology*. Trans. R. F. C. Hull. New York: Meridian, 1956.

Kaplan, Amy. *The Social Construction of American Realism*. Chicago and London: University of Chicago Press, 1988.

———. "The Spectacle of War in Crane's Revision of History." In *New Essays on The Red Badge of Courage*. Ed. Lee Clark Mitchell. Cambridge, Eng.: Cambridge University Press, 1986. 77–108.

Katz, Joseph. " 'The Blue Battalions' and the Uses of Experience." *Studia Neophilologica*, 38, No. 1 (1966), 107–16.

———. Introduction. *The Portable Stephen Crane*. Ed. Joseph Katz. New York: Viking, 1969. vii–xxi.

———. Introduction. *"The Red Badge of Courage" by Stephen Crane: A Facsimile Reproduction of the New York Press Appearance of December 9, 1894*. Gainesville: Scholars' Facsimiles & Reprints, 1967. 9–42.

———. "The *Maggie* Nobody Knows." *Modern Fiction Studies*, 12 (Summer 1966), 200–12.

———, ed. *The Blue Hotel*. Columbus: Merrill, 1969.

Kipling, Rudyard. *"Captains Courageous": A Story of the Grand Banks*. New York: Century, 1897.

Koren, John. "The Liquor Traffic Without Private Profits." *Arena*, 9 (Apr. 1894), 561–70.

LaFrance, Marston. *A Reading of Stephen Crane*. Oxford: Clarendon Press, 1971.

Lender, Mark Edward, and James Kirby Martin. *Drinking in America: A History*. New York: Free Press/London: Collier Macmillan, 1982.

Levenson, J. C. "*The Red Badge of Courage* and *McTeague*: Passage to Modernity." In *The Cambridge Companion to American Realism and Naturalism: Howells to London*. Ed. Donald Pizer. Cambridge, Eng., and New York: Cambridge University Press, 1995. 154–77.

Lincoln, Abraham. "Abraham Lincoln on Temperance." In *Readings and Recitations, No. 5*. Ed. L[izzie] Penney. New York: National Temperance Society and Publication House, 1884. 29–30.

Linson, Corwin K. *My Stephen Crane*. Ed. Edwin H. Cady. Syracuse: Syracuse University Press, 1958.

Longaker, Mark. *Ernest Dowson*. Philadelphia: University of Pennsylvania Press, 1944.

McClurg, A. C. "The Red Badge of Hysteria." *Dial*, 20 (Apr. 16, 1896), 227–28.

McGregor, Rev. Duncan. "What Is Intemperance?" In *Readings and Recitations, No. 4*. Ed. L[izzie] Penney. New York: National Temperance Society and Publication House, 1882. 11–13.

Mackay, Charles. "The Dream of the Reveler." In *Readings and Recitations, No. 3*. Ed. L[izzie] Penney. New York: National Temperance Society and Publication House, 1879. 37–39.

Mariani, Giorgio. *Spectacular Narratives: Representations of Class and War in Stephen Crane and the American 1890s*. New York: Peter Lang, 1992.

Mayer, Charles W. "Two Kids in the House of Chance: Crane's 'The Five White Mice.' " *Research Studies*, 44 (1976), 52–57.

Mayo, Mrs. Claude H. "The New Crusade March." In *The Voice of Song: Songs of the WCTU*. Rev. ed. Evanston: National Woman's Christian Temperance Union, 1960. 11.

Michaels, Walter Benn. *The Gold Standard and the Logic of Naturalism: American Literature at the Turn of the Century*. Berkeley: University of California Press, 1987.

Monteiro, George. "Stephen Crane: A New Appreciation by Edward Garnett." *American Literature*, 50 (Nov. 1978), 465–71.

Moody, D. L. "A Warning Against Wine." In *Readings and Recitations, No. 1*. Ed. L[izzie] Penney. New York: National Temperance Society and Publication House, 1877. 15–16.

Morris, Wright. "Some by That Master, Anon." *New York Times Book Review* (Jan. 20, 1980), 32–33.

Mosher, M. Florence. "It Is Coming." In *Readings and Recitations, No. 5*. Ed. L[izzie] Penney. New York: National Temperance Society and Publication House, 1884. 7–8.

Muir, Henry D. "Stephen Crane." *National Magazine*, 17 (Nov. 1902), 247.

———. "Stephen Crane." In *Songs and Other Fancies*. Chicago: Privately printed, 1901. 107.

Murphy, Brenda. " 'The Blue Hotel': A Source in *Roughing It*." *Studies in Short Fiction*, 20 (Winter 1983), 39–44.

———. "A Woman with Weapons: The Victor in Stephen Crane's *George's Mother*." *Modern Language Studies*, 11 (Spring 1981), 88–93.

Nelson, Harland S. "Stephen Crane's Achievement as a Poet." *Texas Studies in Literature and Language*, 4 (Winter 1963), 564–82.

Bibliography

Nietzsche, Friedrich. *The Birth of Tragedy and The Genealogy of Morals*. Trans. Francis Golffing. Garden City: Doubleday, 1956.

Nordau, Max. *Degeneration*. New York: D. Appleton, 1895.

Norris, Frank. *McTeague: A Story of San Francisco*. New York: Signet, 1981.

Norton, Caroline E. S. *Bingen on the Rhine*. Philadelphia: Porter & Coates, 1883.

Ober, William B. "Swinburne's Masochism: Neuropathology and Psychopathology." In *Boswell's Clap and Other Essays: Medical Analyses of Literary Men's Afflictions*. New York: Harper & Row, 1988. 43–88.

Odell, Ruth. "Nebraska Smart Sayings." *Southern Folklore Quarterly*, 12 (Sept. 1948), 185–95.

"Old Soldier." "Tales of the Revolution." In *Collections, Historical and Miscellaneous*. Ed. J. Farmer and J. B. Moore. Concord, July 1824. III, 210–12.

Oliver, Lawrence J. "Brander Matthews' Re-visioning of Crane's *Maggie*." *American Literature*, 60 (Dec. 1988), 654–58.

Overmyer, Janet. "The Structure of Crane's *Maggie*." *University of Kansas City Review*, 29 (Autumn 1962), 71–72.

Patton, M. Oakman. "Maggie of the 'Dump': An Incident of the Coal Famine." *National Magazine*, 17 (Mar. 1903), 752–55.

Pease, Donald. "Fear, Rage, and the Mistrials of Representation in *The Red Badge of Courage*." In *American Realism: New Essays*. Ed. Eric J. Sundquist. Baltimore and London: Johns Hopkins University Press, 1982. 155–75.

Pentecost, Rev. George F. "God's Clock Strikes." In *Frances E. Willard Recitation Book, Werner's Readings and Recitations, No. 18*. New York: Edgar S. Werner, 1898. 132–34.

Petry, Alice Hall. "*Gin Lane* in the Bowery: Crane's *Maggie* and William Hogarth." *American Literature*, 56 (Oct. 1984), 417–26.

Pilsbury, Caroline T. "Literature" [*The Open Boat and Other Tales of Adventure*]. *Boston Ideas*, 12 (June 18, 1898), 6.

Pollard, Josephine. "The Price of a Drink." In *Readings and Recitations, No. 5*. Ed. L[izzie] Penney. National Temperance Society and Publication House, 1884. 57–58.

———. "Stolen; or, the Mother's Lament." In *Readings and Recitations, No. 4*. Ed. L[izzie] Penney. New York: National Temperance Society and Publication House, 1882. 83–87.

Porter, Horace. "The Philosophy of Courage." *Century*, 36 (June 1888), 246–54.

Pratt, Lyndon Upson. "A Possible Source of *The Red Badge of Courage*." *American Literature*, 11 (Mar. 1939), 1–10.

Quinet, Edgar. *Œuvres complètes de Edgar Quinet*. Paris: Pangerre, 1858.

Reel, Arthur. *Maggie, Girl of the Streets*. Unpublished play, Billy Rose Theatre Collection, New York Public Library. Copyright 1976.

Rexford, E. E. "Your Father's at the Helm." In *Sunshine for Sunday-Schools*. Collected by P. P. Bliss. Cincinnati: John Church/Chicago: George F. Root, 1873. 52–53.

Rimbaud, Arthur. "Sleeper in the Valley." In *Rimbaud: Complete Works, Selected Letters*. Ed. and trans. Wallace Fowlie. Chicago and London: University of Chicago Press, 1966. 57.

Robertson, Michael. *Stephen Crane, Journalism, and the Making of Modern American Literature*. New York: Columbia University Press, 1997.

Rorabaugh, W. J. *The Alcoholic Republic: An American Tradition*. Oxford and New York: Oxford University Press, 1979.

Bibliography

Schaefer, Michael W. *A Reader's Guide to the Short Stories of Stephen Crane*. New York: G. K. Hall, 1996.

Schoberlin, Melvin H. "Flagon of Despair: Stephen Crane." Unpublished manuscript. Schoberlin Collection, Syracuse University Library, Syracuse, New York.

Scudder, Rev. H. M. "The Destroyer." In *Readings and Recitations, No. 1*. Ed. L[izzie] Penney. New York: National Temperance Society and Publication House, 1877. 51–53.

Shannon, Edgar, and Christopher Ricks. " 'The Charge of the Light Brigade': The Creation of a Poem." *Studies in Bibliography*. Charlottesville: University Press of Virginia, 1985. Vol. 38. 1–44.

Shi, David. *Facing Facts: Realism in American Thought and Culture, 1850–1920*. New York and Oxford: Oxford University Press, 1995.

Solomon, Eric. *Stephen Crane: From Parody to Realism*. Cambridge, Mass.: Harvard University Press, 1966.

Sorrentino, Paul. "Newly Discovered Writings of Mary Helen Peck Crane and Agnes Elizabeth Crane." *Syracuse University Library Associates Courier*, 21 (Spring 1986), 103–34.

Soule, Caroline A. "The Cry of the Women." In *Readings and Recitations, No. 1*. Ed. L[izzie] Penney. New York: National Temperance Society and Publication House, 1877. 12–13.

Spinucci, Pietro. "La Poesia di Stephen Crane." *Studi Americani* (Rome), 17 (1971), 93–120.

Stallman, Robert Wooster. *Stephen Crane: A Biography*. New York: Braziller, 1968.

———. *Stephen Crane: An Omnibus*. New York: Knopf, 1952.

Stedman, Laura, and George M. Gould, eds. *Life and Letters of Edmund Clarence Stedman*. New York: Moffat, Yard, 1910.

Stoddard. "The Wine-Cup." In *Swinton's Fifth Reader and Speaker*. New York and Chicago: Ivison, Blakeman, 1883. 404–8.

Stone, Edward. "Crane's 'Soldier of the Legion.' " *American Literature*, 30 (May 1958), 242–44.

Swann, Thomas Burnett. *Ernest Dawson*. New York: Twayne, 1964.

Sweeney, Gerard M. "The Syphilitic World of Stephen Crane's *Maggie*." *American Literary Realism*, 24 (Fall 1991), 79–85.

Swinburne, Algernon Charles. "Dolores." In *Poems*. Intr. Ernest Rhys. New York: Boni and Liveright, 1919. 103–16.

———. *Poems*. Intr. Ernest Rhys. New York: Boni and Liveright, 1919.

———. *The Swinburne Letters, Volume I: 1854–1869*. Ed. Cecil Y. Lang. New Haven: Yale University Press, 1959.

———. *The Swinburne Letters, Volume III: 1875–1877*. Ed. Cecil Y. Lang. New Haven: Yale University Press, 1960.

Talmage, Rev. T. De Witt. "True Help." In *Readings and Recitations, No. 3*. Ed. L[izzie] Penney. New York: National Temperance Society and Publication House, 1879. 18–20.

Tennyson, Alfred Lord. "The Charge of the Light Brigade." In *The Poems of Tennyson*. Ed. Christopher Ricks. London and Harlow: Longmans, 1969. 1034–36.

———. *The Letters of Alfred Lord Tennyson, Volume II: 1851–1870*. Ed. Cecil Y. Lang and Edgar F. Shannon, Jr. Cambridge, Mass.: Harvard University Press, 1987.

Tiffany, O. H. "An Evil Waste." In *Readings and Recitations, No. 4*. Ed. L[izzie] Penney. New York: National Temperance Society and Book Publication House, 1882. 71–74.

Trachtenberg, Alan. "Experiments in Another Country: Stephen Crane's City Sketches." In *American Realism: New Essays*. Ed. Eric J. Sundquist. Baltimore and London: Johns Hopkins Press, 1982. 138–54.

Twain, Mark. *The Adventures of Tom Sawyer*. In *Mississippi Writings*. Ed. Guy Cardwell. New York: Library of America, 1982. 1–125.

———. *Life on the Mississippi*. In *Mississippi Writings*. Ed. Guy Cardwell. New York: Library of America, 1982. 217–616.

Tyler, Helen E. *Where Prayer and Purpose Meet: 1874—The WCTU Story—1949*. Evanston: Signal Press, 1949.

Van Doren, Carl. Introduction. *Twenty Stories by Stephen Crane*. Ed. Carl Van Doren. New York and Cleveland: World, 1945. v–xvii.

Wakeley, Rev. J. B. *The American Temperance Cyclopædia of History, Biography, Anecdote, and Illustration*. New York: National Temperance Society and Publication House, 1875.

Watts, Isaac. "Holy Fortitude; or, the Christian Soldier." In *The Psalms, Hymns, and Spiritual Songs, of the Rev. Isaac Watts, D.D.* Ed. Samuel Worcester. Boston: Crocker and Brewster, 1838. 563.

Webster, H. T. "Wilbur F. Hinman's *Corporal Si Klegg* and Stephen Crane's *The Red Badge of Courage*." *American Literature*, 11 (Nov. 1939), 285–93.

Wentworth, E. "The 'Blue Ribbon.'" In *Readings and Recitations, No. 2*. Ed. L[izzie] Penney. New York: National Temperance Society and Publication House, 1878. 14–15.

Wentworth, Harold, and Stuart Berg Flexner. *Dictionary of American Slang*. 2nd Supplemented ed. New York: Crowell, 1975.

Wertheim, Stanley. "*The Red Badge of Courage* and Personal Narratives of the Civil War." *American Literary Realism*, 6 (Winter 1973), 61–65.

———. "Stephen Crane and the Wrath of Jehovah." *Literary Review*, 7 (Summer 1964), 499–508.

Wertheim, Stanley, and Paul Sorrentino. *The Crane Log: A Documentary Life of Stephen Crane, 1871–1900*. New York: G. K. Hall, 1994.

———. "Thomas Beer: The Clay Feet of Stephen Crane Biography." *American Literary Realism*, 22 (Spring 1990), 2–16.

Wheeler, Mary S. "The Charge of the Rum Brigade." In *Readings and Recitations, No. 1*. Ed. L[izzie] Penney. New York: National Temperance Society and Publication House, 1877. 27–29.

Wheeler, Post, and Hallie Erminie Rives. *Dome of Many-Coloured Glass*. Garden City: Doubleday, 1955.

Wilcox, Ella Wheeler. "Water Power." In *World Book of Temperance*. 3rd enlarged and rev. ed. Compiled by Dr. and Mrs. Wilbur F. Crafts. Washington, D.C.: International Reform Bureau, 1911. 176.

Willard, Frances E. "Everybody's War." In *Readings and Recitations, No. 4*. Ed. L[izzie] Penney. New York: National Temperance Society and Publication House, 1882. 54–57.

———. "The Great Evil." In *Readings and Recitations, No. 5*. Ed. L[izzie] Penney. New York: National Temperance Society and Publication House, 1884. 68–70.

———. "Saloons Must Go!" In *Frances E. Willard Recitation Book, Werner's Readings and Recitations, No. 18*. New York: Edgar S. Werner, 1898. 178–79.

———. "Which Shall Win?" In *Readings and Recitations, No. 1*. Ed. L[izzie] Penney. New York: National Temperance Society and Publication House, 1877. 9–10.

———. "The Widening Horizon." In *Frances E. Willard Recitation Book, Werner's Readings and Recitations, No. 18*. New York: Edgar S. Werner, 1898. 91.

———. *Woman and Temperance: or, The Work and Workers of the Woman's Christian Temperance Union*. Hartford: Park Publishing, 1883.

Willard, Frances E., and Mary A. Livermore, eds. *A Woman of the Century: Fourteen Hundred-Seventy Biographical Sketches Accompanied by Portraits of Leading American Women in All Walks of Life*. Buffalo, Chicago, and New York: Charles Wells Moulton, 1893.

Wister, Owen. *Lin McLean*. New York and London: Harper, 1908.

Wyndham, George. "A Remarkable Book." *New Review* (London), 14 (Jan. 1896), 30–40.

Zara, Louis. *Dark Rider: A Novel Based on the Life of Stephen Crane*. Cleveland and New York: World, 1961.

Index